PLAYED UP **POMPEY**

24 FRATTON PARK FAVOURITES REFLECT ON THEIR BLUES CAREERS

BY **NEIL ALLEN**

Published in 2015 by Johnston Press plc

Orchard Brae House,
30 Queensferry Road,
Edinburgh
EH4 2HS

A CIP catalogue record is available for this book from the British Library.

ISBN 191042105-7

Printed and bound in Great Britain by Bishops Printers, Portsmouth.

Johnston Press plc is the publisher of The News, Portsmouth

To Tony Goodall, Ken Malley and Eddy Wilson.
They gave everything to their club.

Contents

Acknowledgements

My thanks to the 24 former Pompey players who sacrificed their time to contribute towards this book.

None had to be coerced, none had to be paid, all were enthusiastic volunteers, willing to reminisce over their Fratton Park days, usually with brutal honesty.

To a man they continue to relish their association with the club, irrespective of success or longevity on the south coast.

Without their assistance this book would have failed to emerge. Thank you.

Just as crucial has been the support, advice and immeasurable patience of my wife, Emma, throughout the process.

She has read every word contained within, often twice over, while accepting my diminished spare time towards her and our children Abi and Greg without complaint.

My parents, Keith and Daisy, have also offered boundless backing from the days of writing Bedworth United match reports to this point of publishing my first book.

Similarly Tony Parratt, former editor of the Heartland Evening News, who provided my first opportunity in newspapers.

In terms of this book, a sterling performer has been Roger Holmes, whose encyclopedic Pompey knowledge and personal newspaper collection have proven absolutely invaluable.

Roger has penned several Pompey books himself and his guidance throughout and keen eye for statistical accuracies cannot be praised enough.

My army of proofreaders have also contained Steve Bone, Matt Reeder, Dave Allen, Neil Weld and Johnny Moore.

A huge thanks to Alex Crook for convincing me to write Played Up Pompey after I had previously shrugged off the idea on several occasions, and also for his frequent advice.

Elsewhere, Barry Harris kindly contributed the foreword and provided his usual brand of infectious enthusiasm into all things Pompey along with his incredible memory.

Immense gratitude also goes to those who provided essential assistance in tracking down many of the players interviewed in this book.

In particular, Jake Payne warrants a special mention for his inexhaustible contacts list and devotion to recognising Pompey's proud history.

Others deserving a hearty pat on the back are Darren Bentley and David Hynds from Burnley FC, Gareth Edwards, Helen Mayo and Dominique Grant from Everton FC, Steve Kattenhorn, Daniel Kovacevic, Mark McAdam, Pat Neil, Darren Simmons and Mike Vimpany.

Not forgetting club photographer Joe Pepler, who has kindly supplied many of the photographs used within this book, along with The News.

Any other photographer whose work is involved is invited to contact the publishers in writing providing proof of copyright.

Finally, I wish to deliver my thanks to The News' editor Mark Waldron, Bishops Printers managing director Gareth Roberts and designer Andy Sanders for their unwavering help and support.

Statistics in this book include the Full Members Cup and its guises of the Simod Cup and Zenith Data Systems Cup, in addition to the Anglo-Italian Cup.

Such fixtures previously haven't been taken into account in player records by other Pompey publications.

Foreword - **Barry Harris**

I have laughed, I have cried, I have been angry and I've had some lovely, lovely times. I owe Pompey a lot.

It began on my eighth birthday, the date February 23, 1952.

My dad, Bill, decided to take myself and my brother, Cyril, to Fratton Park for an FA Cup fifth round fixture with Doncaster Rovers.

We were among 44,392 who witnessed Bob Jackson's side win 4-0 through goals from Peter Harris, Len Phillips, Marcel Gaillard and a Herbert Rouse own goal.

I can recall Doncaster's wing-half and skipper Dave Miller did Jimmy Scoular with a tackle, studding him down the leg, and was sent off for the foul.

Jimmy Stewart, the old trainer, was cleaning up Scoular who shouted in that Scottish voice of his 'Don't send him off ref, leave him on, I'll deal with him'.

That was it for me, I was hooked, and from then on used to sit on the wall beside the home dugout, where I befriended Reg Flewin.

Reg had been Pompey's captain in their two title-winning sides yet was injured and in the process of packing up to help in the backroom. One day he turned to me and said 'We'll get you fixed up son, you can be our mascot'.

So for the first game of the 1952-53 campaign, at home to Stanley Matthews' Blackpool, I was mascot with the responsibility of leading the players on to the pitch and shaking hands with the captains, as well as helping in the dressing room.

It was a job which continued over the next few seasons, but at the age of 10 my commitment to Pompey would earn me the cane in front of my school.

We had an FA Cup replay against Bolton Wanderers in February 1954 and the day before the headmaster at the Fareham County Primary School, 'Fatty' Fulford, warned us in assembly that any boys taking half-a-day off to watch the match would be punished.

I thought 'Fair enough, I'll get caned'.

There were 10 of us who went to the match, a 2-1 defeat, and in assembly the following day 'Fatty' Fulford called us up one-by-one.

I was the last and he said: 'You had the whole day off and not a half like the rest of them, what's your explanation?'. I replied 'I had things to do!'.

Well, he didn't like that and gave me two swipes - more than anybody else - before asking whether it hurt.

'Not as much as Pompey losing yesterday!' was my response.

'Fatty' Fulford was horrible and it turned out he also got on the blower to Reg Mulcock, the Pompey secretary and an absolute gentleman.

That Saturday we were at home to Burnley and when I arrived to serve as mascot the trainer-cum-kitman Billy Wright said: 'You had better go upstairs, Mr Mulcock wants to see you, stand by and be prepared to be told off'.

So I went in and he warned 'Any more of these antics from you and you won't be walking down this road to go to these games. Don't do that anymore'. It made me cry, but never stopped me.

I would later be the Pompey sailor for 21 years, trained for the club as a physio for a while and then moved onto kit duties.

For a long time now Kev McCormack has worked with me, he comes over all bolshie but when you get to know him he would do anything for you and when I broke my left ankle in a hit-and-run in October 2007, he along with Sean Davis were the first people to visit me in hospital.

Scoular remains my all-time hero, even if he did leave at the end of my second season of watching Pompey. I wish I had seen him when I was older.

He put so much in, he was a leader who possessed passing ability, work-rate, an excellent general attitude to the game and a gentleman as soon as the whistle went. I tried to model myself on him, but couldn't tackle!

The most skilful player I have seen for us is Len Phillips, without a shadow of a doubt. People talk about Robert Prosinecki, who we had at the end of his career, but he wasn't fit to lace Len's boots.

Len always had space, time on the ball, and his passing was immaculate, he would put the ball over the top of the full-back for Peter Harris to run onto.

I have seen 31 permanent managers come and go at Fratton Park, but Harry Redknapp is my favourite.

People say he put this club into trouble with his spending but he also sold on the likes of Lassana Diarra, Glen Johnson, Niko Kranjcar, Sulley Muntari and Sylvain Distin. He knew what a player could do.

Harry's a lovely man, on Friday nights before an away game we would talk for hours and I still keep in touch now.

He was a man who took defeat very badly, you would have to keep out of his way for however long it took. He had the hump and would go quite quiet when coming home after an away loss.

The owner who I liked the most was Milan Mandaric. John Deacon didn't mix much, but Milan was very approachable, honest and a thoroughly pleasant man. Another bad loser, though!

Winning the FA Cup in 2008 was my favourite moment, as a fan to have the cup in my hand on the Wembley pitch was special.

Then there was winning at Old Trafford in the quarter-finals during that run, when Sylvain Distin said 'Come on, we'll have some fun Baz'.

Now, bearing in mind the season before he joined us he was Manchester City's captain, he lifted me up in front of the Stretford End to celebrate and wind them up. They weren't impressed!

Defeating Tottenham Hotspur in the 2010 FA Cup semi-final at Wembley was a memorable occasion, nobody expected us to do that to Harry's side.

Ricardo Rocha was made man-of-the-match and I remember in the final against Chelsea he was so upset afterwards, crying.

He was great to have around the place, always pleasant to me, and whenever Kev would start up on me having a bit of fun, as he does, Ricardo would joke 'Have a bit of respect for your elders'.

Apart from Lindy Delapenha, I have watched and worked with all the footballers interviewed in this book.

I never got to know Prosinecki that well, he wasn't around long enough to get that understanding really, but was one hell of a player.

He liked a cigarette at half-time in games, sometimes in the changing room toilet. I remember Kev having a cigarette ready for him in the tunnel during half-time in one match. Honestly!

Arjan De Zeeuw was a lovely man and when we beat Southampton 4-1 in April 2005, on the morning of the game I did a sponsored walk from St Mary's Stadium to Fratton Park in aid of the Tom Prince Cancer Trust and he organised a whip round which helped take the total to £4,000.

That was him, a leader, and he wouldn't let people rest on the pitch, he would let them know if someone wasn't doing it. It is always important to have a good leader on the pitch.

The craziest player I have come across was Hermann Hreidarsson, that one was mad.

During the 2008 pre-season, we travelled to South Africa and were on safari in a jeep when he nicked the driver's gun and got a right telling off. It was loaded and although the trigger was on a lock the driver wasn't impressed!

Hermann was a good man to have in the dressing room, always up to mischief, he used to thump people, punch you in the ribs or pick you up, even getting me in a headlock once. He never did anything to Kev, though!

I would say Lomana Lualua was his own worst enemy, what skill, he should have gone further in the game, but didn't always believe in himself.

Matt Taylor was a good player, a sensible person who scored some lovely goals for us at Sunderland and also at home to Everton. I thought he left us a bit too early.

I always remember him at Old Trafford in the FA Cup in January 2003 when we lost 4-1, he was so nervous he was all over the place for the first 20 minutes, I think the stage was too big for him that day.

One former player I have always been close to is Alan Knight, we still have a really good relationship and he regularly says to me in that dull voice of his 'What do you want, Harris?'.

Knightsie has pulled himself around and you have to admire what he has done, getting his life out of a mess and giving up alcohol and the fags.

Andy Awford always jokes that he wouldn't go for crosses, but what a shot stopper. He should have achieved more, and I think if he had gone on to a bigger club he might have done, but he stayed at Pompey.

I used to say Mick Kennedy was an unskilful Scoular, but he is one of my favourites and they both played the game in the same way.

We played Wimbledon in September 1987 and he and Vinnie Jones had a niggle in the first half so at the end of the interval Micky was stood waiting outside the door for him.

I was behind him and heard him say 'You, if you go anywhere near me this half I will put a hole in you'. Then just walked away.

Jones didn't go near him after that, Micky tackled him a few times that game but the Wimbledon midfielder didn't want to know.

During those days I was living in Fareham and ran Fareham Park Lane Boys' under-11s to under-14s and Micky and Mick Quinn would come over on a Tuesday night to coach them in the gym before we all went for a drink afterwards.

Alan McLoughlin was very thorough as a footballer, very thorough as a person and a great coach who always had time to talk you about the game.

I used to really enjoy his company in the hotel on a Friday night going through a few things. We all think we know the game and then you speak to people like him, so methodical on the game.

As a player he was a bit like Len Phillips in that he always had space. He wasn't the best at tackling but that didn't matter with his passing ability and I remember that hat-trick at Blackburn in the FA Cup.

One very, very skilful player at Pompey was Alan Rogers, although a full-back could frighten him by getting into him early on!

He could play, though, was one hell of a player with a clever step over and once scored directly from a corner against Huddersfield. Frank Burrows had a lot of faith in him.

I could tell you some stories about Paul Merson, a player with unbelievable skill and the one whose passing ability took us up in 2002-03.

Merse was funny, off the pitch he would pick up on people's weaknesses for a bit of fun and Nigel Quashie was always an easy target.

Now Nigel was a nice man, but everything had to be right, he was funny like that.

One time we had just played Wolverhampton Wanderers on the Wednesday night in November 2002 and were staying at a hotel near Telford as we were playing Derby County the following Saturday.

Merse wanted a wind-up with somebody and beside the driveway there was a big lake with moorhens on it so he called me over.

'In a minute,' he said, 'I am going to ask you what those birds are on that lake and you are to say they are 'morons' and see how Nigel reacts'.

So I was reading a book and when Merse asked the question I looked up and responded 'morons'. Sure enough, Nigel angrily piped up and shouted 'You're a moron, you can't talk properly'.

Merse always got up for breakfast, a lot of players didn't, Yoshi Kawaguchi always got up, me, Kev and most of the staff also did, while Harry would have it in his room.

Something else which got Nigel mad would be if you stirred your tea and tapped the spoon on the cup, he hated it.

Merse picked up on that and one morning at breakfast he arranged that all eight of us would do it when Nigel came into the room! He was easy to wind up.

I never got to know Mark Hateley that well, he was a great goalscorer, though, and it was a pity he wasn't with us longer before his move to AC Milan.

He and Alan Biley were really good for us in that 1983-84 season, Mark with his strong, hold-up play was superb and became the first Pompey player since Jimmy Dickinson to represent England.

Another great goalscorer was Ron Saunders, whose record spoke for itself and a man who always had time for people, which I respected.

He would score out of nothing, although funnily enough was often moaned at for missing a lot of chances, but his positional sense in the box was incredible.

Billy Wilson is a lovely man, a typical pub landlord, always friendly and bubbly and I wasn't surprised when he went into the pub trade, he's so good with people.

As a player you could put him as a holding midfield player or at left-back, he would get the ball for you and also use it well, which was important.

Another who had time for people was Noel Blake. He went through a rough time with the racism problem and that was wrong, but he fought it and the following year was made The News/Sports Mail's Player of the Season.

Blakey was a strong character, a powerful and intimidating player who although lacked pace but could score a goal and the central defensive partnership with Billy Gilbert complemented each other.

Just like Jimmy Scoular, he was a different man off the pitch to the one portrayed on it, and was actually quite gentle.

We were very lucky to get Norman Piper from Plymouth Argyle, he was a great signing, not the strongest, not the bravest but made up for it in other ways.

He could pass a ball, had superb positional sense and could play in several roles, ending up playing at full-back for Pompey.

Guy Whittingham is a lovely man and the season he scored 47 goals for us we should have gone into the Premier League - instead he moved to Aston Villa.

What a good goalscorer, in the box feeding off defenders' mistakes and Paul Walsh helped him a lot that campaign.

Another prolific striker was Dave Kemp, who I thought was lazy but would get you goals so was a favourite among the Pompey fans.

I thought he left us in a mess when he joined Carlisle United and could have stayed to keep us in Division Three, while a lot of his goals came as consolations in defeat such as 6-1 at Shrewsbury Town and 3-1 at Preston North End.

His strength was playing with his back to the goal and turning, he could score in the box for you and goalscorers are always popular.

I have known Andy Awford since he was a boy in the youth team, he's a good football man who packed up playing too early after a lot of injuries.

Kit Symons was the forceful one in their central-defensive partnership, Andy was always covering and had the football brain and a special positional sense. If he had moved on he probably would have played for England.

I first saw Ron Newman when he played for Fareham, later moving to Pompey and was someone who would run through a wall for you - and very quickly!

On match days I would catch the 10.08am from Fareham and Ron would be on the same train so we would travel together and talk. What a nice man.

Alan Biley was a showman who you can only talk about with admiration considering all the good things he did at Pompey, although to this day I don't know what caused the fall-out with Alan Ball.

Back in those days I used to make home brew, it was a bitter-cum-lager which was a bit strong, and I was allowed to take 8-10 bottles on the team coach for the players to have on the way back, with Biley very partial!

I never got to know Mike Barnard very well, but as a player he was steady and very reliable, you never saw him have a bad game even if Pompey were declining a bit at that stage.

There have been so many players over the years, many I count among my friends, and that is why Pompey is such a special club to me.

ty
6
6
17

The News, Monday, March 3, 2003

FOOTBALL: Mark McGhee forces his players to sit through recording of 5-0 thrashing – simply so his team can

VIDEO NASTY? MORE LIKE AN OSCAR WINNER

MARK McGHEE made his Millwall side watch a video of their 5-0 thrashing – to show how good Pompey are.

by MARK STOREY reporting from the Den

Millwall's manager believes his players can learn from a Blues display which rivalled anything they have produced in an already phenomenal season.

'You can never stop picking up things from good sides,' admitted Lions striker Steve Claridge, who sat through all 90 minutes at training yesterday.

'Portsmouth are superb. We lost 5-0, but the thing is we didn't play that badly.'

Pompey's excellence just made Millwall look poor. They always had players spare and Paul Merson enjoyed enough space in the hole behind the front two to pitch a marquee.

Every Pompey attack in the first half seemed to lead to a goal. It was like watching a butcher cleave a carcass – quick, efficient and ruthless, the blood Millwall's.

'Watching the video will help us learn from this defeat,' said McGhee. 'But not just to see where we went wrong, but where they went right.

'It was all over by half-time. We seemed to get punished every time we lost the ball and they went forward. They're a quality team and always found the spare man.'

There had been a symbolic moment after six minutes, when Merson threw off his black woolly gloves.

The Millwall crowd laughed, failing to read it as a signal of intent from Pompey's skipper, instead calling him a fairy for wearing them in the first place.

It was those same fans, however, who were ...

Pompey managed. But it was punished by Merson, who was left unattended for most of the 82 minutes he was on the pitch.

With Tim Sherwood and Nigel Quashie blotting out David Livermore and Wise in midfield, Merson was free to roam.

Millwall could not hide behind the excuse of tactics for Pompey's opener on 15 minutes, however. They simply allowed Yakubu enough time to write a letter back to Nigeria before stroking in Kevin Harper's low cross.

The Den is a strange place. Despite the small crowd, an air of brooding hostility can make it one of the most intimidating places to play.

But when things go wrong, that malevolence can make Millwall implode. You can quite imagine how they lost 6-0 to Rotherham on the opening day of the season.

The silence when Pompey scored – John Westwood must have had his mouth taped up in the directors' box – only seemed to heighten the Den's self-destructive traits.

Warner's save from Todorov at 1-0 appeared significant until Merson produced a replica pass to send him clear again. This time, the ...

> It was like watching a butcher cleave a carcass – quick, efficient and ruthless, the blood Millwall's.

Neil Harris volleying over from three yards before Sherwood headed home his first Pompey goal after Todorov and Harper had combined.

Wise underlined Millwall's frustrations by scraping his studs down Nigel Quashie's calf, earning a booking. Sherwood raised his arms at Wise in response, but Quashie got the yellow.

McGhee said: 'The difference of opinion between Dennis Wise and Tim Sherwood looked like handbags to me.

'Dennis should know better than to get involved, but he's a quality player who arrived here with a certain temperament which makes him susceptible to boiling over. But it's the first time we've had anything like that in 20 games.'

Pompey's fourth in first-half injury-time persuaded some Millwall fans to go home. Todorov's emphatic thump past Tony Warner from Merson's pass perfectly reflecting Pompey's dominance.

Millwall deserved a goal for their pressure after the break. But Shaka Hislop had other ideas with a brilliant save from Kiner's free-kick which snuffed out the the last embers of life in McGhee's side.

Yakubu had another chance for a hat-trick when Paul Robinson brought him down in the second half. But Redknapp pointed at Merson to take the penalty, which he deposited firmly in the corner with Warner guessing wrong.

Todorov failed to ...

MILLWALL 0
POMPEY 5

Attendance: 9,697

STAT ATTACK

SHOTS ON TARGET	
MILLWALL	6
POMPEY	8
SHOTS OFF TARGET	
MILLWALL	11
POMPEY	2
CORNERS	
MILLWALL	4
POMPEY	1
FOULS	
MILLWALL	5
POMPEY	5

Arjan **De Zeeuw**

118 games, five goals (June 2002 - August 2005)

Millwall 0
Pompey 5 (Yakubu 2, Sherwood, Todorov, Merson)

Division One, The Den, Saturday, March 1, 2003

Pompey: Hislop, Primus, De Zeeuw, Festa, Harper (59 mins Crowe), Taylor, Sherwood, Quashie, Merson (81 mins Diabate), Todorov (77 mins Pericard), Yakubu.

Subs Not Used: Kawaguchi, O'Neil.

Attendance; 9,697

That day at The Den, Paul Merson was unbelievable, like a conductor, and we were in his orchestra.

There was such a flow to our game, we kept on scoring goals, producing wonderful attacks, Millwall could not handle us and we absolutely annihilated them.

Nobody cheered through. A goal went in and you could hear only one or two people celebrating, it was like playing in a Sunday League fixture.

It was such a surreal game, we put on one of our best performances of that 2002-03 promotion season and there were barely any Pompey fans present to see it because they had been banned.

There were some who had crept in, we could hear the odd few, but it was very limited and I didn't see any of them, so it was extremely weird.

I had never, ever played in a game with that sort of feeling, perhaps that is why it sticks in my memory as my favourite Pompey game. I have such good memories of that performance.

We played brilliantly in that March 2003 match, an important fixture in our promotion push and it was a shame there weren't many of our fans there because they would have loved every minute of it - like we did.

I don't think Millwall were playing that well at the time but from the start to the end we performed like it was no effort whatsoever. When we left that pitch it was 'Yeah, that was okay'.

Normally when you come off after a match you are tired, yet it was one of those where we thought 'What a lovely game'. It was like playing in the park.

Merson was brilliant, that stood out as one of the games where I thought 'Wow, this guy can play'. You could imagine what he must have been like in his prime.

He was a strange guy, a very loveable fella and a big name, but a really nice down-to-earth guy with no arrogance whatsoever.

If anything, he felt a bit awkward with strange people. He liked it when the team was around, was more comfortable with people he knew, and really great to have in the dressing room.

At the training ground Merson was rubbish! He would hide on the side of the pitch, playing right-wing but trying not to touch the ball too much - although every time he did touch the ball it was brilliant.

Overall he didn't seem to want to get involved too much - but in the games was outstanding.

We knew he wouldn't track back and wouldn't defend but that was okay, give him the ball and he would be creative so other people around him had to run a little bit faster and a little bit harder.

It wasn't a problem, though, because he could make something happen so you didn't mind doing a bit more for him.

He was a league above and really important in winning promotion.

That season the games went so thick and fast, I remember Kevin Harper scoring a ridiculous goal at Walsall which he was never going to score again, I netted a header from a Merson free-kick against Gillingham, but I can't recall everything.

We had begun the campaign against Nottingham Forest with eight new players in the starting XI and it just gelled from day one.

Don't get me wrong, not everybody was best friends off the pitch, there were people in the team I didn't get along that well with but, as a group, there was a really good spirit and that was crucial.

We had a good mixture of old and young, funny characters in the dressing room like Hayden Foxe and Merson, there were creative people and there were hard-working players like myself and Linvoy Primus.

People would not hold back against each other, if I was not happy with something I would tell that person, and it also worked the other way around. You had the odd clash in the changing room but that was always in front of everybody, then it would be out of the system and you carried on.

It was so enjoyable to be part of that. Winning every week, the fans getting more and more excited because they can see you are going for promotion, everything about the club was positive and it is rare you have that.

I also had that with Barnsley under Danny Wilson. We won promotion in 1996-97 right at the end with second place, but with Pompey we just went through Division One. There was not another team threatening us.

When I went back to Wigan Athletic we made it to the Carling Cup final and at one stage reached second in the Premier League, but the Pompey promotion campaign was one of the most enjoyable I ever had.

My arrival at Fratton Park in June 2002 from Wigan had been unexpected.

Harry Redknapp rang me up and more or less said 'Hi, it's Harry, would you like to come and play for us?'

I just thought 'Who is this guy?', I didn't know much about him and looked at the league table to see Pompey had only just escaped relegation the season before. I wasn't sure - but chatted to him anyway.

He had such a charming personality, explained the way he wanted to play and that was it, suddenly I was really looking forward to this new challenge, although wasn't sure how good we actually were.

Then that season we absolutely blitzed it.

Harry got the most out of us, he took this struggling football club into the Premier League and then kept us there. He worked wonders.

I will never forget playing Arsenal at Fratton Park in the FA Cup in March 2004 and it wasn't because we played really well! We got hammered 5-1.

The thing that stuck out from that game were our fans. We were losing 5-0 at one stage and they were singing, still behind us every step of the way, chanting 'We're going to win 6-5'.

Thierry Henry, who scored twice, turned to me and said: 'Your fans are mad, they are brilliant, they keep on singing'.

It's easy to have a laugh when you are 5-0 up but he had a point, we were being destroyed by Arsenal in the FA Cup and our supporters were ridiculously good.

Another sensational atmosphere at Fratton Park was the following season when we slaughtered Southampton 4-1 in April 2005. By that stage Harry was in their dugout and we had a new manager in Alain Perrin.

That was such a ridiculous game, there was so much riding on it for both teams and there were moments you stood on the field and could feel the enthusiasm and passion of all the fans present.

Yakubu scored a penalty, I netted with a header and Lomana Lualua grabbed two then got injured in the celebration, the idiot, but that is him!

The result meant more or less we were staying up and Southampton were going down. They were one of our rivals in the relegation dogfight so it was perfect for us to win.

Football fans in general still associate me with the El Hadji Diouf spitting incident at Bolton Wanderers in November 2004 and, funnily enough, it has really been good for my image as a player considering I didn't react in a way everybody would expect.

Diouf got even more criticism because of my actions - and to this day has never apologised.

I remember four years later being approached in an airport by a teacher from Northern Ireland leading a school trip.

He wanted to shake my hand and asked if I would be willing to have my photograph taken with his class. Obviously I agreed but enquired why.

The teacher replied: 'I'm a football fan and I have used the way you dealt with Diouf that day as an example to my class how violence does not have to be retaliated with violence.'

From that point of view I had done something really outstanding!

If it happened again you might turn round and smack him, but at that time there was too much riding on it, we needed three points to help in our relegation battle.

Besides, we had a manager who asked me to be responsible for the team because he was struggling big time.

Velimir Zajec had been a big player in Yugoslavia, captaining them in the 1982 World Cup, but he wasn't managerial material. He didn't like speaking in front of the group, so instead asked me to carry the team.

I had scored the goal just before half-time to give us the lead and with five minutes to go the scoreline was still 1-0 and you are thinking how important these points could be to us.

And then it happened.

Diouf tried to get a penalty and there was absolutely nothing happening. He had run into the box, I was next to him, and all of a sudden he fell down. It was just ridiculous.

My response was asking him if he should pack football in and work in theatre in the West End, something like that, I didn't even swear at him.

Then I turned and walked away and all of a sudden he was stood next to me and made a noise and spat straight into my face - and ran off.

I was angry, really angry, the ball was somewhere else so I chased him initially to try to smack him yet while I was doing that it occurred to me I shouldn't allow myself to be sent off by this fool. He was not going to get what he wanted.

Even now there are moments when I've thought 'I should have smacked him' but I didn't - and I am glad.

A few months after it occurred I was still receiving letters from Bolton fans apologising - and I have kept those letters.

Many of them were saying they were ashamed of Diouf and thought the way I reacted was brilliant. That meant a lot to me, they weren't even Pompey fans.

The return fixture was played in May 2005, our last Fratton Park match of the season, and the fair play thing had just started where the players lined-up and shook hands with the opposition before the game.

I refused to shake his hand. Diouf never apologised, even before the game he hadn't come up to me and the one thing I wasn't going to do was shake his hand.

Why should I shake somebody's hand who doesn't know the meaning of fair play? It turned out quite a few of my team-mates wouldn't do it either, not that I had asked them to, it was up to them how they felt about it.

That turned out to be my last-ever Pompey league appearance at Fratton Park - three months later I had joined Wigan for a second spell.

When Perrin took over in April 2005, I walked over and introduced myself and from the first moment we shook hands he backed away a little bit and I thought 'I am not sure about this guy'.

I went home later that day and told my wife my fears. Sometimes you shake somebody's hand and look them in the eye and think 'okay' - but not with him.

Something clicked with Harry and other managers, their job is to make tough decisions, decisions sometimes you don't appreciate, but that's okay.

The year we won promotion to the Premier League, Harry looked at Linvoy Primus and thought 'Hmm I don't think he is good enough', but the players knew if we showed we were up to it he would give us a chance.

Linvoy went on to play nearly every game at the back with me that season.

With Perrin I never had that feeling for one second and was proven right, which was a shame. The way he talked to me, how looked at me, the things he said, you could tell.

I loved it at Pompey, I had no intention of leaving, but when you get a manager who doesn't play you and there's another manager who would love to have you in his Premier League team then you have to think about it.

When a new manager comes in it's understandable he wants to follow his own mind and do what he thinks is best for the team. But one of the biggest problems with Perrin was he would say something to you and then do something else.

For example, the manager says 'Listen, I am not going to play you but you are very important to me and you will be featuring in the next game'. Then the next game you aren't featuring, nor the game after that.

Then you go back to him and he says 'I need you, you are just not fit enough', so you prove you are fit enough and he still doesn't play you.

You do that to a player and it won't be long before he can't trust the manager.

The worst thing you can do as a manager is not tell the truth, the best thing you can do is say 'I'm not playing you today because I think the other guy is better' or whatever.

It is hard to take as a player, you want to know where you stand, but it became impossible with Perrin, he was so two-faced.

People like myself, Steve Stone and Linvoy had been there before so when you get a slap on the cheek you can take that as long as you get a chance to go forward.

However, if you keep being lied to that is ridiculous. You think to yourself 'I'm not putting it in for this guy anymore because I don't get anything from him'.

You lose the dressing room, as they say, and he did that big time.

Perrin would speak a lot of French with his little squadron of French players. Now there was nothing wrong with these players, some of them were pretty good, but as a manager you cannot speak to players in French but then not speak to the English ones.

It causes upset, you had to involve everybody.

There have been a few clubs he has been at now where he has not finished the job, you have to wonder why.

He kept telling me 'You are very important, you are my captain, you will feature in my team', yet for the whole of his first pre-season in the summer of 2005 I started three matches.

I came on as a substitute and scored against Bournemouth late on and the fans were brilliant to be fair.

The next game I got five minutes against Inter Milan, just to make sure I wasn't on the pitch long enough to score again, and I thought 'Right this is not going anywhere', while people were also asking what was happening to me.

I was at an age where I had to play. When you come to a certain age and spend too much time on the bench you are not going to get in the team again.

When you are young you can wait your time, but I was an established first-team player and the current The News/Sports Mail Player of the Season. I just didn't get any chance to show what I could do.

So in the August I told Perrin: 'If you are not going to play me just let me go. I want to play and would love to play at Pompey but you are never going to give me a chance. You have told me you would and you haven't, so I can't trust you anymore'.

Around that time I knew Wigan had put an offer in for me. Their manager, Paul Jewell, was aware I wasn't going to be playing and did it the way it should be done and approached the club.

I met our chairman, Milan Mandaric, and asked if he would please let me go, I wanted to play and there was no way I was going to get a chance under this guy.

After a bit he said 'It's okay, you can go, it's a shame because I want you to stay at the club'.

Great, he had agreed, but then Perrin wouldn't sign the form to release me, instead insisting I sat on the bench for the opening game of the season against Tottenham Hotspur!

Wigan wanted me signed so I could play against Chelsea that same weekend - and he refused. Even though the chairman agreed, Perrin had refused.

We had a bit of an argument in his office at the Wellington Sports Ground, I actually really lost my temper. It was the first time I have called a manager proper names, never before had that happened.

Eventually he signed the form that same day but instructed I left there and then and not show my face at the training ground again.

By that time the lads had already started training, so I had to leave through the back door to avoid any confrontations. That was it, I was out.

I obviously met a few of the lads afterwards, but never really had chance to say goodbye, not to the fans either. It was really odd - and that day I drove to Wigan and signed for them.

Going to the DW Stadium turned out to be a good move for me but wasn't the way I wanted to leave Pompey because I had such a good time there. It felt really bad departing like that, almost in a sinister way.

Around four months later Perrin got the sack and Harry had returned to the club.

Towards the end of that season, in April 2006, Pompey visited us knowing a win would secure their Premier League future.

I was actually out injured after breaking my collarbone two weeks earlier at Newcastle United and in a way that was good.

It turned out to be perfect for me because I didn't have to play my old team and potentially be part of them going down. I didn't choose to be injured but was happy to be for that game, I had no part in anything and luckily it was good enough for Pompey to stay up.

After the game I went down to congratulate them all, I was very happy for my old club and the supporters.

A few months after I left Pompey, Tony Blair named me as one of his unsung heroes of the Premier League, which came out of the blue!

He was on BBC's Football Focus and told Manish Bhasin: 'He's really strong, never gives up. I could do with him at the whips' office'.

I was quite amazed and obviously the first question I got afterwards was 'Do you vote Labour?' - which I didn't. I didn't vote Labour but the Prime Minister voted for me!

At the time I had lived in England for 10 years so was allowed to vote and had gone for the Liberal Democrats.

Shortly after Blair said those lovely things about me I was approached by the local Labour party in Wigan who were having a conference, with the Prime Minister attending as an honorary guest - I declined the invite!

I didn't want to get involved. You go and shake his hand and it would be like you were supporting Labour and at the time I was not politically involved, even though I thought he was a very good character.

I did vote Labour later, however, although that wasn't because of Blair!

Looking back, those days at Fratton were wonderful and as long as the fans know I appreciated them very much, that is the main thing.

As supporters go, there are not many I have met better than Pompey's.

BISHOPS
PRINTERS
8

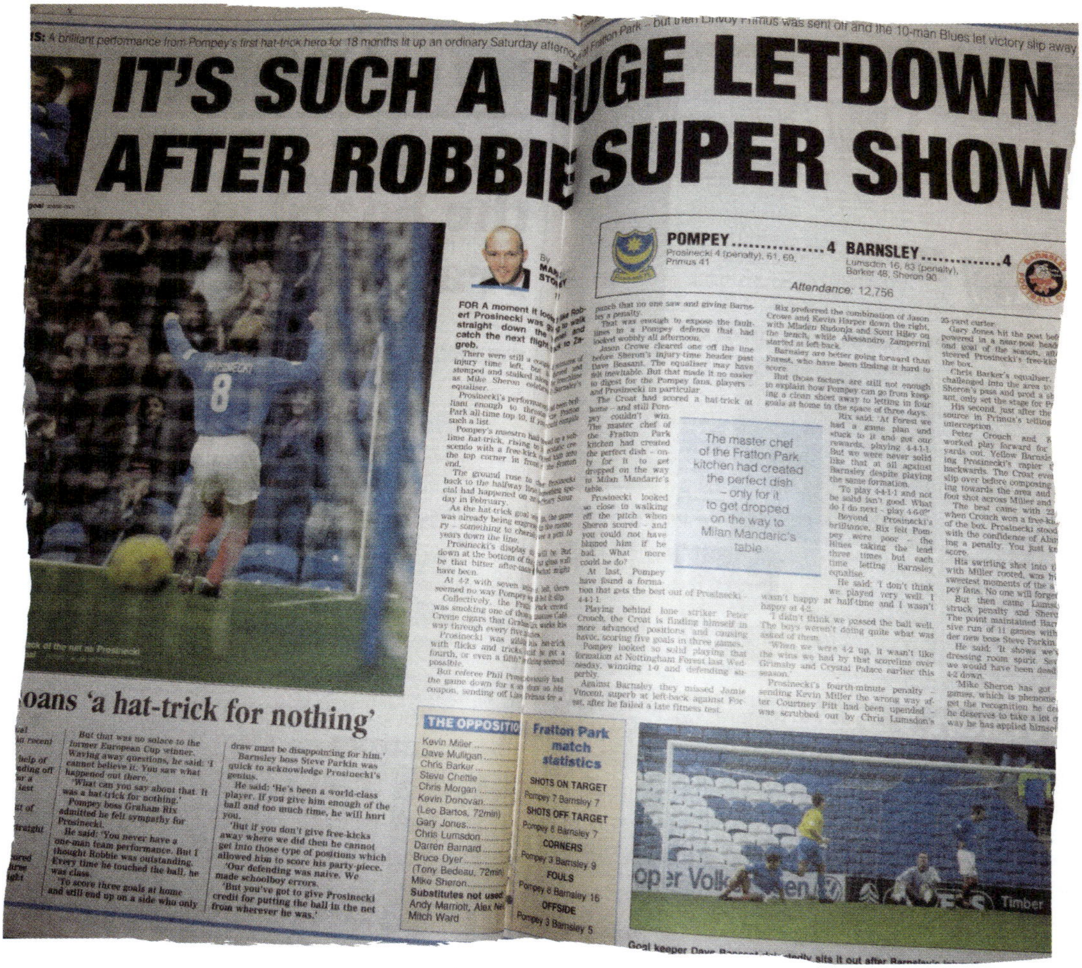

IT'S SUCH A HUGE LETDOWN AFTER ROBBIE SUPER SHOW

POMPEY .... 4 BARNSLEY 4

Prosinecki 4 (penalty), 61, 69, Primus 41

Lumsdon 16, 83 (penalty), Barker 48, Sheron 90

Attendance: 12,756

The master chef of the Fratton Park kitchen had created the perfect dish - only for it to get dropped on the way to Milan Mandaric's table.

...oans 'a hat-trick for nothing'

THE OPPOSITION

Kevin Miller, Dave Mulligan, Chris Barker, Steve Chettle, Chris Morgan, Kevin Donovan (Leo Bartos, 72min), Gary Jones, Chris Lumsdon, Darren Barnard, Bruce Dyer (Tony Bedeau, 72min), Mike Sheron

Substitutes not used: Andy Marriott, Alex Ne..., Mitch Ward

Fratton Park match statistics

SHOTS ON TARGET	Pompey 7 Barnsley 7
SHOTS OFF TARGET	Pompey 6 Barnsley 7
CORNERS	Pompey 3 Barnsley 9
FOULS	Pompey 6 Barnsley 16
OFFSIDE	Pompey 3 Barnsley 5

Robert **Prosinecki**

35 games, nine goals (August 2001 - April 2002)

Pompey 4 (Prosinecki 3, Primus)
Barnsley 4 (Lumsdon 2, Barker, Sheron)

Division One, Fratton Park, Saturday, February 2, 2002

Pompey: Beasant, Crowe, Primus, Buxton, Zamperini, Harper, Derry, O'Neil, Pitt (85 mins Hiley), Prosinecki, Crouch.

Subs Not Used: Tardif, Curtis, Rudonja, Lovell.

Attendance; 12,756

Football took me to Barcelona, Real Madrid, Red Star Belgrade as well as the World Cup finals three times.

Yet it was Fratton Park which staged the only hat-trick of my playing career.

I had scored two goals in a game plenty of times but never three - until Barnsley visited in February 2002.

It would also prove to be the final occasion I achieved it before my retirement.

My good friend Milan Mandaric had brought me to Pompey on a free transfer in August 2001 when he learned I wanted a fresh challenge after spending the previous season with Standard Liege in Belgium.

Playing in England interested me, although I did represent Croatia in this country at the 1996 European Championships.

Milan is a great man and a good person who I still keep in touch with, at the time it seemed the right decision to come to the south coast and join his new football club.

He described me as 'a gift to the fans' when I signed. I'm not sure about that!

However, he explained what was going to happen at the club and I liked the sound of it. It really appealed to me and I knew it was time to leave Belgium after 21 games and four goals for Liege.

After I signed I was given a tour of the city along with my family, we also visited Chichester and Port Solent, we liked looking around the marina, and Portsmouth was a very pretty city, somewhere I wanted to be.

I really enjoyed my year with the Blues and felt I had a very good relationship with those noisy supporters. I can still hear them now singing 'Play up Pompey'!

Coming into that Barnsley game I had scored in successive matches - a 3-2 defeat at home to Wolverhampton Wanderers and a late winner in a 1-0 victory at Nottingham Forest.

Then it was onto the Tykes and a fixture during which I would score a hat-trick for nothing. I didn't even want the match ball after the final whistle!

It would take just four minutes for us to break the deadlock, Courtney Pitt being fouled and I sent Kevin Miller the wrong way from the penalty spot.

We would have the lead for just 12 minutes before Chris Lumsdon curled in an equaliser from 25-yards. It was a good goal, a really good goal.

Just before half-time we were back in front when Pitt steered my free-kick back into the box and Linvoy Primus headed home at the near post.

The match was up and down and Chris Barker equalised for Barnsley on 48 minutes when he collected Mike Sheron's pass and slotted the ball past Dave Beasant.

We were attacking the Fratton end in that second half and it makes me happy to remember my second and third goals came during that period, ensuring my hat-trick would come in front of the home supporters.

My second goal - which gave us a 3-2 lead - arrived on 61 minutes when Peter Crouch and Kevin Harper worked the ball to me 30-yards out.

It was pleasing to see the Barnsley defenders standing off and allowing me room, I even slipped at one point, but was able to carry on and then hit a left-foot shot.

My attempt struck the inside of the post on its way into the net and the cheer was deafening. The fans seemed to enjoy that one!

The hat-trick, my first and only ever hat-trick, was completed in the 69th minute after Crouch had been fouled just outside the penalty area.

I knew what to do and sent a right-foot shot into the top corner with the goalkeeper, Miller, unable to move and the score was 4-2.

How I wish the match could have ended there and then, I am sure the fans felt the same, but there were 21 minutes remaining and it didn't turn out that happy for any of us.

You wonder how you can score three goals and still not win a match? You don't think it is possible, but it happened that day, and in the last seven minutes of the match. Incredible.

In the 83rd minute Primus was sent off for apparently throwing a punch at one of their players with Lumsdon scoring from the penalty and also leaving us to play with 10 men.

Then in stoppage time, Sheron scored a header and we no longer had a win, it was a point.

I was a little bit angry afterwards, I admit that, and didn't even ask to keep the match ball. We didn't win so it didn't seem right. I was very annoyed.

To be 4-2 up and draw 4-4 is football, that is life, but it would be the only hat-trick of my career, the first and last time, and I couldn't celebrate also getting a win. I was not happy!

I left the dressing room very quickly with Mladen Rudonja, who I am still friends with, he lives in Slovenia now and we talk every single day.

Looking back, though, my memories of this game are very good, despite how it ended. The entire stadium were cheering my name and that is something I will never forget.

My stay at Pompey was only a year but I played good, people liked me and they were really friendly. I had a very, very nice time and thank everyone for that.

When I came to England I was aged 32, Milan was very persuasive and Pompey was the right club for me, it was an enjoyable season and also allowed me to work with Harry Redknapp, who I consider a great manager.

Graham Rix was in charge when I arrived, although I almost didn't get here because there was a problem getting a work permit.

I was told I did not satisfy Home Office criteria that all non-EC nationals should have played in 75 per cent of their country's games over the past two years.

That was stupid. I had stopped playing for Croatia after the 1998 World Cup finals and then changed my mind two years later to play six of their eight most recent games - and was also captain.

However, the Department of Employment ruled I should not get a permit because I'd appeared in only six of Croatia's last 17 matches in total, which was 35 per cent!

The club appealed and Harry attended a tribunal in Manchester, with Scotland manager Craig Brown also writing a letter, and finally I was allowed to play in this country.

The delay, though, and a game for Croatia against the Republic of Ireland meant I missed the first match of the 2001-02 season at Wolves.

By the time it came to the second game against Bradford City at Fratton Park, I had trained only twice for my new club and was named as substitute that day.

I came on for the final 16 minutes for Shaun Derry and it was disappointing because we lost 1-0 through an Eoin Jess goal. All the same, I had experienced the ground for the first time and that was a special feeling.

One of my earliest matches which stands out for me was a 4-2 win over Grimsby Town in August 2001 after I had got into an argument with the Croatian football Federation.

I had turned down training with the national side ahead of a World Cup qualifier with Scotland to play for my club and am so glad I did.

Mark Burchill and Peter Crouch each scored twice, and I had a hand in both of Peter's goals in the second half. It was a super match, the fans were so noisy and I really enjoyed it.

I was starting to love the Fratton Park atmosphere and couldn't believe during the visit of Colchester United in our previous home game how the supporters were still trying to encourage us when we were losing.

We weren't proud of that performance and lost 2-1, but they still backed us. You don't see that at many places.

I had always respected English football as among the best in the world and it didn't worry me the ground was different to the Bernabeu or Nou Camp where I had played before.

I remember once watching Pompey play on television with my brother, Daniel, and the fans did not stop singing and clapping throughout the game - even when they let in a goal.

There is that passion also at Barcelona and Madrid but, of course, there are many more fans in a bigger ground in Spain.

Yet passion for the club comes from the heart in the same way it does over there.

In the end we weren't doing well enough under Rix so he left in March 2002 following a goalless Fratton Park draw with Sheffield Wednesday in which I was a substitute.

Harry, who had been the club's director of football, took over for the final five matches, although I missed his first match away at Preston North End as I was playing for Croatia against Slovenia.

I was also away on international duty for a fixture against Watford, but played in his other three games that season, including the final match at Manchester City.

During that time I could see Harry was very good at his job and it was no surprise to me he managed to take the club into the Premier League the following season when they won the Division One title in style.

When my countryman Niko Kranjcar had the chance to come to Pompey in August 2006 and work with Harry, I advised him to take it up and not let the chance pass him by. I knew the club would be right for him.

I was assistant to head coach Slaven Bilic for Croatia at the time and was happy he listened to me - I proved I was right!

Niko went on to do very well at Fratton Park, winning the FA Cup in 2008, and later followed Harry to Tottenham Hotspur and QPR.

At the end of that 2001-02 season, Harry wanted me to stay with Pompey and I was still contracted for another year, but wanted to try Japan and Grampus Eight were interested.

I had a one-year get-out clause in my Blues contract and the plan was I would stay in Japan after the 2002 World Cup finals and play in the J-League where I would get a longer deal and another challenge.

Unfortunately, that fell through and with my father ill back home in Zagreb I wanted to be closer to him so joined NK Olimpija Ljubljana, who played in Slovenia, a country which borders Croatia.

It wasn't that I was desperate to leave Pompey, I was settled in Fareham with my wife, Vlatka, and two-year-old daughter, Leonarda, and the climate was not too bad. In England there is too much rain, but Portsmouth was okay!

My wife speaks perfect English, which helped us during our year on the south coast. We now have two daughters, both of which attend an international school in Zagreb so can speak English.

I am the only one in our family who has a problem with it, I can speak a little bit!

For me England is a footballing country, with lots of supporters, and Fratton Park may be little but I thought the ground was perfect, it could get so loud sometimes, especially when they sang 'Play up Pompey'.

We finished 17th in my only season at the club and had good players like Crouch, Harper, Derry, Primus and Nigel Quashie, I enjoyed playing with them.

Behind the scenes we had the kitman Kev McCormack, a big man and former boxer. I really liked him, a very good man who made us smile a lot.

Pompey still has a place in my heart, I had a very happy year, I was made to feel very welcome by the fans, the players and all the staff, they looked after me and I appreciated that.

Even now I look out for their results, I can promise the wonderful fans I have not forgotten about you.

And yes, I still smoke!

PORTSMOUTH F.C.

News Sport

SOUTH COAST KINGS

Pompey take chances to grab Dell glory

SAINTS 0, POMPEY 2

POMPEY handed Saints a lesson in soccer's most priceless art of chance taking to win yesterday's High Noon clash at the Dell.

Barry Horne and Terry Connor struck clinical goals to give the Fratton fans the victory they most wanted against their South Coast neighbours.

By MIKE NEASOM

But before, between, and after their first half strikes Saints drove their supporters to despair by tossing away a series of gilt-edged opportunities — and then completed the job in the second half when they twice failed to hit an empty net from ten yards.

So, in the end Saints could not complain at becoming the fall-guys in Pompey's second away win of the season.

For much of a match lacking the frenzy and passion which so often goes with derbies, they never managed to stamp any authority on things.

They failed because their midfield was never allowed a moment's respite by the busy work of Mick Kennedy, Horne, and Kevin Dillon — and because a lively, and towards the end outrageously cheeky, Vince Hilaire tormented the hapless Steve Baker.

They also failed because Danny Wallace, looking far from fully fit after his ...

Yet for all that, had Clarke and Wallace, two men in the First Division's list of top marksmen, finished with even Fourth Division proficiency, they might still have denied Alan Ball's men the win they so desperately needed.

They had seven or perhaps eight glorious chances but only once managed even to get a shot on target.

Pompey were significantly more efficient. They had perhaps the two they took and an early half-chance in the first half; two more in the second, one of which John Burridge saved with a desperately lunging boot and the other which skimmed an inch or so wide of the post.

So Pompey deserved their first victory at the Dell since February 1964 — and the points which lifted them out of the bottom three and level with Coventry, Derby ...

● LOOK WHAT I'VE DONE ... Pompey's Barry Horne waits for the accolade after opening the scoring at the Dell yesterday. Photo sales no.— B2003-1.

...RATION TIME ... Terry Connor turns away in triumph after scoring Pompey's ...al at The Dell yesterday. Picture by MURRAY SANDERS. Photo sales no. — C2003-4.

...ll's special day

Bradford in shock move for Kennedy

POMPEY are prepared to sell Kennedy to Second Division promotion Bradford City for £250,000.

No comment

Sex tycoon

Mick **Kennedy**

149 games, five goals (June 1984 - January 1988)

Southampton 0
Pompey 2 (Horne, Connor)

Division One, The Dell, Sunday, January 3, 1988

Pompey: Knight, Whitehead, Ball, Blake, Hardyman, Dillon, Kennedy, Horne, Hilaire, Quinn, Connor.

Subs Not Used: Gilbert, Baird.

Attendance; 17,002

Alan Ball walked into The Pompey pub, glanced over to me and uttered 'You're gone'.

It was a Tuesday, that was always a bitch of a day, we knew what was coming from the manager, he would train us hard, give us a really tough running session.

Still, we had the Wednesday off so us players would start drinking from the afternoon onwards, commencing in the pub next to Fratton Park, although we would begin by ordering only halves, what with it being so close to the club.

That particular Tuesday, Bally had made his way down from the office, came through the pub and just turned round to me in front of everyone and said 'You're gone'.

My first thought was 'What's he on about there?'. I would later discover I was being sold to Bradford City.

Not that Bally wanted me to leave, our chairman, John Deacon, was bailing out, he wanted his money back and having originally paid £100,000 had the chance to cash in on £250,000.

We were a cool bunch and when he said those words to me I didn't twig, I thought I was there for life.

I was three-and-a-half years into a four-year deal and thought there was a contract around the corner for me. Obviously not.

At the time I was only 26, so my legs couldn't have gone, but it was for other reasons and the way Bally said those words sticks in the mind. That was him though, always straight.

Regardless, I didn't know Southampton at The Dell was going to be my last game.

We were in the dressing room before that January 1988 match and Kenny Swain had been dropped so I had the captaincy given to me - after it had been taken off me in the first place!

Kenny had the biggest hump that game, but when they took the captaincy off me almost 18 months earlier he was the one who came up and said 'Mick, it's only a toss of a coin mate, don't be putting transfer requests in!'.

Work that one out, but that was Bally, he was like that, you never knew what was going to happen the next day, but he was honest, straight as a die, called a spade a spade.

So there I was, captain again in a big fixture like Southampton and up against one of my idols in Jimmy Case.

I don't think we played well in that game, we were lucky, it was just one of those matches where it went for us and we won 2-0.

Maybe with me going it was on the cards and God was looking down on me to get us the win, but we didn't play that well.

Barry Horne opened the scoring on 16 minutes, then Terry Connor got another seven minutes later and that was it, we had our victory in the local derby.

Bally had bought Barry for £60,000 from Wrexham, that was his eye for a player, and he went on to be a right decent midfielder, willing to run, wasn't frightened of hard work and would get 59 caps for Wales.

I recall Kevin Dillon giving me a ball in the last minute of the game and it was short. Case came in and booted me.

I turned round to Dill and shouted 'Are you some kind of idiot or what?', Dill wouldn't say a word though.

Boy was I sore, that hurt me, especially as it came from Jimmy, I didn't want him to kick me. I wouldn't have minded kicking him, but for him to kick you, well he knew how to kick a player.

The referee never blew his whistle either - and I came off limping thanks to Dill.

Yet I didn't know it was going to be my last game, weird isn't it?

On the Tuesday, Kenny Swain was going up to Liverpool so I got a lift to Heathrow with him to catch a plane to Leeds Bradford Airport. By the Friday I had joined the Bantams.

I had played at Halifax Town and Huddersfield Town so knew the area, in that respect it wasn't a big move for me. I was also married at the time and my wife was from Middlesbrough so she was happy with it being nearer her home.

Bradford were a talented team, good players like Stuart McCall, John Hendrie and Ian Ormondroyd, and if we had drawn the last game of the season at home to Ipswich Town we would have got promoted to the First Division - we lost it.

I didn't want to leave Pompey, though, I was sad to go, I had made a lot of friends.

Jack Charlton had a saying 'Three-and-a-half to four years at one club is long enough'. I never felt like that at Fratton Park, I honestly thought I would stay forever.

It was only because of the chairman bailing out that I went, don't forget Mr Deacon was 75 years of age trying to get every penny he could back into his own pocket.

Yes, I was upset, but it was out of my hands and I was heading back to a place I knew.

Maybe I would have been bitter if I was going to Wales, but I was moving to Yorkshire and knew all about that area, I had friends there, it wasn't as if I was starting all over again.

I had been Bally's third signing upon becoming manager in June 1984 and that was down to Mickey Baxter.

God bless him, he was a great friend of mine and later died of Hodgkin's disease in 1989.

After leaving Middlesbrough and signing for Pompey that summer he put a good word in and, with Boro having to sell because they were skint, two weeks later I was also recruited.

He must have told Bally I was a right, horrible so-and-so who liked winning - and boy did I like winning!

You can ask all the players in that team, speak to them one-by-one from that era, they hated training against me, and yet if I didn't do it Bally would be on my case.

He loved to see me kicking everyone, Kevin Dillon wouldn't come near me on the training pitch, he would say 'You are mad'!

Bally was a star in my eyes and I will never forget our fourth game back in Division One in August 1987.

We got hammered at Arsenal 6-0 and afterwards he sat on a medical table in the middle of the Highbury dressing room and said 'Gentlemen, welcome to the First Division!'.

In other words wake up, this isn't Division Two any more, this is a big league - and he had his flat cap on and was pulling it down as he spoke.

I had his father as a manager as well when first starting out as a 16-year-old at Halifax, they were a ringer for each other, had the same habits.

Alan Ball Senior was a character in his own right and would shout at me every, single day 'Mick, where's my oil?'

In the treatment room there was a bottle of cooking oil the lads would put on their legs, but he would get me to squeeze it into his hand so he could rub it onto his ginger head.

When I was at Pompey under his son years later, I was always the brunt of everything. I remember being 4-0 up at home to Fulham on New Year's Day 1985, yet it ended 4-4 and we were fuming when we came in - Bally blamed me!

There were little things like that. I never used to answer him back, nobody did actually, but there was a spell of six months when I didn't talk to him.

It was over him taking the captaincy off me in July 1986, I had the hump with that.

One night a gang of us were out in Portsmouth and Bally just came out with it 'You might not be skipper next year', I said 'You are joking aren't you?' and he replied 'No, the chairman thinks your disciplinary record isn't good enough'.

I went home, got a pen and bit of paper out and wrote a letter saying I wanted to leave the club because I wasn't happy. I'd made up my mind, I was off, and handed it to him the next day.

Do you think he would let me go? Not a hope, and he didn't care if I spoke to him or not as long as I went out on the park on a Saturday and grafted.

He knew if I didn't graft and get around the park and tackle people I wasn't worth it - and he knew I wouldn't let him down.

The reason about the disciplinary record was a load of rubbish, it was about him thinking I would be a better player without the responsibility of being skipper. That was my assumption, but I know it was for that reason.

After six months of me not talking to him we did make our peace, though.

Under Bally we would finish in the top four of Division Two for three successive years, that takes some doing, an achievement on its own.

We had a good squad, we were young, we were fit, had a great manager and let's not forget Graham Paddon either, who was Bally's assistant and didn't get enough credit.

We had a great camaraderie and as long as you didn't go out together on a Thursday or Friday night it didn't matter to Bally because he was twice as bad as us - 'socialising' he called it!

Bally saw it as building team spirit and the modern players still do that now, they tell the chairmen and directors they are going away training for a few days for a change of scenery, but it is nothing of the sort!

There were times we would visit Jersey for three days and Gordon Neave would pack the boots, training kit and balls, but none of them would leave the coach!

We never saw Bally for three days, while we would be on the lash all the time. Then we would return on the Thursday, go out on the Saturday for the match and win.

Although once we travelled to Jersey to watch Steve Davis play an exhibition snooker match and got bladdered, coming back the next day and straight into training, but none of us could stand up let alone train!

Bally got the hump and turned round and shouted 'Clear off, I don't want to see you until tomorrow'. I think we had only been at the training ground for 10 minutes.

I can't recall if we won, lost or drew that next match, maybe I would have remembered if we lost.

They were incredible times, but we were all together. On Wednesdays we drank at the Sportsman's Rest in Copnor Road, it's not there any more.

There were never any women in there, while all the men were tattooed up to the nines, but we knew it wouldn't get back to Bally, I bet he didn't even know where it was.

Running the Sportsman's were two Welsh lads who would make a plate of ham sandwiches for us out the back and we would spend all day there.

On one occasion, there was a yard of ale hanging on the wall and Gary Stanley - a great lad - came up with the idea of us all going for it.

There were about 10 of us, each trying to neck it in one, and Gary was the only one who did it.

The Bird In The Hand at Lovedean was another, we used to slaughter that place, it was our Sunday gaff. The three humdingers of myself, Mick Tait and Alan Knight were always there, while on Wednesdays we would also go to the Cowplain Social Club.

Most of us lived around those areas, with myself, Noel Blake and Kevin O'Callaghan on the same estate in Lovedean and we would take it in turns driving to training in the morning.

Another favourite drinking time was on the bus coming back from games, with every trip five, six or seven hours, so by the time we got home we were hammered.

During my first three seasons at the club we never lost many games, so as captain it was fine me going up to Bally on the coach, usually with Knightsie by my side, and say 'Gaffer, can we stop off at an off licence?'.

He would allow it as long as we got him two bottles of red wine and two big cigars!

We were earning decent money then and everyone had to put £20 in the kitty, you imagine how much beer that would buy. Although young lads like Paul Hardyman or Kevin Ball didn't put in.

So we would get 48 cans of lager, white wine, the gaffer wanted his two bottles of red, Graham Paddon liked a red wine, Peter Osgood would drink cat's wee, it didn't matter to him.

You had to get Kenny Swain a bottle of red wine, he had to be seen doing the same as Brian Clough.

Knightsie and I would also sit on the backseat of the coach and smoked, there were a lot of smokers in that group believe it or not, five or six of us in total.

Jim Sloan was a director and would come to chat with us with this big cigar on him and was always drunk. It wouldn't be Jim if he wasn't drunk, he would be drunk before we left the ground.

He would come to the back of the bus and call me 'Kennedy' and I would say 'Jim, will you stop calling me Kennedy and just call me Mick will you' and he replied 'Respect son, respect'.

Jim was an Army man and when he died in January 2011 I got a document through which stated he was born in Belfast. I had a lot of time for the fella and he never told me that, being a Paddy myself I would have been happy as a pig in mud knowing that!

There was such a wonderful camaraderie at the club between everyone, including the staff in The Pompey pub, while there were great characters like Jim and Mr Deacon - who I had great respect for.

I have to say, though, I did bring good habits to the club, Kevin Ball wouldn't have been a player without me, that is where I give myself a bit of credit, and Paul Hardyman as well. I looked after the young lads.

Admittedly I was horrible, a nasty piece of work, but wasn't off the park and people couldn't understand that.

You know they say when some people cross the white line they turn into a monster, well that was me from day one, right from as a kid.

My parents are Irish farmers so I was brought up tough and also raised in Salford, I could look after myself.

I had two good feet and was quick over five yards, lightning, nobody could touch me over that distance, and as soon as I got that tackle in players knew about it.

What I did was scare opponents by my reputation, while I would also say nasty things to them, anything that got me an advantage I would say. It didn't matter who they were.

Once I asked a player, who I won't name, 'Can you open a tin of beans for me?' because he had a right beak on him. That was only three on a scale of 10 of what I used to say to opponents!

I could upset the Queen. Bally knew that, he didn't give me grief over it, he wanted me to, he knew if I was doing those sort of things the chances were we would win.

Kevin Dillon used to laugh at some of the stuff I came out with towards opponents, Mick Tait was the same, he found it really funny.

I never went to a PFA awards or anything like that. I wouldn't go, I thought I would probably get a good hiding if I did. Not that I ever got voted in any representative teams, but I never went, all the other lads did, though.

If I had gone there would have been a war on. It's alright sitting in that room, but come 11pm or midnight it could easily start up.

Vinnie Jones was frightened of his life with me.

When I was at Stoke City years after Pompey, myself, Wayne Biggins and Billy Whitehurst were drinking in the players' lounge at Sheffield United and Vinnie came in and was looking at me in admiration as if 'Oh look, it's Mick Kennedy'.

It was embarrassing really, he was like a little puppy, I couldn't believe it. We were drinking pints of lagers and port and brandy, maybe that frightened him.

While at Pompey I won two caps for the Republic of Ireland under Jack Charlton, who had previously managed me at Middlesbrough.

Now Jack couldn't coach a fish supper, but just had something about him.

He would wear a pair of wellingtons at training, a khaki green jacket and checked shirt and never coached, not once.

In May 1986 I received a call-up to a triangular tournament held in Reykjavik also involving Iceland and Czechoslovakia, as they were named at the time.

It was a great trip, a fantastic booze-up, even though there was no drink in Iceland at the time, everything was non-alcoholic. Not that it stopped us getting our hands on it.

Now I was quick getting dressed after a game but you have never seen anything like Paul McGrath, he would be stood at the bar having a pint of lager containing an Irish drink called Poitin, which is the colour of vodka and twice as strong. We all got smashed that night.

We beat Iceland 2-1 and then defeated Czechoslovakia 1-0 and all the Eire directors were over the moon, it was the first thing they had won in their life, although I fell out with Jack and never played for them again.

In that Czech game I battered someone, broke him in two, and had his tooth stuck in my elbow.

After the match a couple of their players thought they were dining in the same room as us and who should come through this door but this fella.

Gerry Daly spotted him and shouted 'Do you want a bowl of soup?'. We were in bits, although obviously they couldn't understand Gerry!

Over the years I have been told of the Pompey fans' affection for me but I never thought for one minute I did anything different, I just thought I was Joe Soap, I really did.

I never got carried away with it, I had a couple of decent games against Glenn Hoddle and the like so you think you have shown up well.

In my career I ended up playing more than 550 games so can't have been that bad, it's just I never thought I was that good, simply part of the team.

I would class Kevin O'Callaghan and Vince Hilaire as top quality. I used to enjoy playing with them, it was great for me, just give them the ball and watch them do the magic.

Micky Quinn wasn't the greatest player in the world but knew where the goal was, Kenny Swain was a fantastic pro, I enjoyed Taity's presence around me, he was as strong as an ox, as brave as a lion.

Dill had that special thing about him like Cally and Vince, he could also score a penalty. I often joked with him 'If you couldn't take a penalty you wouldn't be in the team you fat so-and-so'.

Blakey could kill you, the only one who could get away with murder with him was me. I used to slaughter him!

They were great times and while I didn't get the chance to say goodbye, hopefully the fans know I didn't want to leave after that Southampton match.

ty
10

24 The News, Monday, August 19, 2002

POMPEY: There were echoes of seasons past as two goals were shipped before half-time, but that only served to set up a stirring comeback at Selhurst

C PALACE .. 2
Dougie Freedman 40
Tony Popovic 42

POMPEY .. 3
Hayden Foxe 68
Jason Crowe 69, 72

Attendance: 18,315

Scenes of pure joy at Selhurst Park as Pompey stage a brilliant comeback...

Left: Hayden Foxe lands on the back of Arjan De Zeeuw as he celebrates his first goal for Pompey – giving Redknapp's men a lifeline at 2-1

Right: Jason Crowe is hauled back by Richard Hughes and Matthew Taylor after netting Pompey's winner

Far right: That man Crowe's jumping for joy after putting Pompey level following his second-half introduction

PICTURES: STEVE REID

STAT ATTACK

SHOTS ON TARGET	
PALACE	4
POMPEY	6
SHOTS OFF TARGET	
PALACE	5
POMPEY	3
CORNERS	
PALACE	4
POMPEY	2
FOULS	
PALACE	16
POMPEY	10
OFFSIDE	
PALACE	2
POMPEY	2

CRYSTAL PALACE

SOMETHING TO CROWE ABOUT..

by MARK STOREY reporting from Selhurst Park

FOR MORE than an hour at Selhurst Park, it looked like Pompey had been kidding themselves about title hopes.

Reality seemed to have come crashing down over Pompey's heads in the shape of a Shaun Derry-inspired Crystal Palace.

Promotion? Pompey looked more like a bunch of expensive misfits wilting like spring flowers in the 90 degree south ...

... slowly and silently along the touchline ...

... back and they were dictating things to us. We were second best.

'I wasn't very happy with the defending in the first half or the way we played in the middle of the park.

'So I changed the shape at half-time. I switched it to wing-backs, and we looked much better balanced. The wing-backs pushed up, and it worked a treat.'

Midway through the second half, things had still looked bleak. Svetoslav Todorov, Paul Merson and Taylor had all ...

... Granville before finding ...

... striker went around ... up for help. Who ... Crowe, who bulleted a ... of Palace defenders.

... be too surprised. ... as a striker and once ... goals in a season as a kid.

He now ... to start his first game of the ... against Watford ... Park on Saturday ...

Paul **Merson**

48 games, 12 goals (August 2002 - July 2003)

Crystal Palace 2 (Freedman, Popovic)
Pompey 3 (Foxe, Crowe 2)

Division One, Selhurst Park, Saturday, August 17, 2002.

Pompey: Hislop, Primus, De Zeeuw, Foxe, Taylor, Quashie, O'Neil (46 mins Crowe), Robinson (46 mins Hughes), Merson, Burton, Pericard (22 mins Todorov).

Subs Not Used: Kawaguchi, Burchill.

Attendance; 18,315

I won everything in football at Arsenal bar the Champions League.

There was the FA Cup, the League Cup, the old Division One - which is really a name change from the Premier League - the Cup Winners Cup and the Community Shield.

Yet that 2002-3 season when we won the Division One title at Pompey still goes down as the biggest thing I achieved in my footballing career, without a doubt.

You have got to remember where the club was for the previous 14 years, they hadn't been in the Premier League and spent plenty of that time fighting relegation.

So for Harry Redknapp to put a team together of eight free transfers and play football in the style we did was incredible. We scored bundles and bundles and bundles of goals, everywhere we went we had a go.

Don't get me wrong, the Arsenal team were 100 times better than Pompey, of course we were, it was a different standard of football.

However, for the feat of promotion and getting that many players together to gel that quickly with everybody performing to their ability through the whole season was just phenomenal.

The game I'll always remember was travelling to Crystal Palace for the third game of the season.

My debut was against Nottingham Forest at Fratton Park with a crowd of 18,910 and I have never played in front of anything like that in my life.

I've turned out in a stadium with a crowd of 100,000, appeared in front of 40-50,000 week in, week out, but had never performed to anything like that before.

We won 2-0 that day and the following match was a mid-week 1-1 draw at Sheffield United - then it was onto Selhurst Park.

Now Pompey weren't the best team in the world, I follow my football and they'd always finished in the bottom six or seven, always scrapping, never near the top.

After the first couple of games we'd collected four points and I was thinking 'Here we go, this isn't a bad team at all', I was really encouraged by it.

Then at Palace I'm walking off the pitch at half-time wearing an all-gold kit and we were 2-0 down - honestly it could have been 100-0.

Dougie Freedman was ripping us apart, I will never forget that, he was slaughtering us and had scored the opener while Tony Popovic had grabbed the other.

I headed towards the dressing room thinking 'What the hell have I done? I have come here and it looks like we are going to win a home game every now and again and then get absolutely battered away every week'.

Inside, Harry came steaming into the dressing room, he was fuming. We had been terrible, all over the place, really, really poor, it was unreal.

He shouted: 'Right, you off and you off, we're going three at the back, Jason Crowe you go right wing-back, Matty Taylor you go left wing-back, Merse you in the hole and let's give it a go - get out there and have a right go'.

We went back out for the second half and it was wallop, crash, we absolutely battered them and won 3-2, Hayden Foxe scored and then our substitute Crowe got two, the winner 18 minutes from time.

There must have been thousands of our fans down there at the side of the pitch and they were going completely crazy.

We played three at the back for the rest of the campaign, Linvoy Primus was one of them and never looked back, he was one of the best players that season and I cannot remember when we lost a game after that.

That day at Selhurst Park was down to Harry and people are so disrespectful to him saying he is a wheeler dealer and all that. So disrespectful.

I have worked under a lot of managers in the game and he is one of the most tactically-astute I have played under.

He doesn't mess about. People go on about Jose Mourinho making changes, well Harry didn't waste any time, this game happened before Mourinho came over, he went bang, bang, three at the back - bang.

Harry would always have a go, no matter where we went, the team never sat back, ever, even when we played Manchester United in the FA Cup when we lost 4-1.

I loved working under Harry, he was a different class.

The other game that season which I won't forget was at Millwall in March 2003 where Pompey fans weren't allowed in after crowd trouble the previous campaign.

I was lucky enough to get a standing ovation from the home fans when substituted nine minutes from the end for Lassina Diabate and I still see Millwall fans who say they have been going forever and have never, ever seen that. Never.

We won 5-0 and had four by half-time courtesy of Yakubu (two), Tim Sherwood and Svetoslav Todorov, then I wrapped it up with a second-half penalty.

It was one of those games where everybody played well and everything came off. It wouldn't have mattered who we were playing, we would have beaten them.

Some days you get that, once in a blue moon. That day was like the Harlem Globetrotters.

I am lucky enough when at Aston Villa getting one at Maine Road after beating Manchester City 3-1, but at Millwall? Well, it's a hard place to please and they had no liking for Pompey either, the clubs are big enemies.

After the game I was getting onto the team bus and a 70-year-old bloke came up to me and said 'Blimey Merson, I have been coming to Millwall all my life and have never before seen that'.

You don't forget moments like that, big parts of your footballing career when another team's fans stand up and clap you off. What a compliment.

It's just a shame none of our fans were allowed in because we were so good. Then again, we were a very good team.

Pompey had a lot of money to spend the year before under Graham Rix, buying players for big cash and it never worked out, they struggled badly.

Then all of a sudden Harry came in and goes 'Right I'll get him, you come in and play in the hole, I'll have him and he'll play centre half'.

He doesn't just go out and buy Tom, Dick and Harry and then when he gets them thinks 'Oh no, where am I going to play them all?'. He goes out and gets his team - and that is where he is very good.

As the season went on we also recruited Steve Stone and Tim Sherwood, top, top footballers coming in to play for Harry. They wanted to work with him and the challenge was there to get the club promoted.

I had joined Pompey in August 2002, Graham Taylor didn't want me at Aston Villa, he thought I was a bit too big for the club, he probably assumed I had a big influence there and wanted me out - then Harry rang.

He said: 'I've just come in and got rid of a load of players, I want you to come down for a couple of years and we'll give it a right go'.

There were no other clubs interested in me and it happened so quickly that everyone was shocked. It was the same at Middlesbrough when I left Arsenal and joined them under Bryan Robson, that happened quickly too.

I did have concerns though - I didn't like training.

My wife had just had twins so I didn't really want to move to the south coast for two years, I had already done the travelling lark years before at Middlesbrough.

I wasn't keen on travelling down every day at my age so when Harry contacted me I told him: 'Harry, it's too far from Birmingham, I don't want to be staying away from the wife - at the time - and the kids'.

He said: 'I'll tell you what son, don't train Mondays, don't train Wednesdays, train Fridays when we play up north, but make sure you turn it on on a Saturday'.

I replied: 'Alright, I'll be down in the morning' and that was it.

Harry kept his word from day one. I never trained Mondays, never trained Wednesdays and only trained Fridays when we were up north. I made 48 appearances that season, playing every game bar one, which was away at Forest when I was having injections in my ankle.

When I moved to Walsall a year later I told the manager, Colin Lee, I would also use that schedule there and he said it wasn't a problem, but a couple of the lads got the hump, so I trained every day and hardly played a match. That is why Harry is different class.

At Pompey I stayed at the Solent Hotel in Whiteley every now and again, but generally drove down in the morning from Sutton Coldfield and then back again afterwards.

When we played away I met them on the motorway after training and then we all travelled together to the game.

When I did train I didn't do a lot, played in 8v8s and that was it. You don't need to do a lot, this league is ruthless, game after game after game after game, that is what it is.

After we got knocked out of the FA Cup in January 2003 by Manchester United, when the next round came along we didn't have a fixture so had a free weekend, effectively making it a fortnight without a match.

So I went in to see Harry and said 'I'm struggling with the gambling, can I go into Tony Adams' Sporting Chance Clinic for a week?'. He said: 'Not a problem Merse, of course you can, I'll see you a week on Monday when we'll get ready for the next game'.

I got home and said to the wife 'Pack your bags, we're going to Barbados,' - there was nothing wrong with me!

So we went to Barbados and one day I was walking along the seafront with the wife and the twins and bumped into this Cockney geezer.

He said: 'Hello Merse, how are you?'. I went 'Alright mate, good'. He replied: 'Do you reckon you'll go up?' and I said 'Hopefully we'll hold on, see you later have a nice holiday'.

Now I didn't know this at the time, but he was Harry's best mate and goes straight back to his villa and rings him up.

'Alright Harry, how are you?', he said. 'Okay Dave what about you?', 'Well, I've just been speaking to one of your players, Paul Merson'.

Now Harry thinks I'm having treatment and turns round to him and says 'Dave, what's wrong with you?', 'What do you mean?' 'Well, Merson's in treatment' - 'No he's not, he's in Barbados with his wife!'

Harry never said a word but told me four years later that he knew.

Still, I came back on the Monday and on the Saturday was part of Pompey's side which beat Grimsby Town 3-0 at Fratton Park. That is what he was like, he thought I was happy so let me be.

On match days I didn't usually come out and warm up. It happened only very rarely, I didn't like it, getting all sweaty and then coming back in and sitting around for another 10 minutes before going back out again.

Instead before kick-off I would sit down and have a cup of tea and a chat with Harry!

I remember my first day at Pompey, finishing training and throwing my kit on the floor - suddenly everybody started laughing.

I said 'What are you laughing at?', I was told 'We wash our own kit here'.

My response was 'You are joking aren't you? Where are we? We are Portsmouth Football Club in Division One, we can't wash our own kit!'

I was told we either washed our own kit or the kit man - 'Big' Kev McCormack - did it for £30 a week.

So being clever like I think I am I said 'Right Kev, I'll do you a deal. Clean my kit for nothing and if we go up I'll give you £10,000. If we don't you won't get anything'.

I had to give him £10,000 at the end of the season when we achieved promotion by six clear points!

When you play for Arsenal you win things, so I went to clubs to also try to win things, that was the challenge for me at Pompey, not the money.

I did it with Middlesbrough before in the 1997-98 season when we went on to finish second in the old Division One behind Nottingham Forest and had to win five of our last six games to clinch it, but we did it.

So when I arrived at Fratton Park I knew what you had to do to win at that level and would always look at other teams' scores, watching how they got on and even had my own wall chart.

I would write down results of teams around us who I thought had a chance of being rivals for promotion, like Leicester City, Sheffield United, Reading, teams like that.

Whatever club I played for I could always tell you their fixtures a month in advance. That is our job, that is where you work and you have to be prepared.

When I was manager at Walsall and asked the players who we had the following week they wouldn't have a clue, it was a joke, unbelievable. You should always know who you are playing.

I always say you are only as good as the players around you and at Pompey that season we had good players who I would say all played well above their potential.

You look at Linvoy, if you had said to him before the start of the season he would be starting virtually every game and be the best player he would have laughed at you and said 'I probably won't be here at Christmas if I am being honest'.

He was a million miles away from playing, so to turn it round and come in and play all campaign the way he did was an absolute credit - and they are the stories I like. Phenomenal.

That was the thing, Harry could spot a good player.

We had Matt Taylor who, for me, was an out-and-out winger. He was great going forwards, didn't really want to defend but was brilliant attacking and scored some big goals such as Leicester away and Forest away.

There were three proper central defenders, Harry picking from Arjan De Zeeuw, Linvoy, Hayden Foxe and Gianluca Festa. They all wanted to defend, no airs and graces, that was the way it was.

You had midfielders like Stone, Sherwood and Gary O'Neil, very, very good players who could provide goals.

Then up front there were Yakubu and Toddy who couldn't stop scoring, if you have players who score goals you are always going to be there or thereabouts. It was perfect.

As for me, I had a free role to go and play behind, I was allowed to do whatever I wanted, with defensive midfield players around me who would get you the ball, and it worked, it worked.

When I signed I took a massive wage cut so the deal was if we got promoted Pompey would give me £250,000 as a bonus - and we were head and shoulders above any team in that division.

At the end of that season I had a year left on my contract but it was obvious being back in the Premier League would involve me training a lot more, travelling a lot more and needing to stay down more.

With the greatest respect to the south coast, I didn't want to stay there all the time, my family were in Sutton Coldfield. Besides, I knew it was going to be a lot harder playing-wise.

Our chairman, Milan Mandaric, had already copped the hump with me because I didn't turn up for the end of season open-top bus thing, but my kid was playing football and my family come first. I had done my job anyway.

That was his problem, it wasn't mine, but after returning to pre-season training me and Harry sat down and I said 'Look, I have found my standard of football, mate'.

He had just brought in Teddy Sheringham, which was obviously a really good signing, and it was time for me to leave. No-one threw me out, it was my decision.

Perhaps at the back of my mind there was the temptation of going out at the top with Pompey having secured promotion in style, but it was mainly to do with the family.

I did it at Middlesbrough as well, I went up in the first season and then left for Villa, for me that was job done.

So I departed Fratton Park in July 2003 with the club's blessing, my contract was cancelled, although I had already filmed the Match of the Day opening credits wearing Pompey colours!

It's funny, the other season I was at Northampton Town to watch Pompey play in League Two and supporters were coming up telling me that promotion season was the best they had ever had seen.

You have got to remember the club later won the FA Cup and played in Europe, but people still talk about that campaign, it was so special.

Winning matches, scoring goals wherever we went, packing out houses at home, it was unbelievable.

I loved it.

15

POMPEY IN EUROPE

Not quite a fairy tale ending, but Pompey can hold their heads high

Adams' heroes so close to incredible European upset

NEIL ALLEN at Fratton Park

Kanu turns in Glen Johnson's cross to put Pompey 2-0 up and send Fratton Park ecstatic in the Uefa Cup group game last night

A crestfallen David James after AC Milan's late equaliser

POMPEY 2
Kaboul 62, Kanu 73
AC MILAN 2
Ronaldinho 84, Inzaghi 90
Att: 20,403

MAN IN THE MIDDLE
SERGE GUMIENNY (Belgium)

Sylvain **Distin**

96 games, 0 goals (May 2007 - August 2009)

Pompey 2 (Kaboul, Kanu)
AC Milan 2 (Ronaldinho, Inzaghi)

UEFA Cup, Fratton Park, Thursday, November 27, 2008

Pompey: James, Johnson, Kaboul, Distin, Belhadj, Little (66 mins Mvuemba), Diop, Hughes, A.Traore, Crouch, Kanu (81 mins Davis).

Subs Not Used: Ashdown, Hreidarsson, Pamarot, Wilson.

Attendance; 20,403

When I saw Ronaldinho lining up that free-kick I thought 'That's it, that's it'. You could feel he was going to score - and that is exactly what happened.

I had played with the Brazilian at Paris Saint-Germain for a season years earlier and knew very well what he could produce from that situation.

After training sessions he would stay behind to practice, taking 20-25 free-kicks and hitting them into the top corner of the goal every single time. It was incredible to watch.

Then he was at Fratton Park, yes AC Milan at Fratton, something you would never expect to happen.

I remember before the draw for the group stages of the UEFA Cup the players were talking about the prospect, can you imagine that, playing AC Milan at Fratton Park? We laughed - then later realised it was going to happen.

On that November 2008 night we were 2-0 up when Glen Johnson was adjudged to have fouled Ronaldinho around 30-yards from goal in the 84th minute.

I knew he would score - and seconds later he struck a right-foot shot into the far corner of the net, David James had no chance.

Then two minutes into stoppage-time, Gianluca Zambrotta clipped the ball into the box and Filippo Inzaghi controlled it before poking home the equaliser.

I am not going to lie, at the final whistle it still felt like we had won that game, we were proud to play against a team like AC Milan and very proud to compete against them, which was most important of all. We had competed.

Obviously 2-0 up with six minutes to go you feel you could have won it, but altogether it was a good game for us, there was nothing to regret. What a match.

The atmosphere was always amazing at Fratton Park but the fact we were playing a club like AC Milan sent the fans crazy, with the Milan fans also very good. The whole place was really friendly and really enjoyable.

I can recall it wasn't possible to hear anything between the players when speaking on the pitch, Fratton Park is a small stadium and the supporters are so close so when they are loud, it really is loud.

It felt strange us scoring against them, you don't expect it, you see their players and during the game we were looking at them going 'Wow, I am playing against these guys!'.

What is weird is I can't actually remember our goals! Obviously Younes Kaboul headed home Johnson's right-wing cross in the 62nd minute and then Kanu bundled home another Johnson cross in the 73rd minute, but I've had to look it up since!

What I can recall, though, is the feeling of 'What's going on? Milan are at Fratton Park and we are 2-0 up', you just don't believe it.

I think that is what cost us, we were dreaming and they came back to get the draw.

Despite losing that lead I found it altogether really enjoyable and it is the Pompey match which sticks most in my mind, ahead of Old Trafford, ahead of the 2008 FA Cup final - two fixtures we won.

That European campaign was something amazing for the club, for the fans travelling and for us players. We had a lot of international players, but not many of us had played in Europe so it also meant something to us.

After AC Milan we travelled to Wolfsburg in December and lost 3-2, but that wasn't an enjoyable game. The hotel we stayed in was not great, it was cold and also the first time

I had played against Edin Dzeko, who gave us a good game.

Nothing could match that special atmosphere against AC Milan, though.

People still talk about my tackle in the FA Cup quarter-final at Manchester United in March 2008, but for me I didn't do anything special.

It is not even a tackle to be honest, it wasn't like a sliding challenge where I stretch my leg and hook the ball away from the opposition player.

I couldn't believe Michael Carrick didn't shoot, it was an open goal, he took too much time and missed his opportunity.

In the 70th minute he went past David James and I just went for it, but it wasn't like I could get the ball from his foot, I wasn't close enough, then he just delayed it for a second.

Maybe he didn't see me coming, but it gave me time to put my leg in front and he kicked the ball against me and it bounced away - that's it.

I really didn't feel like that was a good tackle. Sometimes as a defender you do something and think 'Yes, that was good' but in this instance I didn't believe it was anything special, I just went for it, Carrick has taken his time and I got it.

It was 0-0 when it happened, they had been on top and if they had scored that goal it was game over, but it was not down to me, it was down to him missing.

That was a really good and strong United team, 10 of them would be in the side which won the Champions League final against Chelsea two-and-a-half months later and they dominated against us.

Going into it we felt we could win, we were on a decent run with good spirit through the team and knew we could compete, but after 15 minutes realised we would have to defend the whole match.

I cannot remember if we even had a shot on goal before Sulley Muntari netted the winner from the penalty spot in the 78th minute, but we knew we were strong defensively so just kept at it hoping we could counter and score.

Just playing against Manchester United was special at the time and it was an amazing, amazing experience winning there.

Their fans expected a victory and, as they were also well on top of us, expected to score soon. It didn't happen though and all of a sudden we scored a penalty after Tomasz Kuszczak had brought down Milan Baros - then it went quiet!

We had won at Old Trafford, not too many players in the game can say they did that, especially against a Sir Alex Ferguson side.

In the semi-final we saw off West Bromwich Albion 1-0 and funnily enough in the final were in the same position Manchester United had been in when they faced us earlier in the competition.

Everybody expected us to beat Cardiff City at Wembley, but it was a tough game against the Championship side, we had only a few chances, although they also didn't have many themselves.

We didn't have a lot to defend against, while they were really compact so it was difficult for us to break them down.

Maybe for the first 30 minutes you feel like you were going to score one or two goals and come back at half-time 2-0 up, but it didn't happen. Then you start to realise if you want this you have to work hard for it.

Kanu scored the winner in the 37th minute when he finished John Utaka's right-wing cross at the near post and then did that victory dance. Although I am still not sure if he was dancing or actually trying to walk away, he had a very dodgy knee!

Lassana Diarra was, for me, our man of the match at Wembley, what an amazing player he was.

When he signed for us in the January of that season I wasn't sure. He's a good player but I didn't think the type of player we needed at the club.

After three training sessions I was like 'Wow', he just never lost the ball, tackled really well, his passing was amazing, he was a great guy. He had everything.

I got it wrong!

Lass was the engine of the team, he was tackling, scoring goals, passing, getting assists, he was doing everything and looking back at my career was one of the best to have been on my team.

I have played with so many great players over different generations and when people ask me about strikers I often talk about Alan Shearer because for me he was the most impressive one.

You can compare him to Didier Drogba and Thierry Henry and people don't really get it, but I played with him at Newcastle United and against him and I can say he was one of the finest.

In terms of midfielders, Lass is right up there.

He used to just come, train and go. Obviously we always had a laugh, but he wasn't one for talking loudly in the dressing room, he was just quiet, did his job and left.

Lass had so much energy, he dribbled past players easily, he really had everything and that centre midfield of him and Sulley was an amazing partnership.

As a defender, when you have those in front of you you feel you can win anything, Sulley could put in some really strong tackles and hit the ball so hard. He also could take penalties at Old Trafford!

As for Kanu, he is a mystery, the only player I have seen play on one leg.

His knee would not allow him to walk, run or do anything, but at training when you played a one-versus-one you could not get the ball off him. He was amazingly gifted and very strong as well.

When you look at him he is gangly but you couldn't dispossess him, it was impossible. Technically I haven't seen anyone as good as him.

You could go through the whole squad, we had the right players in the right positions at the right time and it was great. I wouldn't say we were the best of friends outside of the football club, but once we came together it was superb.

Actually most of the players kept themselves to themselves, apart from Hermann Hreidarsson. Nobody was as loud or as crazy as Hermann.

The night before the FA Cup final we went to an Italian restaurant in Bray, near our hotel, The Oakley Court in Windsor. We were the only ones there and there was karaoke.

Hermann went to the toilet and came back dressed as Elvis Presley, then started to sing and dance. I didn't understand half the words in that song, his dancing was good but the singing was not great.

Everybody was expecting high standards when they saw that fantastic costume, but no. It was hilarious though and a good night, a really good night.

That FA Cup win was my first trophy in England. I had captured silverware in France before - the French League Cup with Gueugnon in 2000 - but, no disrespect to Pompey, you don't expect to win a trophy with them and you don't expect to finish in the top eight in the Premier League.

Having said that, when I was at the end of my contract at Manchester City in the summer of 2007 and approached by Harry Redknapp I thought it could be a good challenge moving to Fratton Park.

At the time he was trying to build a team which looked quite interesting to me, there were a lot of international players and it excited me, perhaps we could achieve something.

The big mistake I made was not visiting the training ground at Eastleigh first, it was awful!

I had a few options but Pompey was the ideal choice and when the manager talked to you it was difficult to say no.

Harry makes you feel like you are the best player in the world, you come out of a meeting with him and think 'I want to play there'. His man management is really, really good.

It was good for me coming down south as well, a part of England I hadn't lived in before, and we won the FA Cup, finished eighth and played in Europe.

The procession the day after the cup final was also a new experience to me. When we won the trophy at Gueugnon we didn't do that, it is a really small town, we went to the stadium and didn't go through the city on an open-topped bus, so that day in Portsmouth was pretty special.

I cannot remember much because I was still hungover from the previous night, but can recall the sea of people everywhere around the city and that is a sight I keep in my mind even now.

Hermann was still drunk and we caught him a few times when he nearly fell off the bus. He was standing up on the bars on the top deck, if nobody had held him he would have fallen, he was hammered, dangerously hammered.

We had to keep an eye on him that day, we had to babysit him, he actually needs a bodyguard 24 hours a day, he is just crazy. He doesn't even have to drink to be like that!

He tried to throw the owner, Sacha Gaydamak, off the stage on Southsea Common. What seems crazy to us seems normal to him!

Do you know what, though, I didn't expect to see so many people that day, I really didn't, and the stage felt small in the middle of them all. Great memories, but occasions like that are always too short.

The following day everybody went on holiday and that is it, it had lasted two days maximum. I have never seen Milan Baros since the final, there are other players as well.

You always feel like you enjoy it and are making the most of it, but really you don't. Mind you, what are you supposed to do, you are not going to spend a week together because you have won the cup!

It is afterwards when you realise 'Wow, that's just a one off'. It went so fast.

Around five months later Harry had gone and Tony Adams was manager but the machine was broken and it was a tough time for him.

As a centre back, to me he is a legend, an amazing person, so I automatically had a lot of respect for him as soon as he arrived to the club initially as assistant manager, I listened to him like a kid.

When he went Paul Hart stepped up to keep us in the Premier League, but there was less expectation on him than Tony, at the time he had nothing to lose. It was a completely different situation.

I left for Everton in a £5m deal in August 2009 after only two seasons but it felt like it had been six or seven because we went so high so quickly and then so low so swiftly - maybe twice as fast.

It was tough, a rollercoaster, you go from winning the FA Cup and playing in Europe to selling all your players one-by-one.

In the build-up to me moving to Goodison Park I was actually really close to extending my contract with Pompey, but it was just not possible so I went, it wasn't an easy decision though.

We were talking and then every week bad news was coming in to the point they needed to get some more money. I was one of the last ones they could receive a transfer fee for and left as well.

As much as it was nice to go to Everton and have a new challenge, I wasn't happy to leave because I knew the club were in a bad situation, you could feel it and I left good friends there, not just players - they can always play somewhere else in the lower leagues or whatever - but there were a lot of people in the offices who lost their jobs.

As I was leaving I was contemplating whether it was the right thing - you kind of want to stay and fight but there is nothing you can do, even if you win every single game.

If the money is gone the money is gone, so the best thing for me to do was go, after all it would bring money into the club.

We played away at Arsenal - our third match of the season - and I kind of sensed it would be my last for Pompey. Nothing was done but you feel it because of the talk you have with your manager, if you weren't the last one to be sold you were the last before one.

Obviously you cannot come out and say you are leaving before the match, it was just a strange feeling.

We lost 4-1 that day at the Emirates Stadium and I was the last to leave the field. In the space of three months everybody had gone, everybody, I was one of the final ones and it was weird.

Sulley, Glen Johnson, Sol Campbell, Peter Crouch, Sean Davis, Noe Pamarot and Lauren had all gone that summer, we barely had enough players to make a squad - Niko Kranjcar left five days after me.

You would receive frequent letters from the club saying you won't get paid this month, but as a player you think 'It's okay, I can help them'.

Then you open the papers and see crazy stuff, you are watching television and there's more bad news. You just feel like it's bad news after bad news after bad news and cannot see the end of it.

I don't have any regrets going to Everton, not at all, and found a club very similar to Pompey in terms of the atmosphere and felt very comfortable there right away.

I sometimes still think about Pompey, there are always reminders on television, or you look for a player you knew you played with and realise there is absolutely no-one left.

There are occasions when you sit down and think about your past and what you achieved and the question comes up of 'What if?'. What if we kept those players and carried on what we started?

But we will never know.

EVENING NEWS, MONDAY, OCTOBER 28, 1963

Vinger plays big part in superb recovery at Leyton

ILL'S JIG OF TRIUMPH FOR SIX-GOAL POMPEY

e want Ron
nders" chant
supporters

(By LINESMAN)

y must have the most
l" supporters in the
A brand new Beatles-
nt developed from them
the second-half excite-
Brisbane Road on

the match, Leyton
who have strong show
connexions, had a
f young entertainers
out some pop songs
h in the manner of The

mpey supporters could
themselves heard as
to set up the Chimes
ompey chant, based on
a-cha.

second half, the big
Pompey fans in the
d suddenly remem-
of the songs which the
pounded out.

de up their own ver-
Beatles's "She Loves
h, I am told, is No. 3
rts. It came out as
yeah, yeah, yeah."
g repeated several
on caught on.

match, the supporters
und the players' en-
ve a rousing send-off

nt Ron" was the
went up now. And
-forward Ron Saun-
appear, the crowd
ard, ruffled his hair,
d him on the back

"I've scored, I've scored" he shouts

(By LINESMAN)

Pompey, the only League team to experience last week's mini-quake, certainly sent a few tremors through Brisbane Road on Saturday with their great 6—3 win over Leyton Orient.

Leyton had only let in two goals at home this season, and were unbeaten before their own supporters.

Just before half-time they were 3—0 in front and, after a most promising start, Pompey had drifted into what looked to be a hopeless position.

No-one could have forecast such a superb come-back. Two goals just on the interval by centre-forward Ron Saunders changed all that. And ten minutes into the second-half, Mickey Lill had scored twice and his partner Albert McCann once.

Thirteen minutes from the end Saunders completed his second "hat trick" in successive weeks to round off an all-action match the like of which we are unlikely to see for many years.

Quite fantastic

It was quite fantastic. Saunders was desperately unlucky with two early attempts and a shot from McCann scraped the wrong side of the Leyton post.

Quite unexpectedly, the Orient took the lead after 14 minutes with a goal in a thousand from the skipper and right-back Stan clumsily turned it past Davies to make it 1—3.

The clock was showing 43 minutes at this stage, but there had to be a liberal allowance for injuries.

In Pompey's very next raid, Saunders almost scored again from another McClelland cross.

He was soon back again sending a fine drive past Davies and into the roof the net.

Glory for Lill

The first ten minutes of the second-half brought the glory which has eluded Lill for so long.

Wilson laid on a "hat trick" chance for Saunders but, for once, the centre-forward did not accept it. He missed his kick and the ball ran on to Lill, another who had not scored this season.

The winger hit it into the net and stood momentarily looking straight ahead of him as though he could not believe his eyes.

Then, he leapt into the air, his arms raised. "I've scored. I've scored," he shouted excitedly as he went rushing upfield, jumping repeatedly as his colleagues tried to congratulate ...

match, came on the scene.

The talk continued, and when the referee did persuade Armstrong to take up position, the Orient left-back fired the ball against the outside of the post and behind.

The Saunders "hat trick" was completed 13 minutes from the end. Lunniss came up to get in a header from McClelland's corner, and, with the ball travelling wide, Saunders flicked it past Davies with his head.

Gordon was a disappointed man after the match not to have joined in the goalscoring, but this was not due to any lack of effort.

The amazing transformation in Pompey's finishing power has brought them 11 goals in two matches, after failing to get more than two in any of their previous League matches.

They are having a four-day break at Saltdean this week—and they will still be practising their shooting.

RON SAUNDERS who performed his second "hat trick" in successive weeks.

Leyton Orient. — Davies; Charlton, Lewis (E.); Lucas, Bishop, Lea; White, Musgrove, Bolland, Ward, Mason.

Portsmouth. — Armstrong; Wilson, Lunniss; Campbell, Dickinson, Lewis (B.); McClelland, Gordon, Saunders, McCann, Lill.

Referee: Mr. J. Lowry, of Neath. Attendance. 12,705.

McFarland saves

Saints side must be changed, after this

(BY JANUS)

Leeds for promotion? Few the 18,000 crowd at The on Saturday who saw this cle tough side send fumbling So ampton crashing to a 4—1 de will disagree.

But Leeds will lose m friends if they continue to all "strong arm" tactics to cr into their game.

Admittedly, Terry Pain name was the first to go in the notebook of Referee Mr. R. Loynton, but three Le players were later "booked" Norman Hunter, Ian Lawson, a Billy Bremner.

Southampton were alw struggling against the promoti candidates, who brought a la number of supporters with the

PRESENTATION TO PAINE

After the match Terry Pain was presented with two gift which were given to all th players who appeared in th England v. Rest of the Worl match at Wembley la Wednesday.

At a ceremony in the board room, Mr. George Read (Southampton's ...

Ron **Saunders**

261 games, 162 goals (September 1958 - August 1964)

Leyton Orient 3 (Charlton, Bolland 2)
Pompey 6 (Saunders 3, Lill 2, McCann)

Division Two, Brisbane Road, Saturday, October 26, 1963

Pompey: Armstrong, Wilson, Lunniss, Campbell, Dickinson, Lewis, McClelland, Gordon, Saunders, McCann, Lill.

Attendance; 12,705

It made the headlines as one of the most spectacular storms of the century, sparking lightning and widespread flooding across England.

Certainly the weather on the night of Friday, September 5, 1958, made life difficult for this footballer who had been lined-up to journey from Gillingham to Fratton Park the following morning to sign.

As it was, with road and rail routes rendered non-negotiable by storm damage, travel plans had to be altered at the last minute to enable me to fulfil my Pompey debut against Chelsea.

That meant catching a Dove aircraft to take the 25-minute flight from Croydon to Portsmouth Airport - and then receiving a police escort along the Eastern Road to the match!

To think the previous day I had been ordered home from training by Gillingham boss Harry Barratt with a heavy cold.

Still, I arrived at Fratton Park at 2.20pm and would spend the next six years on the south coast.

The £10,000 deal would also establish me as the first player to ever move from Division Four into the top flight - and for me the start of bigger things.

I finished as Pompey's top-scorer in six successive seasons, totalling 162 goals in 261 games, and appeared in three different divisions, winning promotion once and suffering two relegations.

I'm also informed only Peter Harris and Johnny Weddle have netted more times than me in the club's history.

I was a goalscorer. Most of it was based on natural ability, goalscorers either have it or don't have it. My game was to score goals - and I did it reasonably well.

Freddie Cox recruited me to Fratton Park, a manager who had taken over from Eddie Lever the previous month.

I don't honestly know if they were the only club in for me, in those days it was nothing like today when everything is headlines. It just happened - I was a Pompey player.

By that stage, four matches of the campaign had passed, Pompey winning just one of them, and Freddie, who was a smashing fella, decided to sign me.

I had only been with Gillingham a season, scoring 20 goals in 49 matches, with Archie Clark having plucked me from Southern League side Tonbridge Angels the previous summer.

As far as I was concerned, it was fantastic to be playing in Division One a little more than a year having featured in non-league football and held down a part-time job to help my earnings.

There were 31,815 at Fratton Park for my debut as we drew against Chelsea 2-2, Harry Harris netting twice with me having a hand in both of them. It was a decent way to start life at a new club.

Meanwhile, the directors' box contained club president Field Marshal Montgomery, First Viscount Montgomery of Alamein and singer and actor Tommy Steele!

Suddenly I had the likes of Jimmy Dickinson as a team-mate, and everything people say about him is spot on. A lovely fella and very good footballer.

He had no weaknesses to his game, was a good tackler and one of the league's top players in no matter what division you played in, what more can I say?

I would score a 29-minute hat-trick in his 500th appearance for Pompey later that season, a 4-4 draw at Tottenham Hotspur in February 1959.

It was my first treble for the club, with Harry Harris getting the other, but Bobby Smith grabbed a last-minute equaliser for the White Hart Lane club to ruin the occasion for Jimmy.

Regardless, that result was unexpected and one of only three games we avoided defeat on our travels from November until the end of the season - all of them draws.

My career had actually started in Division One with Everton in 1951, although I would make just the three appearances for them.

During my time at Goodison Park I went into the Army, did National Service and came back but, by that stage, like a lot of clubs in those days the Toffeemen were struggling financially and put around 15 players on the transfer list.

It was more or less the whole of the reserve team - which included me.

I then had a lot of people from different clubs phone, plenty of different managers, but Dougie Hunt from Tonbridge was the one that caught my eye.

Of course, in those days the wages were strictly limited, but he suggested I went and gave it a go, even if it was non-league football, so I joined in July 1956.

I would score 39 goals that season and in May 1957 was back in the Football League with Gillingham for the princely sum of £800.

A year later I was in the top flight, this time for Pompey, although it would prove to be relatively short-lived at that level, unfortunately.

As mentioned before, Cox was our manager and I liked him, a brilliant coach and real gentleman who was an absolute pleasure to play for.

Life is what you make it and that is particularly apt for football. They were a good set of lads, despite our poor league position throughout my maiden campaign with the club.

In that first season I was still comparatively inexperienced as you would imagine, while having initially dropped out of the Football League then come back into it had left me very grateful.

Then there were those big gates, definitely my first regular experience of being asked to cope with such pressures - and I believe that is what I did.

For me I was back playing in what you might call the big time again. Everything was big, everyone was big and it was that much different.

However, I didn't have too much time to adjust as we were soon in the thick of a relegation fight.

I would top our scoring charts with 24 goals in 40 games that first campaign, but it wasn't enough to prevent us being relegated after 32 years in the top flight, including winning the title twice.

After a 4-2 home victory over Burnley in November 1958, in which I scored twice, we didn't win another league game for the remainder of the season. That was four draws and 20 losses over the final 24 league matches.

Unsurprisingly, we were bottom in 22nd spot, having won only six times in the league and conceded 112 times.

We would also struggle in Division Two and, at the end of the 1960-61 campaign, were relegated in 21st spot, when I scored 23 goals in 36 games.

It was under George Smith, who had arrived in April 1961 to replace Cox, who steered us to the Division Three title the following season, having started the campaign with a 14-match unbeaten run in all competitions.

At Christmas we were at the top of the table, although there was a bit of a stutter with a poor five-match run in early April 1962 when we scored once and picked up only one point.

Still, I netted both goals in a 2-1 Easter Monday win against Watford at Fratton Park and we ended up finishing five points clear, winning 12 out of 23 away games.

Our team was excellent, with Jimmy Dickinson, Johnny Gordon, Dick Beattie, Alex Wilson and Cyril Rutter the mainstays, while in the December Tony Barton arrived from Nottingham Forest and Dave Dodson from Swansea City to help us on our way.

Barton, who I later took to Aston Villa where he would become my assistant, had a lot of ability, he just more or less went out and played, as most of us did in those days. It all came very naturally.

The next season Albie McCann joined from Coventry City and was a lovely little fella. Very, very quick and extremely sharp, a really good player.

I can remember very few of my goals over my career, likewise my games, as I have a poor memory these days. Anyhow, I was paid to score goals and if I didn't they would employ someone who could, it was my job.

However, one of my most memorable Pompey matches was in October 1963 at Leyton Orient in Division Two.

It wasn't merely the feat of netting a second successive hat-trick which stands out for me, but the manner of those three goals as we fought back from 3-0 down to win 6-3.

Entering that fixture, Orient were unbeaten at home having conceded only twice in the process, while we arrived on the back of a 5-2 Fratton Park win over Newcastle United.

It started disastrously, though, when right-back Stan Charlton thundered in a long-range shot which John Armstrong couldn't keep out. They doubled their lead when Bobby Mason's centre was glanced home by Gordon Bolland.

Then Bolland made it 3-0 to Orient after taking the ball around Armstrong and finishing into an empty net.

However, we managed to pull back two goals in the final two minutes of the first half, with me getting both.

The first was when I converted a low, hard John McClelland cross and the next was a drive past Reg Davies into the roof of the net.

We were superb after the interval and Micky Lill levelled when he finished off Alex Wilson's pass.

Lill then put us in front for the first time with his second, before he pulled it back for Albie McCann to net via the inside of the far post to make it 5-3.

I managed to complete my hat-trick in the 77th minute when Roy Lunniss got a header to McClelland's corner and I flicked it past Davies with my head.

It's funny, The Beatles were number three in the charts at the time with 'She Loves You' and the away fans gave their own rendition of 'Pompey, yeah, yeah, yeah' during the second half, which made some of us smile.

And to cap it off, afterwards we were given a four-day break in Saltdean in East Sussex!

That Orient result meant we had scored 11 goals in two matches after failing to get more than two in the previous 14 league fixtures that season.

We would, though, finish only ninth, even if it was my best goal-scoring season and an improvement on 16th place the previous campaign.

However, I had to leave Pompey in August 1964 following a disagreement with George Smith. Although we won't go too much into the whys and wherefores.

George was a great big fella, about 6ft 6in, and a very good coach, but I had reason to fall out with him and that was it. I asked to go on the transfer list and within 16 days had been sold to Watford.

The manager told me a few lies and I found out and told him I didn't want to play for him. He had lost my respect.

In fact, not only did I not want to play for him - but I definitely wasn't going to play for him.

It stemmed from him leaving me out for our final match of the pre-season, with Arsenal coming to Fratton Park.

Despite the campaign not having even kicked off, I found myself dropped along with Brian Lewis and Tony Barton following a friendly against Aldershot. I had scored 33 goals the previous season.

While the first-team lost 5-1 to the Division One Gunners that Saturday, I was playing for our reserves at Bournemouth and scored twice in a 4-1 victory.

That was the first time I had ever had any set-to with any manager, I had always got on with managers, had no problems whatsoever.

I don't want to go into the full details and I still started the opening three matches regardless, but what he did left me determined not to play under him ever again.

I was upset to go, of course I was. We also had our first house so didn't want to leave that either. It was at 27 Fortunes Way, Bedhampton, a lovely place, you looked across to Hayling Island from the windows, it was beautiful.

But there you go, that is what the game is all about and Watford paid £15,000 for me.

My last Pompey match turned out to be a 3-2 home defeat to Charlton Athletic in Division Two, in which I scored twice - 48 hours later I had gone.

My previous season saw me net 33 goals and register three hat-tricks so I gather it was seen by supporters as a controversial decision for me to leave, but I just couldn't stay with Smith there.

I would spend a year at Vicarage Road and then got very lucky by moving to Charlton, where Bob Stokoe was my manager for two years and he was a very good golfer as well.

We had quite a few games of golf together with our England international midfielder Mick Bailey and England's cricket captain Colin Cowdrey, although not always with Colin because he had different schedules to us.

Overall, though, I don't think I carried on scoring too many after I left, and in April 1967 retired from full-time football to become player/boss of non-league Yeovil Town.

Pompey were the best days of my career because I was there longer than any of the other clubs.

I've had a few problems with my health over the years and am struggling to remember things, then little bonuses like being inducted into the Pompey Hall of Fame arrive and are gratefully received.

The fans are fantastic and I never cease to marvel at all the football clubs up and down the country who have all these groups of supporters prepared to keep on turning up, no matter how much more expensive it is these days.

Just imagine the state of the game if nobody bothered to go and watch.

Anyhow, I was informed of my Hall of Fame honour in 2014 but was having a bad time physically around that period and unfortunately couldn't go back to the club to accept it, which was disappointing.

Regardless, it was an honour to see my name alongside team-mates such as Jimmy Dickinson and Albie McCann. I thank the fans for that.

One thing you learn when you are a competitor all your life is that there are things that are going to happen and a lot of things that are not going to happen that you would like to happen.

You have to come to terms with the fact that whatever it is you are carrying on your shoulders it is going to happen and when it does you get on with it - then you become a happy person.

I don't watch much football nowadays, I'm not interested in it, although when Randy Lerner turned up as Aston Villa's owner in August 2006, they invited me down to watch a match.

It was a big day out, we have 10 grand kids and five great grand kids and maybe one or two more. They fixed me up with tickets so we all sat together, it was a fantastic day, really good.

But like I say, I don't follow football anymore.

asics
Goodmans

BARCLAYS LEAGUE: Fratton hit-men makes Rovers return home in despair

Pompey's two W's beginning to click

Guy's goals and Walsh wizardry

POMPEY 4 BRISTOL ROVERS 1

POMPEY'S variation on soccer's traditional W-formation destroyed Bristol Rovers on Boxing Day.

The two W's – Walsh and Whittingham – sent Rovers back to the west country wondering what hit them.

Walsh's waspish effort unsettled a defence that had brought a record of four consecutive clean sheets to the match. And Whittingham made a mockery of it by scoring all four goals.

By MIKE NEASOM

It was his third hat-trick of the season and his seventh as a Pompey player. Now only the fabled Wyndham "Farmer" Haines is ahead of him as a scorer of trebles.

This latest blast from Corporal Punishment took him to [illegible] league goals in as many appearances and to 27 in all 30 matches.

And he might easily have had a fifth.

Midway through the first half as Pompey threatened to tear Rovers apart, he was played clear by Alan McLoughlin and Brian Park[illegible] managed to block his shot.

Whittingham said: "I could have chipped him."

Yet curiously after the Rovers defence had donated the [illegible] two goals to the preda[illegible] [illegible]-year-old, Pompey then [illegible] hell-bent on tossing [illegible] away.

[illegible] dominating the [illegible]

when he pulled his cross behind Whittingham.

But Chris Burns retrieved it and got in a shot that Parkin failed to hold and Whittingham was in like a flash to whisk it home.

Seven minutes later Paul Hardyman's hometown return was blighted as his backpass fell short leaving Whittingham clear to grab his second.

For a spell it was one-way traffic. Pompey's ninth corner came in the 23rd minute and shortly afterwards the season's best crowd – 14,288 – was ready to acclaim Whittingham's hat-trick until Parkin redeemed himself by blocking the shot.

Suddenly things changed.

CELEBRIT[illegible] ON THE SP[illegible]

Alan Robinson, from F[illegible] ham, is a former FIFA re[illegible] who has officiated at the [illegible] est level. He now assesses [illegible] ent-day Football League [illegible] ees.

Blowin[illegible] whistl[illegible] on Ma[illegible] troop[illegible]

UNFORTUNATEL[illegible] not had much opp[illegible] to watch Pompey [illegible] season as the maj[illegible] my assessing duti[illegible] taken me to The [illegible]

I was fortunate to [illegible] such a resounding [illegible]

Guy **Whittingham**

225 games, 115 goals (June 1989 - August 1993, January 1999 - March 1999, July 1999 - March 2001)

Pompey 4 (Whittingham 4)
Bristol Rovers 1 (Taylor)

Division One, Fratton Park, Saturday, December 26, 1992

Pompey: Knight, Russell, Symons, Awford, Daniel (81 mins Stimson), Chamberlain (81 mins Clarke), Aspinall, Burns, McLoughlin, Walsh, Whittingham.

Attendance; 14,288

My wife slaughters me because I didn't cry when my three sons were born, yet there I stood on the Fratton Park pitch with my eyes welling up.

I was hurting, the double disappointment of not reaching the play-off final and the realisation it would be my last match for Pompey.

That 1992-93 campaign saw us relatively successful, any other season we would have gone up, with the rules changed that year to focus on goals scored and not goal difference. The following season they reverted back.

We finished level on points with West Ham United, but having scored one more goal they were handed second place ahead of us. So it was off to the play-offs where we faced Leicester at Nottingham Forest's City Ground and lost 1-0.

I had a great chance, a one-on-one with goalkeeper Kevin Poole and missed. I should have scored.

Then it was off to Fratton for the second leg and that night in May 1993 we drew 2-2, with referee Roger Milford not spotting an offside goal from Ian Ormondroyd that I remember to this day.

The aggregate score was a 3-2 defeat, we had missed out on the chance to reach the Premier League.

There was no doubt if we had gone up that season I would not have left Pompey three months later.

I'd had four years with the club, having started late at the age of 24, and was coming up to 29 years old, if I didn't leave after scoring 47 goals in a campaign then I was never going to do it.

It certainly wasn't about money, I could have earned more staying in Division One, the fact was I wanted to test myself at the highest level. Like any profession, I wanted to reach the top.

After that second-leg semi-final result, while applauding the fans I knew that would be it, in my mind it was probably going to be the last time I would do that.

There had been a lot of speculation, obviously, and it does have an effect on players, no matter what anyone says. Back in those days it was just in the papers, now it's all over the Internet.

Regardless, I was still around for Pompey's pre-season training and even went on tour to Finland, then it just happened. I got a phone call and was heading to an Oxford hotel to meet Aston Villa manager Ron Atkinson.

It was a case of 'That will do, get me up there,' seriously, that was it. It didn't take much negotiating that's for sure and in August 1993 I left in a deal valued at £1.2m deal, with Mark Blake coming in the other direction.

For me the move was made even more special as my grandad, Harold, was a Villa supporter. My uncle was a Wolverhampton Wanderers fan and although I never supported a team as a kid, I always looked out for the results of those two clubs.

The first game of the season we won 4-1 against QPR, Dalian Atkinson and Dean Saunders both scoring, while Dwight Yorke was around at the time as well, and I was sat on the bench thinking 'I am never going to get into this side!'.

Before that match I was presented with the silver boot from Uefa in recognition of my goals the previous season for Pompey. It was strange receiving it on the Villa Park pitch and not at Fratton, it was the wrong place really.

As it turned out, my best time in the top flight would be at Sheffield Wednesday, who I joined almost 17 months later in a £700,000 deal after 33 games and six goals at Villa.

Ultimately I think I proved myself in the Premier League during my time at Hillsborough, I don't believe you can play three-and-a-half years solid at that level if you hadn't, even if David Pleat had converted me into a right-sided midfield player!

I wasn't necessarily jinky but could get up and down the pitch, performing as a defender one minute and then in the opposition box the next. Pleat saw it pretty much as having an extra striker in his side and I scored 25 goals in 130 matches for the Owls.

Of course, what I had never expected that play-off night was I would be back at Fratton Park permanently in July 1999.

I first arrived at Pompey in June 1989 having initially been spotted by Alan Ball playing Army football.

I was stationed in Bordon at the School of Electrical and Mechanical Engineering and our football team coach had a son in Pompey's Centre Of Excellence and one day mentioned to Bally there were a couple of lads to come and watch.

Unfortunately he got the sack in the January, but John Gregory instead came to watch a game, liked what he saw and brought me to Fratton Park on trial in three reserve matches from April.

I scored on my reserve debut against Charlton, set up Martin Kuhl for a goal against Wimbledon and also featured against QPR.

Since then I have spoken to John about the day he first watched me and he says he knew in the warm-up it was worth a gamble. Apparently you can just tell by somebody's warm-up, I looked the sort that might be able to make it.

That season I scored 99 goals playing 100 games and representing seven different teams, I kept a record and then typed it out later.

My friend Mickey Spencer, who was also my boss, played a similar number of games and we had a competition to see who could score the most goals in a game and who could get the most nutmegs. He used to win the nutmegs - I used to win the goals!

My job was a Physical Training Instructor (PTI) and that season I turned out for my unit team, regiment team, corps team, then the Army, the combined services, then Waterlooville and Yeovil.

I was aged 23, although hardly trained with my teams because I was playing all the time. So I might have a game on the Wednesday afternoon for my unit, a game the Thursday night for the corps, a game on the Saturday for Yeovil, then on the Monday a game for the Army, it was constant.

I still continued my Army job. As a PTI ranked as Corporal, I was in the gym so if you were away playing for the Army somebody would cover you and then when they had a duty at night you would cover them.

It was all worked out fine, never a problem, and in our gym there was an Army golfer, an Army gymnast and two Army footballers, so people understood the situation.

I had joined the Army aged 17-and-a-half and was given the number 24623795, which I have never forgotten! You had to say it everytime when asked who you were, it's still there in my mind, like an important phone number.

After soldier training for 12 weeks I went to Bordon for my trade training, specialising as an armourer, fixing up small weapons.

I have to admit, though, because of my sport commitments I ended up deferring my training as I wasn't keeping up with my work, so was put back a couple of courses, taking me 18 months rather than 12!

Still, it kept me there for another football season and then I went off to Munster in Germany for two-and-a-half years doing my trade as an armourer - but still playing football.

I never saw real action. I did a two-week rock climbing exercise in Gibraltar - there was a lot of action in that - that was about it really!

There were actually no conflicts involving this country at the time. I joined two-and-a-half years after the Falklands War, and left two-and-half years before the Gulf War, so as far as timing was concerned it was almost as good as my finishing!

What I learned in the Army was massive, it was all about team play, working hard for each other, covering each other and I don't regret coming into the game the way I did because I think it helped me in my football career.

Ultimately if you don't cover someone's back in the Army it can cost lives and, although I never saw real action, that is what I was trained for.

When it came to leaving the Army to become a professional footballer with Pompey in June 1989, I was priced at £450 in recognition of the training they put me through.

The compensation figure depends on how long you signed up for, in my case nine years and I'd done six-and-a-half years.

I paid that £450 myself and when I signed for the club they reimbursed me, it was basically my signing-on fee and was pretty much straight away given back to me.

My full debut was Newcastle United away in September 1989 having come on before as a substitute against Stoke City and Hull City at home, netting in the latter game six minutes after replacing Mark Kelly.

That just gives you the confidence you can score at that level and over three different spells I would make 225 Pompey appearances and record 115 goals.

It would be the 1992-93 campaign which would be my best at the club, with my favourite goal the one which secured my hat-trick in a 4-1 win over Bristol Rovers on Boxing Day 1992.

I netted four in total that day, but that goal in the 64th minute stood out, I cannot even tell you how the other three went in!

It started with me collecting the ball on the edge of our penalty area and then, right under the South stand, playing a series of one-twos with Paul Walsh before he put me in with a perfect ball.

I then clipped it over Rovers' keeper Brian Parkin for my third hat-trick of the season and seventh for the Blues.

It demonstrated the understanding myself and Walshie had, it was just the two of us working our way up the pitch and thankfully he put it inside the box because I wouldn't have finished it if it had been outside!

I didn't score many from outside the box, what's the point? Let other people shoot from there, I'll just get the rebound!

In fairness, I did get one or two outside the penalty area. In my first season we faced Leeds at home in October 1989 and were down 3-1 with a minute to go when I was played in on the edge of the box and curled it past Mervyn Day, I remember that one! We ended up drawing 3-3.

I'm getting old now, the memory is going, I started the season off with a hat-trick against Bristol City, but can only recall two of those goals, it would be nice to say I remember every single one, but I don't.

The relationship I had with Walshie was fantastic, he had a good reputation in the game and, most impressive for me, was his desire and work-rate, that is why when he came and played in Division One he went back up into the Premier League again.

A work ethic is fundamental in any player, that is really what makes the difference between good players and great players.

As soon as pre-season started he was up at the front of the running and you are thinking 'He hasn't come here for an easy time'. He was taking pride in his work.

At the time it was run to cones, run to lines, sprint back, and you can always tell those who are honest and work hard. They go to the line, they don't go short, and he was one of those that went to the line every time, while reaching the full 30 seconds in the running and not starting to stop at 28 or 29 seconds.

Our partnership developed pretty quickly really. Neil Sillett, the physio at the time, had told me Jim Smith recognised my goal-scoring ability and wanted somebody alongside to create the chances for me. He couldn't have picked anyone better.

Walshie was more of a target man than me, even though he was 5ft nothing and his hair made him 6ft!

With his ability on the ball he could suck people into him, manipulate the ball and hold it up, while I made runs off him or off people he played the ball into.

Jim liked wingers getting crosses into the box, Walshie would do all the stuff outside it and I would do it inside it. I played off him really.

He was skillful, two footed, had everything about him and was too good for Division One.

To this day he can't believe he got The News/Sports Mail's Player of the Season and I can't believe it either, yet it showed what an impact he made at the club.

If I hadn't previously received that award I think I would have been a bit upset about it, but fortunately I got it in my first campaign in 1989-90 so I was okay.

You talk about great things Walshie did, but Sunderland in our final away match of the campaign in May 1993 was a real let-down. He got sent off for flattening Martin Gray with his arm after Guy Butters had been dismissed earlier, we ended up down to nine men and losing 4-1.

That made him suspended for the play-offs, which was a massive blow and, to be honest, took the wind out of our sails a little bit. We felt with our strikeforce we had a chance of scoring goals - then suddenly it was just me.

I didn't create many, I got on the end of a few, but didn't create many.

Jim Smith always blamed me for missing a penalty against Peterborough United at home in a night game and you could say that was the goal needed to put us level with West Ham United. Well, I hope he was joking, I got 42 league goals!

There were lots of other people who also spurned good chances, I remember Benny Kristensen in the final league game missing an open one against Grimsby Town.

That previous summer I was concerned with how injuries had been hampering my recent seasons and decided to look outside the box to resolve it. My Pompey career started with 24 goals, then 20 and then 13 and something had to be done.

I had come out of the Army really fit, that is what got me through a campaign, so it was clear to me I maybe wasn't doing enough training and need to get myself fit for that 1992-93 season.

At the time most players would have six weeks off, you don't do that nowadays but it was different then and my idea was to work with a sprint coach over the summer of 1992.

The idea came through a sports masseur at the Mountbatten Centre, she knew Team Solent athletics coach Arvel Lowe and introduced us.

He worked out some training routines, focusing on sprint training, and I concentrated on that side of my game which was very hard, but obviously paid dividends.

I had never considered myself a quick person, a lot of my success was through anticipation, being on the move and making it happen rather than standing still and reacting to it, but the work that summer made me sharper.

I even met up with Olympic medalist Roger Black on a couple of occasions, we never trained together but I would see him around and chat, with him offering me bits of advice on running and the fitness side of things.

That was my own motivation. I think I was a little bit different in a way, a lot of players come through the football system and rely on football people to get them there, but I was thinking for myself.

What happened the following season in terms of my 47-goal haul in 56 games couldn't be put just down to that, neither was it only Walshie's ability or the good team we had - it was a combination of everything.

That campaign also saw me set a Pompey scoring record by netting 42 league goals, beating Billy Haines' tally of 40 set in 1927.

After moving to the Premier League at the end of that season, I returned to Fratton Park five-and-a-half years later when Alan Ball brought me in on loan from Sheffield Wednesday in January 1999.

The club was in administration and in a bit of trouble in Division One, I just think it boosted everyone at the time, even if it was for six weeks before being recalled after seven goals in nine matches.

Pompey had some decent players and were in a bit of a false position, while the expectation didn't bother me. I was in a win/win situation really, I had quite a good rapport with the fans from my previous spell and Bally had confidence in me that I could get the goals.

In July 1999 I rejoined the Blues permanently, making it a third spell, although that didn't go so well.

I knew I was coming to the end of my career, I was aged 34, so to be offered a two-year deal was decent, and with good friends still down here it was a fairly easy decision to return.

Then there was a change in managers with Bally going and Tony Pulis coming in with different ideas. You have to accept that and try to do your best, then if you are not playing and it's towards the end of your career you have to find somewhere else if you can.

I ended up stranded on 99 league goals, which is disappointing. First of all you tend to think 'I wish that manager had put me on in a couple of games', but then it occurs to you that you had nearly six-and-a-half years at Pompey to have scored another goal.

You cannot just blame people for not playing you, I missed goals I should have scored, that is just the way it is.

In October 2000 I was on loan at Oxford United, scoring on my debut in a 2-1 defeat at Swindon Town, then Steve Claridge took over Pompey from Pulis and asked me to come back to assist him - I had only been at Oxford for a week!

Denis Smith, their manager, was disappointed but agreed, however when I returned to Fratton Park I wasn't allowed to play for a while as technically I was still out on a month's loan.

During that spell Steve and I approached it as if he was the manager and I was the coach, that is how it was for three months until he was called into the office by Milan Mandaric and told Graham Rix had been appointed boss.

I was still registered as a player and ended up going to Wycombe Wanderers, which was a bit of a blessing, and playing in an FA Cup semi-final against Liverpool at Villa Park - and losing again!

Once my playing career finished it was never a case of becoming a manager somewhere, I wasn't necessarily interested in that, I knew I wanted to be a coach because I had done my A-licence at Villa when aged 28 so knew that was the way I wanted to go.

Tony Adams brought me back to Fratton Park in January 2009 with the idea of developing the under-21 players, then when Steve Cotterill came in I moved up to the first-team environment as a coach before eventually taking over as caretaker boss when Michael Appleton left for Blackpool.

Having gone through two spells as a caretaker boss and worrying about what was going to happen to me if someone else came in, I then thought why not give it a go as a permanent manager with the understanding we are going take our time and build. I took the board at their word.

I don't regret having done it, they did what they thought was right, I am not going to knock them for that, that is the way it is and I left in November 2013.

You remember the good things, not necessarily all the battles with administration or the struggle against the board and trying to convince them we have just come out of intensive care and need time.

From my post-playing days I recall the atmosphere in the Praca de Santiago square in Guimaraes, the AC Milan game, triumph over Sheffield United after the community takeover and the euphoric victory at Crewe Alexandra after 23 games without a win when the press afterwards cheered and applauded me.

In total I spent eight-and-a-half years coaching and playing at Pompey, I suppose I couldn't resist going back time and time again to that wonderful club.

Promotion spotlight on the South Coast derby

POMPEY FOILED IN TENSE BATTLE

Webb's brilliant goal not enough

POMPEY 1, BRIGHTON 1

OMPEY'S dream of a victory which would have taken even closer to leadership of the Second Division was royed by a bizarre Brighton equalizer shortly before the of a first half which Alan Ball's side had dominated.

By MIKE NEASOM at Fratton Park

Referee: Dennis Hedges (Oxford).

POMPEY: Knight, Stanley, Tait, Dillon, Blake, Gilbert, O'Callaghan, Kennedy, Morgan, Webb, Hilaire. Sub: Doyle.

BRIGHTON: Moseley, Keown, Hutchings, Pearce, Young, O'Reilly, Wilson, Biley, Ferguson, Connor, Smillie. Sub: Kraay.

POMPEY VERDICT

Pompey are now unbeaten in ten matches but satisfaction at that will be slightly blunted.

For they desperately wanted to chalk up their second win of the week against neighbours Brighton.

But they failed to do so in a match of considerable tension, periods of good football, and periods of great scrappiness.

They dominated the first half thanks largely to an inspired performance by Neil Webb.

BIG MATCH ACTION

• Ex-Pompey favourite, Alan Biley, turns away as Kevin Dillon gets in a fierce drive against Brighton at Fratton Park.

Holmes saves it for Saints

NICK HOLMES popped up to hea Saints a late equalize against Watford Vicarage Road th afternoon.

Alan **Biley**

120 games, 57 goals (August 1982 - March 1985)

Pompey 1 (Webb)
Brighton & Hove Albion 1 (Blake OG)

Division Two, Fratton Park, Saturday, April 6, 1985

Brighton: Moseley, Keown, Hutchings, Pearce, Young, O'Reilly, Wilson, Smillie, Ferguson, Connor, Biley.

Sub Not Used: Kraay.

Pompey: Knight, Stanley, Blake, Gilbert, Tait, Hilaire, Dillon, Kennedy, O'Callaghan, Morgan, Webb.

Sub Not Used: Doyle.

Attendance; 22,867

Puerto Banus was the Spanish setting for Pompey players and management to unwind following the culmination of the 1983-84 campaign.

We were in Sinatra Bar beside the marina in the Costa del Sol resort one night and, as ever, I was one of the last ones left, along with the caretaker boss and in-coming manager Alan Ball.

Bless him, he was not very good in drink, often quite retrospective, very dour and a bit sad - or he could get quite aggressive.

On that occasion he was the latter.

Ball walked over to me and said 'I've never rated you, never liked you, you couldn't lace my boots'.

Only a week earlier I had netted a hat-trick in a final-day 5-0 win against Swansea City in his first match in temporary charge following the dismissal of Bobby Campbell. It took my season's tally to 18 goals in 43 games.

My response was something like 'I think you are one of the best one-touch footballers I have seen in my life, you were a fantastic pro, you are a great coach, but a useless manager'.

Nobody has any reason to believe me about that conversation, but his actions backed that up the following season.

Pompey was a three-year box in time and if I could possibly open that box again and recover moments, a day even, then I would die happy.

They were ultra-special days, week after week I couldn't wait to play. I fell in love with the club and it has never gone away.

Then Ball made me leave in March 1985 - and it hurts to think about it even now.

There is footage of me scoring in that famous Santa game and the commentator, Martin Tyler, saying 'There's no way surely that Alan Biley will be allowed to leave Portsmouth now,' but the manager had no intention of keeping me.

I left for Brighton & Hove Albion two-and-a-half months later and the final insult to me was he was prepared to let me go for £50,000. It was a case of getting rid of me at whatever the cost, while in all honesty I probably would have gone anywhere.

It was a combination of things Alan Ball did to me. He isolated me, he pulled me aside and said things, and at training was continually on my back. He did it either to get a reaction or make it clear to other people I was not going to be there much longer.

He didn't bully me, I think he manoeuvred me.

Blowing my own trumpet, I am the easiest person to get on with, I am open, friendly and have no big-time Charlie about me at all. I have kept friends who are Pompey supporters and send them Christmas cards to this day.

Ball had a dislike of me. Whether it was me as a person which tainted his opinion of me as a footballer or whether me as a footballer had tainted his opinion of me as a character, I don't know. Perhaps it was both together.

Everything came to a head one day when training at Fratton Park, while playing a bit of keep ball across the pitch he picked on me and picked on me and picked on me.

In the end the ball came to me, I picked it up, drop kicked it over the Fratton end and shouted 'Stick your ball up your backside' before walking off and leaving training. He was after a bite and got it.

In the aftermath I was called to his office. He was smaller than me but sat on a seat which had been screwed up to a high level, I was opposite almost sitting on the floor in another chair.

I don't know what he said to me in that meeting, truth be told I didn't even want to listen to what he had to say. He had lost my respect.

The on-going situation wasn't sorted out as a manager, he sorted it out as an ex-player would. It was confrontational, it was aggressive, it was sharp and matter of fact from where he was coming from - and it was a closed shop.

The previous summer he had brought in Scott McGarvey for £85,000 from Manchester United. Whether he came in to replace Mark Hateley, who had left 48 hours earlier for AC Milan, or myself, it worked out he was playing instead of me.

Now I really liked Scott, he came and lived at my house in Bishop's Waltham when he first arrived, he's a great lad, but you could see he was struggling.

If you had been a striker at Pompey for the past three years with 50 goals in 100 games and thought you had done reasonably well wouldn't you wonder why you were being dropped for somebody who couldn't hit a barn door?

The reason was Ball wanted me out and I can only assume he didn't like the fact I was popular.

Eventually I put in a transfer request, we had gone a few weeks down the road, I was a substitute and could see the future. The supporters were saying it as well, nobody could understand it.

This despite having scored 13 times in 26 games that campaign, I had even netted the winner in Ball's first match as manager that season, an 87th minute goal against Middlesbrough in August 1984.

I was never given an explanation. There were rumours coming back at me that I was having an affair with Alan Ball's daughter, that I was having an affair with the chairman's wife who was about 74 at the time, that I was going around Portsmouth on a bike trying to pick up girls with sweeties.

I swear to you, at one stage I asked somebody I knew to start a rumour that Luton Town had come in for me and I wanted to go back to my home-town club - and within a week it was all around the city! That's what happens, it is a huge village.

I did an awful lot of naughty, boyish things. I liked to drink, I liked going out, I enjoyed myself, but all of those rumours about potential affairs with young girls and wives made me laugh, despite being serious.

Even if I had been doing that - which I wasn't - I wouldn't have thought it would be a reason to drop someone from the football team.

I don't want to speak harshly of Ball because I really want to remember him as the great player he was and a fantastic, energetic, knowledgeable coach.

However, I have to be honest and if I can say really good things about him I have got to balance it out and say he was an awful man-manager.

He might have been a fantastic man-manager to someone else, I accept that, after all some players may say Bobby Campbell was a dreadful manager, but he was perfect for me.

I couldn't wait to leave and when I joined Brighton never saw him again. When I came back to Fratton Park the following month for a match we didn't speak, I can't even remember seeing him.

The weirdest thing is I have met three or four other people in football, coaches and managers at other clubs, and they had been in Ball's company and apparently he couldn't say anything but nice things about me!

I had arrived at Pompey in August 1982 from Everton for a fee of £100,000 - just three days before the start of the 1982-83 campaign..

At Goodison Park I was one of what was dubbed the 'Magnificent Seven' who had ridden in a year earlier under new manager Howard Kendall.

There was me - who was his first buy - Alan Ainscow, Mickey Thomas, Mike Walsh, Neville Southall, Jim Arnold and Mickey Ferguson, all recruited within a week, except it didn't turn out too magnificently for a few of us who, for different reasons, were not able to get a first-team place.

I would score two goals in my first two games, then not long after Kendall changed my position and started playing me wide right. I scored only once more after that and then lost my place because of it.

My 1981-82 campaign ended on loan at Stoke City where I played in eight matches as they stayed in the top flight under Richie Barker, before returning to Goodison Park.

Then during the summer, Kendall pulled me into his office and said Pompey were interested in taking me.

He handed me a piece of paper with Bobby Campbell's phone number on and I told him I would ring him out of courtesy. With respect to Pompey, I wasn't even aware what league they were in, I was totally in my bubble of trying to save my position with the Toffeemen.

Anyhow, I rang up Bobby and he said 'Son, don't say anything just promise me you will come down for a day'.

That was the gist of it, there wasn't much more than that and being pretty open-minded and willing to give everyone a chance I came down to the south coast for talks with this Division Three club.

'You are the last part of the jigsaw in this puzzle,' I was told by Bobby, 'I don't want you to change, the fans need somebody they can relate to, I don't want you to cut your hair, I don't want you to tuck your shirt in'.

I am sure most of it was buttering up, but I needed to hear something that strong. In those days you didn't have all these substitutes and squad rotations, I just wanted to know I was one of the first XI.

Bobby didn't just give me that promise, I got much more in that I was also integral to his plans, the last part of the jigsaw.

Now he could be abrasive and might be Marmite to some people, something I only found out years later, yet he is right up there as one of the very best managers I've ever worked with.

However, I know of three or four players that really, really didn't get on with him, and that's being polite.

Before I experienced it for myself, I didn't know how good the Pompey supporters were, I didn't know the fervour throughout the city, I actually had no idea about the club's popularity throughout the world through its naval connections.

From day one I felt I was the main man and the number one for that position - and am pretty sure he told the other 10 players the same about their position too. That is what a good manager does.

I would score on my debut for Pompey in a 4-1 win over Sheffield United on the opening day of the 1982-83 campaign, with the sun shining and 13,361 in attendance. We took them apart.

Just before the season started, the summer signings of myself, Neil Webb, Dave Thomas and Ernie Howe were lined-up for television interviews.

Webby was first, a 19-year-old, nervous and not very articulate, but said the right things and it was a good interview.

Then it came to the old heads, Ernie and Dave, standard procedure with 'We're a good side, we're hoping to be successful this season, the introduction of the new players have improved the squad'.

It was my turn next and I said 'We're going to win the league!'. You should have seen their faces, 'Why the hell have you said that?' was the response.

I knew we would win the Division Three title, though, I was as confident as you can be without it being cocky. Looking at my team-mates for the season ahead I was so assured.

In Alan Knight we had the best goalkeeper in the league, while the back four of John McLaughlin, Steve Aizlewood, Ernie and Colin Sullivan had fantastic experience.

Andy Rollings came into the defence at times and did really, really great, then there was Peter Ellis who never, ever let you down and if he wasn't starting was usually the one allotted substitute.

McLaughlin was a really classy full-back, if he had pace he would have played a lot higher, but was a moany old so-and-so.

I used to drive in every morning to training with Aizlewood, sometimes in his wife's Mini, and he would bring a roll of toilet paper. His nose had been broken that many times he struggled to breathe through it and would blow into a tissue every five minutes.

He would then throw the tissue out of the window, I used to say there would be a paper trail from my house to the training ground!

Baz, as we called him, was a lovely lad but uncouth and didn't look after himself enough, if he had been a real fitness fanatic he could have played higher and longer. He had a lovely touch for a big man, I don't think people realised what a good footballer he was.

Mick Tait could do everything and a harder man you couldn't wish to meet, Bobby Doyle was the same and one of the best passers I ever played with, pinpoint. Webby could do everything and was like a gazelle.

Then Kevin Dillon arrived from Birmingham City for the final 11 games and what a wonderful player he was. I love him to bits, a nutcase but a talent who could ping a ball.

You would never see a finer crosser of the ball than Alan Rogers. He was a quiet lad, didn't put himself about, but was silky, he glided across the turf and a sweet left-foot with delivery second to none.

Up front there was Billy Rafferty, such an unselfish striker but his career shows he always got his fair share of goals. What a lovely man, a very, very neat player and great to play alongside.

Then there was me, who possessed the worst haircut in the world according to the News Of The World, I have the article laminated, but am still waiting for my trophy!

The peroxide bog brush wasn't your normal look, I actually looked a right plonker but thought I was the bees knees at the time.

I didn't know it then, but you have to possess a certain amount of confidence to take that onto the pitch, particularly if you are a goal-scoring striker with a barnet like mine. You stick out like a sore thumb.

It wasn't until quite a way through my career and coming to Pompey where I matured and started to understand how the game worked. I realised by having this ridiculous hairstyle if I had a bad game then I have an absolute stinker because I stuck out!

It was influenced by Rod Stewart and Denis Law, my two heroes long before I got involved in football professionally.

It just so happens there is a cohesion between the two, they both have a love of football, are passionate Scots and I loved the hair - something I copied from the age of 17 or 18.

I absolutely adore Rod. Not so long ago I bought the most beautiful old 1962 record player and regularly play 'Smiler', 'Never A Dull Moment' or 'Every Picture Tells A Story', with all the crackles which accompany them.

Everything about him I love, his exuberance, his honesty, the way he is with people and as a singer/songwriter he is the best there has ever been and ever will be.

As for Denis, he was like a panther, 10st wet through, skin and bone, but was tough. He had every bit of skill you could ever wish for and is probably the most devastating finisher ever.

With him being one of my heroes, everybody thought I was copying him by playing with my cuffs down, but it is because I suffer with cold hands! As a young lad I would come in at half-time almost in tears because of poor circulation in my hands.

My haircut was what defined me and it was also what I wanted, it was a choice. At first I dyed it myself, Baby Blonde 101, then a hairdresser would come around my house at whatever club I was at.

I think I can talk on behalf of every other goal-scoring striker that has ever lived, if you are not up your own backside you are never going to be a goal-scoring striker. You have to think you are great - and by that I don't mean you need to go and tell people that.

People also associate me with the Santa match in December 1984. It's a bit like a fisherman's tale, every time you tell it the fish gets bigger - and I love that about it.

It was a game played in atrocious conditions, an Oxford United team right up there with us vying for promotion,and we were 1-0 down to a Kevin Brock goal when somebody dressed as Father Christmas came onto the pitch and delayed the game.

It took a good two minutes before it calmed down again and in that time added on we were lucky enough to get two goals to win 2-1, me netting them both with headers.

It was on my mum Eileen's birthday and what a present. She was there that day, along with my stepdad Brian, they never missed a game. He was a photographer and whenever I got the ball he would stand up and take photographs, thousands and thousands of them in which I look like a little ant!

Then there was away at Bournemouth in February 1983 on my 26th birthday, I scored in a 2-0 win along with Steve Aizlewood and will never forget travelling to Dean Court and for the last mile there were Pompey fans either side of the road.

That same 1982-83 season there was the game against Southend United in May 1983 when we won 2-0 to clinch promotion, with me and Kevin Dillon the scorers in front of a Fratton Park crowd of 18,356.

For the last 10 minutes the supporters had spilled onto the edge of the pitch and I remember saying to the referee 'When it's time for the final whistle can you blow up when we are near the halfway line, we need to get inside before the crowd get on'. He just smiled.

Anyhow, we are comfortable at 2-0 up when the ball gets played towards the old North terrace and people started to come onto the cinder track, including this well-built chap with a denim waistcoat and shirt.

I shouted 'Get off the pitch' and pushed this geezer - he went flying. Years later he came up to me and introduced himself as Johnny Moore, nowadays he is the club's fans liaison officer. Apparently I ripped his waistcoat in the incident as well!

Still, the game carried on and then the ball goes down to the far corner by the Milton End and the referee blows his whistle, with me down there!

Thousands poured onto the pitch and I am running like mad, then all of a sudden I am gone. They nicked my shorts, my boots everything - I ended up getting into the dressing room with just my pants on.

I would also net the match-winner in a 1-0 victory at Plymouth Argyle on the last day of the campaign to secure us the Division Three title. I had already been named The News/ Sports Mail Player of the Season and finished up with 26 goals in 50 matches.

I never wanted to leave in March 1985, I wanted to cement myself in folklore to be one of the club greats. You don't know anything about Pompey until you drive onto that island, you haven't got a clue. When you do, it grabs you forever.

My belief was I would have rotted under Alan Ball if I hadn't left, but by going to Brighton it finished my career anyway because the heart had been ripped out of me.

Chris Cattlin signed me and 29 days later I found myself running out again at Fratton Park - a place I adored.

I'd been playing pretty well for the Seagulls and was coming back home to face Pompey in a Division Two match. Was I looking forward to it? Not at all.

Yet that April 1985 fixture would prove to be my most memorable Blues match, despite being on the opposing side.

Rightly or wrongly my heart wasn't in that game. I should have focused and said 'I am going to show you Alan Ball' - but my feelings for Pompey far outweighed that.

I never expected a boo, not for one minute, the fans are not like that because they really do take to the people who have given for them, but I never anticipated what happened next. All I can say is the warm-up killed me.

Before the match the Brighton fans were acknowledging me with chants of 'There's only one Alan Biley' and it was quite blatantly clear Pompey weren't having that so they joined in. Soon all four sides of Fratton Park were singing my name, that was gold dust.

How many players have you ever known had their name chanted by both sets of supporters? That for me was as close to utopia as you could ever get, it was wondrous and I could have retired there and then - maybe I should have.

It was the most special day of my life, although I would go on to play like a chocolate fireguard. I did nothing, I don't even know if I had a shot that game, I don't think I could have played more average if you had paid me.

It ended in a 1-1 draw and I left Fratton Park that day in tears.

During my time with Pompey I had walked away from the ground a few times in tears, a lot of occasions out of joy, a lot of times drunk as a skunk, the odd moment was out of pride, sometimes it had been prompted by the adulation received at the success we'd had.

Heading out of Fratton afterwards I was absolutely and honestly upset. When you've got a connection like that with a club it will never go.

Put all those memories together over that three-year period and it starts to knit this wonderful picture of so many exceptional times, highs and one-offs. Pompey was - and still is - my club.

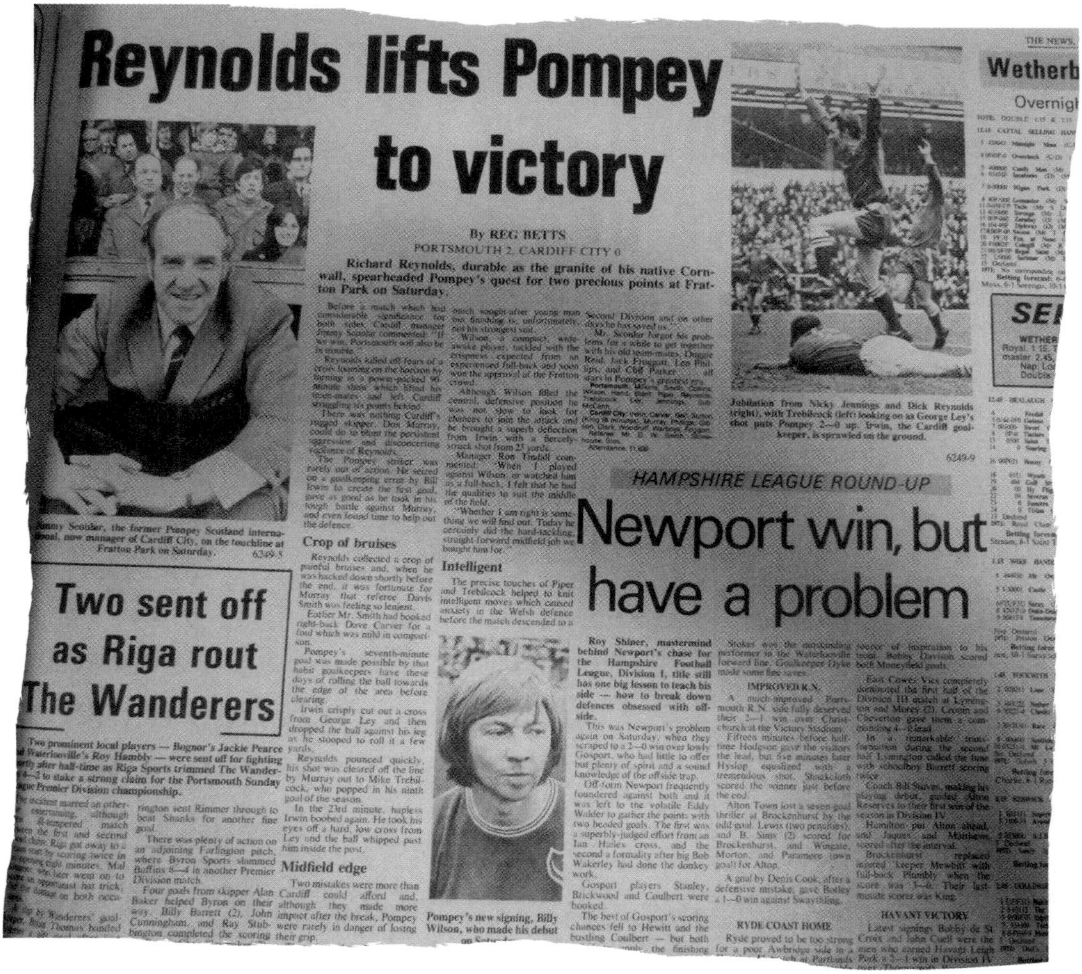

Reynolds lifts Pompey to victory

By REG BETTS

PORTSMOUTH 2, CARDIFF CITY 0

Richard Reynolds, durable as the granite of his native Cornwall, spearheaded Pompey's quest for two precious points at Fratton Park on Saturday.

Before a match which had considerable significance for both sides Cardiff manager Jimmy Scoular commented: "If we win, Portsmouth will also be in trouble."

Reynolds killed off fears of a crisis looming on the horizon by turning in a power-packed 90-minute show which lifted his team-mates and left Cardiff struggling six points behind.

There was nothing Cardiff's rugged skipper, Don Murray, could do to blunt the persistent aggression and disconcerting vigilance of Reynolds.

The Pompey striker was rarely out of action. He seized on a goalkeeping error by Bill Irwin to create the first goal, gave as good as he took in his tough battle against Murray, and even found time to help out the defence.

Crop of bruises

Reynolds collected a crop of painful bruises and, when he was hacked down shortly before the end, it was fortunate for Murray that referee Davis Smith was feeling so lenient.

Earlier Mr. Smith had booked right-back Dave Carver for a foul which was mild in comparison.

Pompey's seventh-minute goal was made possible by that habit goalkeepers have these days of rolling the ball towards the edge of the area before clearing.

Irwin crisply cut out a cross from George Ley and then dropped the ball against his leg as he stooped to roll it a few yards.

Reynolds pounced quickly, his shot was cleared off the line by Murray out to Mike Trebilcock, who popped in his ninth goal of the season.

In the 23rd minute, hapless Irwin boobed again. He took his eyes off a hard, low cross from Ley and the ball whipped past him inside the post.

Midfield edge

Two mistakes were more than Cardiff could afford and, although they made more impact after the break, Pompey were rarely in danger of losing their grip.

Intelligent

The precise touches of Piper and Trebilcock helped to knit intelligent moves which caused anxiety in the Welsh defence before the match descended to a much sought-after young man but finishing is, unfortunately, not his strongest suit.

Wilson, a compact, wide-awake player, tackled with the crispness expected from an experienced full-back and soon won the approval of the Fratton crowd.

Although Wilson filled the central, defensive position he was not slow to look for chances to join the attack and he brought a superb deflection from Irwin with a fiercely-struck shot from 25 yards.

Manager Ron Tindall commented: "When I played against Wilson, or watched him as a full-back, I felt that he had the qualities to suit the middle of the field.

"Whether I am right is something we will find out. Today he certainly did the hard-tackling, straight-forward midfield job we bought him for."

... Second Division and on other days he has saved us."

Mr. Scoular forgot his problems for a while to get together with his old team-mates, Duggie Reid, Jack Froggatt, Len Phillips, and Cliff Parker ... all stars in Pompey's greatest era.

Portsmouth: Milkins, Smith, Collins, Wilson, Hand, Blant, Piper, Reynolds, Trebilcock, Ley, Jennings. Sub: McCann.

Cardiff City: Irwin, Carver, Bell, Sutton (King 86 minutes), Murray, Phillips, Gibson, Clark, Woodruff, Warboys, Foggon.

Referee: Mr. D. W. Smith, Stonehouse, Glos.

Attendance: 11,039

...my Scoular, the former Pompey Scotland international, now manager of Cardiff City, on the touchline at Fratton Park on Saturday. 6249-5

Jubilation from Nicky Jennings and Dick Reynolds (right), with Trebilcock (left) looking on as George Ley's shot puts Pompey 2—0 up. Irwin, the Cardiff goalkeeper, is sprawled on the ground. 6249-9

Pompey's new signing, Billy Wilson, who made his debut on Satur...

Two sent off as Riga rout The Wanderers

HAMPSHIRE LEAGUE ROUND-UP

Newport win, but have a problem

Billy **Wilson**

216 games, six goals (January 1972 - May 1979)

Pompey 2 (Trebilcock, Ley)
Cardiff City 0

Division Two, Fratton Park, Saturday, January 22, 1972

Pompey: Milkins, Smith, Hand, Blant, Collins, Ley, Wilson, Piper, Jennings, Reynolds, Trebilcock.

Sub Not Used: McCann.

Attendance; 11,039

My first day of Pompey training was held indoors and involved Albie McCann kicking lumps out of me.

Nicky Jennings had already warned me. 'Watch your back, I am just telling you' I was informed on that Wednesday having joined from Blackburn Rovers in a £15,000 deal.

The first chance Albie got he gave me a whack up in the air, so I let it go. Then he gave me another whack and I stopped.

'Oi, if you kick me again I will knock your head off,' I snapped at him as I stood my ground.

That night he rang and invited me for a beer at the Green Dragon in Lovedean. He was as good as gold after that.

You see I had taken Albie's place in midfield for the approaching match against Cardiff City which was to serve as my Pompey debut in January 1972.

He didn't like that but it was a surprise to me as well, I'd never before played there. I was a goalkeeper as a kid before working my way up into defence, but had never served in midfield.

As I told Albie: 'It's not my fault I've had number four stuck on my back, I've come down to Pompey as a full-back!'.

I don't know why Ron Tindall put me in midfield to start with, perhaps he wanted somebody with a bit of bite, but I thoroughly enjoyed it.

If you make cock-ups in that role you can repair them and it certainly gets you more involved. It was good getting actually forward and into the opposition penalty area rather than your own.

Everything was left to Norman Piper, though, any free-kicks he was the maestro, he was the caress man.

That day we beat Cardiff 2-0 and I had my first win bonus in ages. It was also my favourite Pompey game, one that has forever remained special.

My move to Fratton Park had come out of the blue, I had to ask my wife, Heather, where Portsmouth even was!

I was having disagreements with the manager, Ken Furphy, we didn't see eye-to-eye, things had gone sour and I would have gone anywhere just to get away.

He had his favourites and I was banging my head against a brick wall trying to get into the team - then I was called into the office and that was it.

I'm on the train to the south coast, getting the hell out of there.

By the end of the week I was lining-up against a Cardiff side managed by former Pompey player Jimmy Scoular and my instructions were to get stuck in.

We smothered them in the first half, grabbed two goals and then sat back and enjoyed it to claim what was a comfortable victory.

Mike Trebilcock grabbed the first on seven minutes when Richie Reynolds' shot was cleared off the line by Cardiff's skipper Don Murray and the ball fell to Trebs to score.

Then in the 23rd minute, their keeper Bill Irwin took his eyes off a hard, low cross from George Ley and it went in at his near post.

I didn't get much time to celebrate, I had to run to catch the 5pm train from Fratton to London otherwise I would miss my connection to take me back to Blackburn to see my family.

Well, I got it by the skin of my teeth, but it was a race every other week for a while, my hair still wet following a post-match bath!

If I ever missed it, I had an hour-and-a-half wait for the next one and there was not a lot to do at Fratton station.

Pompey was a family club, it had a real community feel, and I loved being part of that for the next seven-and-a-half years.

In terms of socialising, the Green Dragon was the boys' haunt. A hell of a lot of us lived in Waterlooville, Norman Piper was just 100 yards from the pub, and we regularly met up there, talking football most of the time.

That was how it was then and I loved chatting to the fans, ideal for somebody who went on to run pubs across the area.

In my first year at Pompey, as a newcomer I got collared to attend the Isle of Wight Pompey Supporters' Club dinner.

My team-mates all tried to get out of going, they wanted to enjoy themselves at night, they weren't keen to get involved in chatting football, but I was put on a good table and thoroughly enjoyed it.

The following year they were looking for volunteers so I stepped forward again. 'What do you want to go there and keep talking about football for?' I was asked by some of the players. My response was 'What do you expect, they are supporters!'

I got to know a really nice family over there and would go every single year. I discovered a lot of Pompey supporters come from the Isle of Wight.

My game was about tackling. The ball could go past and the player could go past, but not at the same time. I wouldn't be allowed past the warm-up these days!

One time I was sent off against Leicester City for crabbing. I went into a tackle and we were both trying to get out and the referee thought we were trying to kick each other so sent us both off.

That is what Tindall brought me in for, to be a backbone to the team. I was a left-back but naturally right footed, I am right handed but play golf left handed.

Looking back at that team when I first arrived, we had Eoin Hand and big Colin Blant at the back, they would have run through brick walls, with little Freddy Smith at right-back.

Mike Trebilcock was good on the ball but left it to other people to actually get it! He was absolutely useless in a tackle, I don't think he could have tackled his missus, but he was a good footballer and scored a lot of goals.

Up front with him was Ray Hiron and they were telepathic as a partnership, they had a link, always knowing what was going to happen.

Tindall was sacked and replaced by John Mortimore, who in turn made way for Ian St John in September 1974 - and I couldn't stand the man.

I have never bumped into him since those days, I even used to switch Saint and Greavsie off when it appeared on my television!

He just wanted the kids in the team because he could boss them around, he used to scream at them, bawling them out.

Those of us who had an opinion and wouldn't be bullied were christened 'The Mafia' by St John, but weren't trouble makers at all.

He didn't like what he heard from us and eventually would walk past me, totally ignoring my presence.

Phil Roberts came to the club as a Welsh under-23 international and left a shaking wreck, St John humiliated him, he reduced him to tears.

Billy Hunter was his assistant, perhaps it was his influence more than anything, he was the ears, but I didn't like either of them.

If ever we were called into the office to see St John we always went in in twos so one would stop the other one from whacking him. Hunter was always there too.

The so-called Mafia was myself, Paul Went, Phil Roberts and Eoin Hand - and I was the one he blamed when the chairman, John Deacon, suspended him and then delivered the sack.

In 1976-77, with about six games to go, he turned round to those of us still there and said 'Get your boots, you lot can clear off, we don't need you'.

Then three days before we were to play at Preston North End, the chairman called asking what the problem was with St John and some of us players.

It turned out that Phil Roberts had earlier rung him up in tears and told him 'You have got to know what's going on'.

In turn the chairman said to me 'I've just had Phil on the phone crying, is it true?'

I said 'Yes, why?' and he replied 'Thank you'. That was it.

Later that day - it was a Wednesday - I was at Frank Vine's, the butchers in Farlington, all the players used to go there, we got him match tickets and he was a big Pompey fan.

'Have you heard the latest?' he said, 'St John has just got the sack'.

I said 'Oi stop taking the mickey, trying to raise my hopes'. He said 'No, it's true' - and it was!

When St John next went in there he blamed me personally for getting him the sack, yet I had done nothing, I'd just told the truth when the chairman asked.

Jimmy Dickinson took over and brought the members of 'The Mafia' that hadn't been moved on - myself and Phil - back into the side for the trip to Preston and we picked up a goalless draw. Luckily we had trained and kept fit.

Then we beat York City 3-1 at Fratton Park and despite losing our last match 4-3 at Swindon Town were safe, the old guard kept them up for another season.

One time under St John, the four of us singled out were training under the reserve-team coach Pat Wright at Eastney.

After a session I said to him 'What's happening now then, Pat?' he replied 'You've got to run a lap'.

Now we didn't have a game until Tuesday the following week so I asked what the point was as we were not even featuring for the first-team.

Pat said: 'I have been told to run you until you are sick,' so I said 'I'll be sick then' and deliberately threw up. Once I had been sick I walked off, went back to the club, got showered and went home. I was fuming.

Later that day, Pat came round our house and apologised saying he was just carrying out his job.

We had been relegated at the end of 1975-76 under St John having finished bottom of Division Two and there were some that didn't give their lot, I don't know why but they were still kept in the side.

If we had 8-10 pulling their weight we wouldn't have gone down, but half of them were just playing for the money and it was frustrating.

That is why I hate Manchester United, I played there many a time for Blackburn and they were so arrogant and when you got stuck in the first thing they would say was 'How much are you on a week, son?'.

Most of the United players would say that, not Bob Charlton, he was too nice.

I really used to hate the smell of their dressing room as well, whatever liniment they used was awful.

The following season at Fratton there were lots of kids coming through and they did well for a while. Then the bubble burst, they all of a sudden lost it, the enthusiasm went, St John started to shout at them and, of course, that didn't help.

In the end we looked like we were going to get relegated before Jimmy Dickinson came in as caretaker manager and we stayed up.

Jimmy was too much of a gentleman to be a manager, a lovely fella who had this thing where he would rub his hands and say 'Right lads, this is what I want you to do'.

At Blackburn one of my managers was Jack Marshall and you used to go into his office and think 'Right I am going to give him a right earful' and when you got through the door it was 'Wils how are you mate? Have a mint'.

By the time you finished sucking the mint you'd forgotten why you had gone in!

Jimmy was the same, so lovely and I had so much respect for him, a true gentleman of football.

I never heard him raise his voice, I don't think he ever shouted at anybody. He wasn't one of those that banged his fist and effed and blinded at players.

He could never be forthright about decisions he made, he wouldn't scream at you, instead he'd ask your opinion to see if he was right - and most of the time he was.

For team talks his approach was 'You all know your jobs, do them to the best of your ability and we should get a result'. It was that simple.

Or he would come in at half-time if something was going wrong and say 'I think you should do this', it was never 'You have to do this'. He was a lovely fella, I can't say enough good things about him.

When Jimmy suffered his heart attack at Barnsley in March 1979, his assistant Frank Burrows stepped up and was superb, you would run through a brick wall for that man.

It was either black or white, you either got a rollicking or a well done. If you got a rollicking you knew it was your fault, he would just tell it as it was and he wouldn't hold back.

We had a house in Talbot Road, Purbrook, and when Frank moved down he rented it until he bought a place in Cowplain. He daredn't drop me in case I put the rent up!

I could never be a manager, you have to be so two-faced because most of them are. Not with Frank, when he spoke that was it, you knew there was nothing more to be said on the subject and that he was right. Nine times out of 10 he was.

I enjoyed playing football again when he was manager but then again it was getting near the end and I was thinking about retiring to run The Pompey pub full time.

In January 1978 I was talking to club director Gordon Gauntlett and he was on about Eve, one of the barmaids, taking over the pub, which in those days was next to the ground.

Before then some couple had it and were useless.

So I told him if I couldn't do a better job than them I would show my backside in Woolworths - and he said 'Okay prove it'.

My wife Heather and I had already been working a couple of nights a week at the Fox & Hounds in Stakes Hill Road, Waterlooville, to get experience and loved it. We used to bring all the lads down for a Thursday night and it would get packed.

I couldn't actually be licensee of The Pompey as that person had to be on the premises at all times, something which was a bit difficult for a professional footballer! So Heather took it on.

We had it for 18 months before leaving in May 1979, it was always our intention to use it as a start in the trade, while it boosted takings for them to have a Pompey footballer behind the bar. And my managers were fine with it.

On a Saturday match day at home, the pub would open at 10.30am and I would always clean the pipes before reporting for the game at 2pm, with old licensing hours dictating it was shut from 2.30-6pm.

I remember us playing Grimsby Town at Fratton Park in February 1979 in what was our first Match of the Day appearance in eight years.

We lost 3-1 and I was responsible for two goals, I gave them away, the first of which I was trying to be clever and it didn't come off. I made two cock ups basically.

So after the game I had a shower, a quick pint of beer upstairs in one of the lounges and then went to The Pompey to open up for 6pm.

They all came in chanting 'There's only one Billy Wilson' and it was packed, lager after lager after lager were served until the chap ordering the round asked 'How much is that?'.

For argument's sake let's say it came to £20, so he counted it out in front of me before handing it over.

'There's far too much there', I said. He replied 'The rest is for you, we want you to buy a length of rope and hang yourself!'

It wasn't done nastily, it was all a joke, you would talk football all night and I didn't mind that at all. I would talk shop all day, me.

We turned that place into a community pub, we had regulars, some of the characters that used to come in were brilliant.

There was one bloke called Jacko who everybody thought was a fisherman, well he said he had his own boat, but he didn't!

He would come in bringing seafood. All the regulars would think 'Jacko is in tonight, we will have something nice and tasty to eat'.

Whenever I was away with Pompey we had to get extra staff in to help serve, but if it was local such as Bournemouth or Brighton & Hove Albion I would come back after the match to help out.

After a Fratton Park game, most of my team-mates would go into one of the lounges first before some came down. I served team-mates many a time!

It didn't clash with my football, though, it couldn't have, you couldn't just drink when you felt like it.

After the game yes, but through the week it would be nothing more than a couple of halves with training the next day.

The worst days were when deliveries arrived first thing in the morning, it was down the cellar, then training, then back behind the bar to serve our customers - but I would remain in the trade for 30 years before retiring in 2006.

Looking back at my footballing days, Pompey was good to start with, then I had that blip in the middle with a certain person I didn't get on with, but overall I loved those times.

OKI
PRINTING SOLUTIONS

Twenty points from nine games

HOW HARRY WON THE WAR

MARK STOREY

WIGAN..............1
Henri Camara 33
POMPEY..........2
Benjani Mwaruwari 62
Matt Taylor (pen) 70
Att: 21,126 (5,300 away fans)

MAN IN THE MIDDLE

Matt **Taylor**

203 games, 29 goals (June 2002 - January 2008)

Wigan Athletic 1 (Camara)
Pompey 2 (Benjani, Taylor)

Premier League, DW Stadium, Saturday, April 29, 2006

Pompey: Kiely, Priske, Stefanovic, Primus, Taylor, O'Neil, Mendes (68 mins Hughes), Davis (45 mins Pamarot), D'Alessandro, Benjani, Todorov (89 mins Routledge).

Subs Not Used: Ashdown, Karadas.

Attendance; 21,126

As the lads celebrated like crazy inside the away dressing room at the DW Stadium, I had serious family matters to attend to.

It was an incredible day, we had just stayed up in the Premier League and I had scored the winning penalty to defeat Wigan Athletic 2-1, running 70 yards to celebrate in front of our fans.

I was on cloud nine - but what I can remember most is the phone conversation with Hannah, my wife to be, who was in a Cornish hospital at the time.

There were several missed calls on my mobile from her when I picked it up after the match, but I didn't think too much of it until listening to a voice message she had left.

Hannah was on her hen do in Newquay but her sister - Deborah - had dislocated her finger while surfing, prompting an ambulance to be called to the beach.

So there I stood in the stadium corridor, speaking to my wife about her sister when I should have been celebrating with the rest of the lads.

Not that it could possibly overshadow the result and an occasion which, for me, stands out more than anything else during my 203 games for Pompey. People labelled it as the Great Escape and it pretty much was.

I firmly believe we deserved to stay up and it was good to do it with one game to go after everybody had written us off having been cast adrift.

It was even more satisfying to achieve away from home because we had sold out at Wigan, which is no mean feat, especially with a 500-mile round trip for the fans, but they were there cheering us on.

At the final whistle we had to wait for the Birmingham City result to come in, we had beaten Wigan and they had to fail to defeat Newcastle United to ensure we stayed in the Premier League with a match to spare.

I remember Harry Redknapp being unsure whether we were saved or not and the relief was immense when it came through the St Andrew's club had drawn 0-0 - then we ran over to the North stand to celebrate with more than 5,000 away followers.

It is all a kind of a blur, but watching it back on YouTube there are things I remember, while also noticing aspects I probably didn't appreciate at the time. I certainly didn't realise how much of an achievement it was to stay up considering where we were at Christmas.

During the match we had the lion's share of possession, dominating the game, but couldn't seem to score, then Wigan went up the other end against the run of play and netted through Henri Camara in the 34th minute.

It was a bit of an anti-climax, all the noise was coming from our fans, everybody was only interested in whether Pompey won or not, they didn't really care about Wigan as they were safe and didn't have a huge amount of fans at the ground anyway.

As ever, though, our supporters got behind us and in the 63rd minute, having been pushed up from left-back by the gaffer, the ball came to me, I hit it and it took a slight deflection off the keeper.

It then struck the inside of the far post and bounced back to where Benjani Mwaruwari was to head home from three yards for the equaliser and his first goal for Pompey after 15 appearances.

Benji is a wonderful person. In life - not just football - you meet people along the way you wish huge success to and it was lovely to see him go on to succeed not just at Pompey but also bigger clubs.

He used to terrorize people on the pitch and, as a left-back or left-sided midfielder, you knew if you played the ball into an area it could actually be made into a good pass because Benji would run after everything.

As a football fan, if you see your team out on the pitch giving 100 per cent you can excuse any mistakes they make because you know they are trying their best for you.

Benji is one of those players I can say only ever gave 100 per cent and that is why so many Pompey fans, even now, still love him.

You knew Benji would always go out and give you every single thing he had. Yes, he might make errors or miss a chance but it didn't affect him, he would just continue attempting the same thing again and again.

If you strip everything else away from it, effort and commitment is what you really want to see on a football pitch and if that is there then supporters can accept if something doesn't quite go right.

Anyhow, we were on level terms and then in the 71st minute Gary Teale used his left hand to block Benji's far-post header from Svetoslav Todorov's cross, earning him a red card and us a penalty.

We had beaten Sunderland the previous week when I scored an 88th minute spot kick - and I put it in exactly the same place, in the bottom right, to beat the keeper.

At the final whistle we couldn't get down the tunnel and then some fans came onto the pitch, carrying me off, it was a wonderful moment not only in my career but my life, those memories stay with you forever.

For the players, afterwards there is a celebration but ultimately it's a huge sigh of relief because we are all professionals, professional people, and ultimately your career is on the line.

Had we got relegated it would have cost everyone financially but, let's not beat around the bush, while money is an important part of football ultimately it is personal pride.

We were fortunate to have some really good leaders in the camp but also had a lot of fearless players, young players not scared and, being one of them, at the time you don't fully understand the situation you are in.

Nowadays I am definitely more aware now of any footballing situation I am in than I ever was at Pompey. As a youngster you are playing football every day, not thinking about anything else, whereas now I am definitely more conscious of everything else which goes on outside of football.

That Great Escape meant so much to us as a team and group of players, nobody gave us a chance so proving so many people wrong by believing in ourselves was self-assuring in a way.

We were near enough written off at Christmas and Harry coming back from Southampton having left us for them a year earlier obviously magnified the situation.

That January 2006 transfer window we recruited some important players, Sean Davis, Pedro Mendes, Noe Pamarot and Andres D'Alessandro, good signings but ultimately we were cast adrift and you have to win some games.

I remember going to Aston Villa in March and losing when we didn't deserve to, then heading into the visit of Manchester City to Fratton Park there were lots of rumours of the manager's position being under threat.

Rather than Harry potentially getting the sack, we were more aware of the fact had we lost that game against City maybe we wouldn't have the chance to stay in the Premier League.

As footballers you are ultimately part of a team, but your role within that team is vitally important and firstly you have to try to do as well as you can individually, then make sure collectively you do well for the side.

The manager's position probably isn't a huge remit within the players' thoughts because you are going out to do the best you can on the pitch - and if you do that then the manager won't be under any pressure anyway.

So I would suggest the biggest thing we were worried about going into that Manchester City fixture was getting a result to give us the best chance of staying in the top flight, not because we were worried about the manager losing his job.

Then Pedro scored that wonderful goal at the end to secure a 2-1 win and spark us on a run of 20 points from a possible 27 to keep us safe with a game to spare.

On that run we were lucky in some respects. I remember going to West Ham United and they had an FA Cup quarter-final against Manchester City just two days afterwards so rested a few players and we won convincingly 4-2.

Take nothing away from us and what we achieved, though, we had some different players but ultimately it was the same core of the team which started the season quite badly, so to come through it the way we did was fantastic.

We picked up a lot of results people wouldn't have expected us to and deservedly stayed up, it wasn't as if we coasted our way to survival that season, and was a tremendously gratifying feeling.

We were nine points adrift from safety with the second-worst goal difference in the league and 10 fixtures remaining going into that Manchester City match - and stayed up at Wigan with a game to spare.

I had arrived at Fratton Park in the summer of 2002 for £400,000 rising to £750,000, although could have gone to West Bromwich Albion, who were in the Premier League and managed by Gary Megson, who would later sign me for Bolton Wanderers.

Luton Town were my club at the time, we had just been promoted from what is now League One but I had the choice to join either Pompey or the Baggies.

I sat down with my dad, Simon, and my then agent and we were of the opinion this was a football move not a money move, certainly I was offered a lot more money elsewhere but we realised at Fratton Park I would be getting the opportunity to play every week.

It was an easy decision but I got really lucky, I was put into a team which played great football and used to run up and down the line where Paul Merson would find me, they were wonderful times.

As a 20-year-old, I had only ever seen guys like Merse on television so for me to be able to play with him week in, week out was superb.

He never used to warm up, he would sit and have a cup of tea with Harry indoors and then all of a sudden it came to 3pm and would turn it on, he was phenomenal.

I missed the last few months of the season through a heel injury, but remember walking onto the pitch with my eldest daughter, Georgia, when we had got promoted to the Premier League and that was a wonderful experience.

Throughout my career it is nice to be able to share these experiences with your family and your children, those memories were wonderful and to share it with those you are closest to is priceless.

I was still injured at the start of our first season in the Premier League and really struggled to get back into the side largely until Christmas, it was difficult.

What it teaches you, though, is character and alerts you to the demands of the Premier League and how football is a squad game. It is not about 11 players on the pitch every Saturday, there will be injuries, there will be loss of form, the manager will change his mind, that is the way of football.

In the end I went on to play a lot of games for Pompey in the top flight and had some wonderful memories, including that Great Escape season a few years later.

My favourite goal for the club was at Sunderland in October 2005, purely and simply for no other reason than I wasn't even in the team the day before the game!

Laurent Robert had been selected and I think the fact he had just left the Black Cats' rivals Newcastle and a few issues with that meant he decided to tell Alain Perrin at midday on the Saturday he wasn't fit so the gaffer basically just said 'Matty you are in'.

We went 1-0 down through a Dean Whitehead penalty, Zvonimir Vukic levelled just after half-time and then I scored to put us in front.

It would be eight minutes later when the ball fell into my path down the left and I struck a 45-yard shot first time which flew into the net. It was 3-1 and I had my favourite goal!

Then I set up the fourth for Dario Silva as we wrapped up a 4-1 victory - I couldn't have had a better game to be honest!

In actual fact, Richard Hughes had given me a dead leg in training the day before so I could hardly move, but the gaffer told me I was playing so I intended to!

Fans also talk about the strike from just past the halfway line against Everton in December 2006 at Fratton Park and ironically it was nothing more than a ricochet off Kanu which set it up for me.

Hughesie was on the bench that day and before the game I told him if I scored I would be going to see him. When it happened, I distinctly remember ignoring the rest of my team-mates and running to the dugout to celebrate with him.

When you are younger you don't really have any fear so you take on things and I probably wouldn't do that shot now if I am honest. At that age you don't really care about missing, though.

Another game which sticks out was the 4-1 win over Southampton in April 2005 in which I may not have scored but took it a little bit far while celebrating Arjan De Zeeuw's headed goal in front of their fans!

I didn't want to leave Pompey but it came to the point where I wasn't playing and had a discussion with the manager - Harry - and a bit of a row.

It was the stage of my career where I needed to play football and fortunately had a few options and a few decisions which made everything slightly easier for me with four clubs to choose from in Sunderland, Middlesbrough, Rangers and Bolton.

Ironically, I suppose because of the experiences I had with Pompey, in January 2008 I joined a team second from bottom in Bolton when I could have moved further north with sides which were more successful that year.

As a southern lad, I didn't want to move a huge distance away from home so chose Manchester. Besides, I had given my word to Megson, we had a bit of a rapport, it was the right decision for me and was completely and utterly proven to be correct.

Earlier that season I nearly signed for Tottenham Hotspur, in fact I thought everything had gone through.

You ask my wife, we were living in the house I am in now just outside Abingdon, Oxfordshire, and we had to go down to the local pub because we had no fax machine at home to send correspondence, but it wasn't meant to be.

I do, however, owe a lot of gratitude to Harry, he put a lot of faith in me and I was very fortunate to sign for the club and then play as much as I did.

Looking back, the thing a lot of people don't realise is within a season of leaving what is now League Two I was playing Premier League football, put that into context these days and not that many players will have done that.

When you start off where I did and suddenly go to the Premier League you become very humble and actually really, really accepting about everything that is done to you.

For me football has not been about money, it has been about football and if you are doing well you will earn the money.

I have been really fortunate to have made the right decisions on a football basis and dad has helped me along the way and remained a big part of my life and career, his opinion really mattered.

I spent the best years of my career at Pompey, not just football-wise, I had my first child when I was there, I got married while I was there, I had a lot of milestones there and really enjoyed my time, it was wonderful.

Last season when interviewed for Burnley's match-day programme I was asked to name the best XI I played with. When you look at the players Pompey have had you actually realise, without being rude, why they were in the financial trouble they were.

You think of the players I played with the club and what they were paying them - then consider how they were trying to fund it.

As a player you are either adored or jeered by fans and I was always treated extremely well by Pompey supporters so it has been upsetting for me, purely as a football fan rather than an ex-player, to see it go the way it did.

It is still a fantastic football club - and I have never had that 'Super Matt' chant sung to me since leaving there.

PORTSMOUTH BUILDIN

16 THE NEWS, TUESDAY, DECEMBER 28, 1976

JUST GREAT, POMPEY

Glorious win for 32,300

POMPEY 1, BRIGHTON 0

...s a win it was famous . . . as an ...sion memorable . . . as an exercise ...e art of winning friends and influ...g people it was textbook.

By Mike Neasom

... about sums up ...'s exploits yester... ...ore the largest ...match crowd at ...Park for nine long ... December '67 ...lackpool's visit ...00 beat it.

...t of table-topping ...resented Ian St ...rgent youngsters ... daunting test of ...ine together — ...t with the assur...ns.

...TRUN

...hey won thanks ...of slackness in ...defence which ...by that ebullient ...Pollock — but ...was the one real ...e occasion.

...e end of this ... and cheering ...mpey had outrun ...t a side rated ... promotion so ... a score of 3—0 ...not have flat...

...the win was so ...ded, the point ...derlooked after... ...about winning.

"We find this, people surpass themselves when they meet us.

"But really we got what we deserved ... after all if you give a goal away and then miss a penalty, you can't really expect to get too much can you?"

That penalty miss — Brian Horton's attempt at a bottom right-hand placement being read brilliantly by Grahame Lloyd, cost the Brighton skipper the job.

"Graham Cross will take the next one ... I wouldn't like to think of the pressure on Horton, or myself, if he ran up to take it after missing his last two," commented Mullery.

That Lloyd save — pretty well the only serious moment of action the Pompey 'keeper was to experience — was a crucial factor in the win.

It came in the 20th minute as Albion were beginning to exert themselves after the deflating experience of seeing David Kemp snap up his third Pompey goal in the seventh minute.

STUNNING

...Pullar was judged to ...

Peter Denyer dives in, as Pompey keep up the second half pressure.

... through a defence in which the fiercely-determined partnership of Paul Cahill and Steve Foster allowed nothing to pass.

These two have been together for only seven matches but they promise to become as effective and destructive a combination as Fratton fans have seen for a very long time.

But above all else this victory, which could herald the start of something really big at Fratton, was a team performance.

Pompey won because they had 11 men prepared to fight and work for everything; Brighton had fewer with that brand of dedication.

Their defence lacked that central core, in midfield they had no one to combat the work of Christ Kamara and Peter Denyer, and up front Pompey held the aces in Pollock, again a non-stop worker, Kemp and Micky Mellows whose driving running on the left had Chris Cattlin struggling.

Only two things blotted the afternoon. Keith Viney and Paul Cahill got themselves booked — Viney for kicking ... three policemen, but its aftermath was the appearance of a dozen or so other youngsters out on the grass despite the moat.

Still nothing could deflate Pompey's delight at the victory all had dreamed of but few had expected.

CLINCHED

It was clinched in the seventh minute as Horton hit a bad back pass. Pollock just beat Peter Grummitt to the ball and touched it into the goalmouth where Kemp was unmarked.

Brighton had just got the shock out of their system when referee Shapter's penalty decision looked like rocking Pompey's self-assurance but Lloyd buoyed it up. For the rest of a first half fought tigerishly and at breakneck speed but littered with stoppages, the nearest either side came to scoring was a 25-yard drive by Cattlin which seared just wide.

After the interval, however, Pompey really took over. They stretched Brighton's defence, exploiting their uncertainty at full back, and driven on by a ... bustle and hustle of Sammy Morgan but even he could not break the hold of the Foster-Cahill duo.

It was all Pompey. Pollock and Mellows carved their way through in the 69th minute but Grummitt stretched into a fine one-handed save. Then it was a Pollock cross and a fine overhead effort by Kemp which set up another chance which Pullar could not accept.

CLIMAX

At last Brighton managed a raid which promised some significant ending — but Lloyd saved splendidly from Tony Towner and the offside whistle made even that exercise by the 'keeper unnecessary.

At the other end, however, it was different for the veteran Grummitt who saved at full strength as Mellows got in a header.

Just to crown the afternoon the teams also stage-managed a magnificent climax.

First in the 87th minute Pollock's glancing header from Norman Piper's cross inched its way wide of Kemp sliding in just too late. Immediately at the other end the potentially ...

A Cross sandwich . . . Graham Cross provides the "fi... Peter Denyer and Steve Foster in an aerial encount...

• RESULTS CHE...

DIVISION I

Birmingham 0, West Ham 0; Coventry 1, Ipswich 1; Derby 1, Leicester 0, Leeds 0; Manchester City 3, Liverpool 4; Stoke 0, Manchester Un. 4, Everton 0; Middlesbrough 3, Aston Villa 2; Newcastle 2, Sunderland 0; Norwich 2, Q.P.R. 0; Tottenham 2, Arsenal 2; West Bromwich 1, Bristol City 1.

DIVISION II

Blackburn 2, Burnley 2; Blackpool 0, Carlisle 0; Bolton 1, Nottingham Forest 1; Bristol Rovers 1, Wolves 5; Cardiff 3, Hereford 1; Chelsea 2, Fulham 0; Millwall 1, Charlton 1; Notts Co. 1, Hull 1; Oldham 1, Sheffield Un. 2; Orient 1, Luton 0; Plymouth 1, Southampton 1.

DIVISION III

Chesterfield 0, Mansfield 1; Gillingham 0, Crystal Palace 3; Lincoln 2, Grimsby 0; Northampton 1, Rotherham 4; Portsmouth 1, Brighton 0; Port Vale 0, Bury 1; Reading 1, Peterborough 0; Sheffield Wed. 3, York 2; Shrewsbury 2, Tranmere 2; ...

Division One

	Home				Goals		Away			Goals		
	P	W	D	L	F	A	W	D	L	F	A	Pts
Liverpool	21	9	1	0	26	5	4	2	5	10	15	29
Ipswich	19	6	4	0	21	6	5	2	2	16	12	28
Man. City	20	6	3	1	15	8	3	6	1	12	7	27
Aston Villa	20	8	1	1	32	12	3	2	5	11	14	25
Newcastle	19	7	3	0	19	7	2	3	4	13	15	24
Arsenal	19	6	2	1	21	9	3	3	4	15	20	23
Middlesbro	19	7	1	2	10	6	2	3	4	5	12	22
Birmingham	21	5	3	2	16	9	3	2	6	16	19	21
Leicester	21	3	5	2	16	16	2	6	3	8	15	21
West Brom	19	5	4	1	21	8	2	2	5	7	16	20
Coventry	18	5	3	3	19	14	1	3	3	5	9	18
Leeds	18	2	5	3	13	18	3	2	3	10	9	17
Norwich	19	4	2	3	10	10	2	3	5	9	15	17
Everton	19	4	3	2	15	11	2	2	6	14	25	17
Man. Utd	17	2	3	3	15	13	3	3	3	13	14	16
[illegible]	18	4	4	1	16	7	0	4	5	6	16	16

Division ...

	P	W	D
Rotherham	20	5	4
Wrexham	20	7	4
Brighton	20	7	1
Preston	20	7	2
Shrewsbury	20	6	
Sheffield W.	20	7	
Mansfield	19	6	
Crystal Pal	19	5	
Bury	20	7	
Tranmere	20	5	
Swindon	20	6	
Lincoln	18	3	
Chesterfield	20	5	
Chester	19	5	
Oxford	21	3	
Reading	20	5	

Dave **Kemp**

74 games, 38 goals (November 1976 - March 1978)

Pompey 1 (Kemp)
Brighton & Hove Albion 0

Division Three, Fratton Park, Monday, December 27, 1976

Pompey: Lloyd, Piper, Foster, Cahill, Viney, Denyer, Kamara, Mellows, Pullar, Kemp, Pollock.

Sub Not Used: Green

Attendance; 32,368

It wasn't a very good idea leaving Pompey, but it is easy to live your life in hindsight.

There was a lot of talk about getting some quite glamorous moves, clubs like Aston Villa, Derby County, Leicester City and QPR, but nothing ever materialised.

Then the final day of the transfer window in March 1978 I was offered the chance to go to fellow Division Three side Carlisle United in a deal worth £75,000.

The agreement would also see midfielder John Lathan coming to Fratton Park, being valued at £25,000.

It was a last-minute thing, it wasn't going well at Pompey, we were struggling against relegation, so I decided to leave. I shouldn't have done.

The concept of freedom of contract was coming into football for the very first time that summer and my Fratton Park deal was running out.

I should have waited until the season's end, then I would have been a free agent and could have had my pick of clubs, but the situation was all new to football.

I tried to get advice and struggled to receive any, everything was up in the air at the time.

Up until the summer of 1978, if your contract ran out the club continued to hold your registration so you had to stay with them whether you were out of contract or not.

Obviously nowadays when your deal runs out you can move on and join whoever you want within reason, yet it wasn't the case back then.

Changes to the system were coming up but I was in unfamiliar territory and made a rash decision I shouldn't have. Like a lot of things in life, I'm very wise after the event.

Carlisle was not a good decision, but I enjoyed my time there. It's not as if I didn't do well, I scored 26 goals in 68 appearances over an 18-month period.

But it wasn't a good career move.

Pompey were going down under Jimmy Dickinson despite me netting 21 times by March and I didn't want to play in Division Four. My contract was running out, and I was thinking 'I could be stuck here' and on the same money, it was a strange time.

Obviously I should have just waited until the end of the season instead of leaving on the last day of the window for Carlisle in the same division, especially when others were definitely interested in me.

A week after I signed for the Cumbrians, Ron Saunders, who was manager of Villa, said to me 'What are you doing, what did you go and do that for? You should have waited and then you could have signed for us'.

I replied 'It's no good telling me now, why didn't you tell me a week ago!'.

If I just waited I would have been a free agent and could have signed for anybody, but I didn't know that. In the current climate I know it is normal practice but those days no-one knew.

There weren't the agents and advisers you get now, you were a young man wanting to play football.

In the end I didn't get higher than the Division Three in my career, I got stuck there, and that was my own fault when I left Pompey to go to Carlisle. I should have moved up and didn't.

Whenever I played against higher level teams in the FA Cup I always scored so I don't think it was a case of I couldn't have done it at a higher level, I'm sure I could.

When the chances came I stuck them in and I remember scoring for Pompey against Leicester City when they were in Division One in a League Cup game at Fratton Park in August 1977.

Clive Green grabbed the other as we beat them 2-0 late on. That was a good night, it gave you a hint of the potential of the club and that is what I remember about the place, a great football city.

At one stage I guested for Derby in a testimonial match for Roy McFarland against Bruges and scored in a 2-0 win.

Derby wanted to sign me but Pompey tried to squeeze more money out of them because I did so well in that match, so the Rams pulled out of the deal.

I loved it at Pompey but unfortunately it was the right club at the wrong time, how I would have relished playing there in a successful team.

However, in those 16 months you could see the incredible potential it possessed, none more so than in a home match with Brighton & Hove Albion held two days after Christmas Day in December 1976.

In my favourite Pompey game we won 1-0, needless to say I scored the goal, but the occasion made me realise how big the club actually was.

They had won the league a couple of times, then 26 years later the club was in the doldrums - yet the incredible fan base was still there.

On that day against Brighton there were 32,368 inside the stadium, while outside 10,000 fans couldn't even get in.

It was the biggest crowd I ever played in front of during my time at the club - home or away - while when we went to their place the attendance was 25,451.

We later discovered it was the largest league crowd at Fratton Park for nine years, when a December 1967 fixture with Blackpool drew 35,000.

The atmosphere against the Seagulls that day was fantastic and travelling to the ground was like going to the FA Cup final, the streets were jammed with people, it wasn't all ticket and everyone was trying to get in.

I knew all about the history of the club, of course I did, but this was only my sixth appearance for them and seeing that level of interest blew me away, it was unbelievable. You can only appreciate it when you are in Portsmouth.

We were up and down under Ian St John and Brighton had a good team in those days, they were top of Division Three at the time under Alan Mullery and I suppose the fact it was around Christmas also increased the crowd.

I remember looking at the crowd when I was out on the pitch and thinking if the club took off you could fill the stadium every week.

We got decent gates anyway, but that was the realisation of what Pompey could become, it really hit home.

The game itself may have finished 1-0 to us but it was action-packed, definitely not dull, with action at both ends, while Grahame Lloyd saved Brian Horton's 20th minute penalty.

My goal was a tap-in on seven minutes. Somebody said to me the following week 'I could have scored that' and I replied 'The trouble is you have actually got to be on the pitch to do it!'

It came from a bad back pass from Horton, Matt Pollock just beating Brighton's keeper Peter Grummitt to the ball and touching it to me to put into the net.

It was the winning goal and an important one. You don't just recall the ones you smash in from the edge of the box, I remember all my goals and they are all important at the time.

Even though it was a tap-in it was an important goal for the club.

Brighton represented the third successive match I had netted and we won them all. Soon the fans started a song about me to the tune of The Scaffold's 'Lily The Pink' entitled 'Dave The Kemp', which made me smile and I really appreciated it.

I'm told even today the Fratton end sing it, even though most of the kids singing wouldn't have been anywhere near born when I was playing! It's nice anyway.

I've been back in recent years to take in a match and somebody I was with pointed it out to me, I thought they were taking the mickey because my hearing is not too good!

It is lovely to be remembered but only the older people sitting in the stadium know who I am. The younger people must think 'Who are they singing about?'

That was the relationship I had with those fantastic fans, you don't realise you are popular until you think back. You certainly don't take things for granted, but that is the world you are in at that time and take it as normal.

I was even a centrefold in Roy of the Rovers because the editor, Ian Vosper, was a Pompey nut and as I was scoring goals for his team started using me as storylines!

I don't know many people who have actually had that. Roy even took the trouble to come down to Fratton to have his picture taken with me and some of my Pompey team-mates. Well, it was a big cardboard cut-out!

When I was assistant manager to Tony Pulis at Stoke City, the boys put a copy of the cartoon on the wall. Times change though, half of them didn't even know who Roy Race was!

It was St John who brought me to Pompey from Crystal Palace in November 1976, in a straight exchange for George Graham who I don't think had been a success.

There wasn't much money down at Fratton Park and I assume my wages were a good deal less than his so the chairman, John Deacon, must have been very happy to reduce costs.

I had broken into the team at Palace, had a good spell but lost my place and then didn't like being out of the side.

It was a bit different from today with the squads, back then you had the first XI and the reserves and I didn't want reserve football, I wanted to be in the first team. If I wasn't going to play I would go.

It's silly when you think about it, I was young, had been in the team and probably didn't handle being out of it very well - and that is how the move to Pompey came about.

I didn't really look too closely into the finances of the club I was joining, I suppose today an agent would do his research but they wanted me, had a fantastic history and I was impressed by St John - so thought let's go and play.

Some of the players didn't like St John - but I enjoyed playing for him.

He went in May 1977 during my first season which was a shame, he did well and inherited an older team which wasn't doing very well, he moved the older players on and started to bring in younger players, local players.

For him it was a chance to build a team and he created a vibrant, young side.

St John had been a manager at Motherwell and was offered a chance at Pompey, probably thinking like I did that it was a great club and could take off. But football can be very difficult with no investment in the team and the club not run properly.

Some may say St John was a bully but he was a manager, that is what managers do sometimes, while moving people on happens in football, that is how it works.

There are senior players who might have felt let down by the way he handled them but the club had been relegated from Division Two the year before and you have got to put yourself in his shoes. He'll be thinking 'The senior players aren't doing it for me, it's not happening so I have got to do something'.

St John was sacked with three games to spare and Jimmy Dickinson came in as caretaker to keep us up - but I believe we would have stayed up under the Scotsman anyway.

Under Dickinson we drew at Preston North End, beat York City 3-1 at home and then lost 4-3 at Swindon Town, with me scoring in the final two matches to finish the season with 17 goals in 33 games.

We got enough points from those games to stay in Division Three. The board had panicked and dismissed St John, but with the fixtures we had we weren't going to get relegated anyway.

In the April under him we had beaten Rotherham United 5-1 at Fratton and they went on to get promoted. We had a young team and I always felt had a chance in those matches.

We could beat Rotherham but then the following week lost 3-0 at home to Tranmere Rovers and that can happen when you have young, inexperienced defenders. We would always be having a go but sometimes didn't have that experience to grind games out.

We could play really well and win quite well, but at the same time could be beaten quite poorly - and definitely would have stayed up even if he had remained in charge.

Jimmy was a legend at the club and a really nice man but being a top player and a manager are completely different, I don't want to disparage him but I don't think management was his game.

Being a Pompey legend doesn't count for anything when you are manager of the club and have to win games, which required different skills. I don't think it was a good move, they should have left St John in charge.

Having said that, despite staying up there was no real investment for the 1977-78 season, I don't think we signed anyone, we had virtually the same people from the season before who hadn't done very well so how were we going to improve?

Of course we struggled, it wasn't good, but I managed to score 21 goals - then in March 1978 left for Carlisle.

It didn't matter if the side I was in was not playing well, I could score goals and I scored goals at whatever club I was at.

I have been coaching longer than I played and there is an argument I have with academy-type coaches who say 'This bloke is a really good player' and I always say 'That's brilliant, what does he do?'.

They tell me 'He controls it and passes it' and my response is 'Yes but what does he do for the team? Does he score goals, does he make goals, does he stop goals? What does this bloke do?'

If they still can't tell you what he does then you haven't really got a player.

When somebody says 'What did David Kemp do?' - well, he scored goals.

If you are signing a defender you want to know if he can stop goals, if he can head it or is a good marker or something. If somebody says he has two good feet and is nice on the ball well brilliant, but what is that going to do for the team?

Someone needs to have an identity and my identity was I scored goals. If somebody signed me they knew I would score 20 goals a season for them.

Not wanting to blow my own trumpet but I was good at getting on the end of crosses, I could score goals by beating players, I could tap them in. I was a poacher, better in the opposition penalty area than anywhere else on the field.

You go back through the history of football, when I scored my goals was the time when the least number were netted in the Football League.

Nowadays the average is three goals a game - when I played it was 1.5 goals a game and the hardest era in football to score.

A lot of my goals I can remember, but not always the ones fans like, they may recall the spectacular, but for me it is more for the importance of the goal at the time.

I played for 15 years and have now coached for more than 30 years. In fact my coaching career has been more successful than my playing career, half my time has been in the Premier League and there has been an FA Cup final, something I didn't do as a player. But I enjoyed my time as a player.

The funny thing is virtually every club I've been at I have been there twice, with Pompey one of them.

There was Wimbledon three times, Plymouth Argyle three times, Stoke twice, Millwall twice, Pompey twice, Palace three times, it is unbelievable.

I was fortunate to be able to go back to Pompey and in January 2000 was first-team coach with Tony Pulis. When I left all those years before I lived in Waterlooville and there was a football ground over the road - not any more, it's a housing estate!

The first training session I took at Fratton Park was surreal really. I had played in that ground and now was there taking training, it just gets you thinking.

Tony and I came together when the club were going to get relegated, it was third from bottom in Division One and we kept them up comfortably, had meetings in the summer and it was all going to take off the way the owner, Milan Mandaric, was talking.

Then as soon as the season started his attitude had changed, I don't know what had happened and we were gone by October.

After that we went to Plymouth who were rooted in the bottom three and going down and kept them up comfortably, Stoke were the same and the same at Palace. We also got Stoke into the Premier League and kept them there.

Looking back at me and Tony at Fratton Park, we signed Linvoy Primus, Nigel Quashie and Kevin Harper, who were both part of the Harry Redknapp's side who won the Division One title, and overall in the transfer market we did great.

Where it all went wrong I have no idea because it was all going swimmingly, we had those meetings in the summer and it was going to be wonderful the next season and as soon as we came back to work something had changed, I don't know what and how but it was a struggle.

That's football, you don't dwell on things like that, life isn't fair let alone football, you just accept it, that is the way it was. It could have all been so different, no question.

The history of Pompey is terrible in terms of their finances, they have been taken to the cleaners so many times, virtually all of my lifetime. They have been so poorly run so often by so many different people, I just feel sorry for the city and the fans.

If they could have just struck lucky once with one owner it could have been a most fantastic club.

So many times in this period the club could have taken off. Can you imagine if Pompey had kept pace with everybody else and had a beautiful new stadium, were somewhere up the leagues and well run? You would struggle to get a ticket.

They always seem to get themselves in bad situations, nobody has ever grasped it properly.

I loved it at Pompey, I just wish it was with a better team and we could have been successful. I would have loved to have been part of a successful Pompey team.

PREMIERSHIP POMPEY

GOAL ONE: Yakubu puts Pompey in front from the spot

GOAL TWO: Arjan De Zeeuw heads home Patrik Berger's free-kick

GOAL THREE: Lomana Lualua beats Antti Niemi

GOAL FOUR: Lualua fires home his dream second

IT DOESN'T GET ANY BETTER

by STEVE BONE at Fratton Park

POMPEY ....4 SOUTHAMPTON 1

Yakubu Ayegbeni (pen) 3, Arjan De Zeeuw 17, Lomana Lualua 22, 26

Henri Camara 20

Att: 20,210

FOUR-ONE. Say it. Then say it again – as many times as you like.

Can there ever have been a more remarkable opening half-hour at Fratton Park?

MAN IN THE MIDDLE

STEVE DUNN (Gloucs)

Let it flow and got the big decisions right – but he should have booked Niemi for

Lomana **Lualua**

91 games, 19 goals (February 2004 - August 2007)

Pompey 4 (Lualua 2, Yakubu, De Zeeuw)
Southampton 1 (Camara)

Premier League, Fratton Park, Sunday, April 24, 2005

Pompey: Ashdown, Griffin, De Zeeuw, Stefanovic, Taylor, Stone, O'Neil, Hughes, Berger (57 mins Cisse), Yakubu (78 mins Skopelitis), Lualua (28 mins Kamara).

Subs Not Used: Hislop, Fuller.

Attendance; 20,210

It was a victory I dreamt was going to happen, a sleep-induced vision arriving the night before.

Normally if I know I am going to play in a match I kind of visualise an outcome, I imagine myself scoring in different scenarios, it's how I like to prepare.

Sometimes I see things in my sleep, it depends how much stress I'm under and what my mind is focused on during the build-up.

The visit of Southampton in April 2005 was massive, a big, big game and I would get the reminder of its importance from people whenever I went into town.

Everybody was talking about it, you had no choice but to dream about playing Southampton when the day came around.

On that Saturday night before the fixture, I dreamt Pompey would win 2-0 with myself and my friend Yakubu scoring.

I wasn't far wrong, although I never quite visualised leaving the pitch after 28 minutes having scored twice and won a penalty!

It was an amazing match, a perfect day and I thank God for giving me the opportunity to be involved in an occasion which is so special to Pompey fans.

I will never, ever forget being in that game and it means everything to me knowing I played my part in a 4-1 win against my club's biggest rivals.

It was also a relegation fight, they were third from bottom and we were only two places ahead with seven more points. We couldn't let them close the gap on us with only four matches remaining.

As a footballer, I always get nervous before a game and remember driving to Fratton Park on this overcast day, then we got changed and came out for the warm-up and you could see how packed the ground was.

You could feel the passion, it was everywhere, such an amazing feeling, and it gave us an extra 10 per cent of energy.

I was so proud of my team-mates that day, we could have let the fans down but knew how important that game was for the city. We just had to beat Harry Redknapp and our local rivals.

In the week beforehand every time you went into town everybody was talking about it. They were saying 'You need to win, it means a lot to us, please beat this team'.

It was a kind of wake-up call, although at one stage I didn't want to go out because it made you feel under so much pressure. We understood though, you knew you had to be right on your toes for this match.

In training ahead of the fixture, I was actually suffering from a little bit of an injury. I had a problem with my hamstring, but didn't want to miss that game for anything, especially with Harry coming back.

I had no problems with Harry, he was the one who took me to Pompey from Newcastle United in February 2004 initially on loan, I have so much respect for him.

In football I am not one of those people who wants to wait, I want to play and had the opportunity to go to Leeds United but decided against it because I knew the type of player Harry likes and knew I would play under him.

It was a gamble to come to Fratton Park, especially when at the time they were one place above the relegation zone, but I knew I would enjoy my football under him and he provided me with the opportunity to show everyone I could play in the Premier League.

I would score on my Pompey debut too, coming on as a substitute for Amdy Faye in a 4-3 defeat at Tottenham Hotspur that same month and netting with a right-foot shot from just outside the area.

Gus Poyet grabbed an 89th minute winner for David Pleat's side, with Jermain Defoe, making his debut for Spurs, also getting a goal.

I ended that season with four goals in 15 matches as we finished our first Premier League campaign in 13th place, 12 points clear of the relegation zone, earning me a permanent move to Fratton Park.

So there Harry was the following season and now manager of Southampton coming back to play us - facing your ex-manager always gives you that extra buzz, even if you still liked him.

Not that we spoke before the game, the atmosphere was so tense we weren't trying to think about him, our focus was on giving 150 per cent and fighting, fighting hard, this was a win we really, really wanted.

It took just four minutes to gain the lead following a mistake by Antti Niemi.

I don't think I would have scored, I was going wide so the keeper actually helped me in the situation. When I saw that ball coming through I thought I would try to race him to get it.

I managed to get a touch, Niemi brought me down and Yakubu calmly stroked the penalty down the middle to break the deadlock.

By winning that spot kick after Niemi had gone through me, though, my hamstring had gone, but it wasn't going to stop me.

On 17 minutes it was 2-0 when Patrik Berger took a free-kick from the right and our skipper Arjan De Zeeuw was at the far post with a diving header.

Just three minutes later it was 2-1 when Henri Camara pulled one back with a low shot into the far bottom corner of Jamie Ashdown's net and the atmosphere was terrific.

Then arrived my two goals in five minutes.

The first was a long cross-field ball delivered by Berger from the left, I saw the keeper coming and my main feeling was to try to scare him off to win the ball as I knew he couldn't touch it outside the box.

Luckily it worked, he missed it and I swivelled and put it into the net with a right-foot shot from outside the box and celebrated with a flip!

It's funny because with the second goal on 27 minutes I wasn't even supposed to be on the pitch because I was injured!

When I scored I contemplated doing another flip, but if you look back at the footage you can see the pain in my face, my hamstring was giving me agony.

After the first goal I was actually going to go off, but it was decided between us to give it another five minutes to see how it went and carry on playing for a little longer.

It was a good second goal as well, Yakubu squared a pass to Steve Stone and Danny Higginbotham slid in with a tackle which resulted in the ball springing loose.

I was waiting outside the box and took one touch before curling it home right-footed, via the inside of the post, but there was to be no flip, my body wasn't going to let me!

A minute later I had to come off, my hamstring had gone and that was to be my last appearance of the season, missing the final three matches.

I was gutted to come off, I wanted to stay there and carry on playing, I was on a hat-trick, and as I left the pitch I suppose you can say I took the goals with me, the match remaining 4-1 until the final whistle.

I gave everything I had within me for those 28 minutes and for the rest of the game sat on the bench cheering us on, I couldn't go back to the dressing room for treatment and miss any of it. I had to stay and support the boys.

The goals and scoreline I dreamed about didn't quite happen - we did even better than that - and I was so thankful for being part of the Pompey team which made that happen.

Living in Port Solent and playing for them I became a fan, it was my team. They weren't my employers, they were the club I supported and wanted to see do really well.

You ask anybody, all the time I was out in the city meeting people, mixing socially and taking part in a lot of charity work with Linvoy Primus. I was a fan of the city and knew how much that match meant to everybody.

It was the best day. I had played for Newcastle against Sunderland but that derby was nothing like the south-coast fixture, that day was unbelievable, just crazy, and '(Is This The Way To) Amarillo' going around Fratton Park - I can still hear it.

Southampton would go on to be relegated three games later after finishing the season in bottom place, while we ended up 16th in the table.

I will never forget that match, I have played in different countries across the world - Greece, Cyprus, Qatar and Turkey - but have never scored twice and got an assist in 28 minutes on the pitch. Incredible.

That game was probably my favourite in my entire career, you just don't do that.

Alain Perrin was our manager that day, regardless I don't think anyone in that team would have good things to say about him.

He came into the club and it didn't work for him because he tried treating English players the French way when it came to training, it didn't go down well with certain players.

He would often run us hard in the morning and then repeat it in the afternoon, it was like a pre-season every single day and not what we were used to in this country.

We would say 'Okay coach but we're not used to this' and he would mock, accusing us of being like a bunch of babies complaining, that sort of thing.

He ended up overtraining us so we were going into games tired, you could see the way it affected our results, we won only four games under him.

Perrin was trying to change us, alter the way we did things, which is okay but you shouldn't try to be a dictator when you have experienced and older players around who you can talk to.

With him it was 'You need to stop this, this is my way so stop yours' but he did it without knowing the history and why we did certain things, such as some of the players with injury records not training every day.

Sometimes it is always better to ask experienced players how things go so they can tell you. I didn't have too many problems with him but certain things he was doing were crazy.

For instance, he banned me having mayonnaise on my food, which didn't make any sense.

I loved mayonnaise, I had to have it, for me some food doesn't taste good unless it is poured on it.

One day we were on the coach going to a game and he stood up and said 'No more mayonnaise', without any explanation. From then on no prepared meals would be allowed to have it on.

He never told me why, he's a very intelligent man but his way of doing things was really strange, I couldn't get my head around it.

The funny thing is I don't eat mayonnaise that much any more, it was a phase I was going through at that time, and if I met him now I would tell him he cured me!

That wasn't the only thing, in the 2005 pre-season we spent a week in France and during some spare time I was watching videos of the Brazilian pair Ronaldo and Ronaldinho on the Internet.

Now Ronaldo is phenomenal, this is the person who made me fall in love with football and before every match I would watch a video of his best bits, it would inspire me.

Anyhow, that day I was watching them on the computer and Perrin comes in and said 'You see, this is the problem'.

I didn't understand so replied 'Why?' and he answered 'You shouldn't be watching them', so I got up and walked off.

I like watching these people, I wasn't doing anything wrong, but didn't want to argue and in instances like those it was best to just walk away.

Thankfully Harry came back in December 2005 and he is a legend, an amazing manager. My times under him were the best I had in football.

At Pompey with him in charge we had a great atmosphere, a superb team spirit, Harry had this magic about him, you ask anybody who knows him.

He makes you feel the best player in the world. Imagine going onto the field with it in your head that you are the best and nobody can stop you that day - that is what he made me believe.

I wasn't the only one, he would have that effect on other players in your team. He is a top man, I still have a lot of respect and love for him.

I never wanted to move from Pompey, I had just scored a hat-trick in a pre-season game against Bournemouth in August 2007 and my friend and team-mate Benjani Mwaruwari had also been trying to convince me to stay.

The problem was I started falling out of love with football and needed something to get me going again. I felt I had to leave.

Different players had come into the club, there had been injuries to me and my 18-month-old son, Jesus, had died of pneumonia, so I wanted to just go and get my head right.

Benjani was saying to me 'Don't go, don't go, just stay, what are you going for, just stay and things will change'.

Harry understood, though, he was very good and said I could leave, he recognised I needed a fresh start to get everything going again.

However, the Blues wouldn't sell me to another Premier League team - so I joined Olympiacos.

There are times when I wish I hadn't left, but Olympiacos made me fall in love with football again so everything was perfect once more.

It has never stopped me missing Pompey, though, just little things like visiting Commercial Road or arriving at Fratton Park for the game, leaving your car outside the ground and the fans coming over to talk to you.

I still have my place in Port Solent and perhaps one day will head back and live there again, it is something I have thought about many times.

Yakubu is one of my best friends in football and we still talk all the time.

Back in May 2012 we played together again at Benjani's testimonial match in Harare, Zimbabwe, and, while reminiscing on our Pompey days, agreed it was the best time we had in football, we enjoyed it so much.

When I joined Pompey, people thought me and the Yak would be fighting for a place, that it was a case of either he plays or I play, but we became such good friends out of football and it helped on the pitch.

You could see it in the way we linked up, I knew what he wanted and he knew what I wanted and it worked well.

The Yak had the strength and power and would finish, I would run, produce skills and work for him.

In September 2011, I came back to England after leaving AC Omonia in Cyprus and was supposed to sign for Birmingham after training there but they had problems with their owner, Carson Yeung, so it couldn't happen.

Then I had talks with Pompey about a possible return but Steve Cotterill decided he didn't want me.

While I was at Birmingham we played a friendly game against Tottenham and Harry was there, I scored twice and he said 'You can still play, you still have it, I know someone who will take you and loves you so much'.

So he put me in touch with Milan Mandaric, then chairman at Sheffield Wednesday, and offered me a very, very good contract.

The problem was I didn't want to play in League One, I wanted to be in the Championship or Premier League. Then in the October Ian Holloway called and took me to Blackpool where I played 32 games and scored six goals.

I still have that Southampton match on DVD and whenever I need happy memories to cheer me up I get it out and watch it.

My kids have seen it plenty of times, that was one of my happiest times in football and I am so grateful to God for letting me be part of such a wonderful occasion.

14—EVENING NEWS, MONDAY, MARCH 26, 1956.

Changed Half-Back Trio "Came-Off"

POMPEY FORWARD LINE STILL A PROBLEM

(By NIMROD)

THERE were two aspects of Saturday's match between Portsmouth and Preston North End, the outcome of which were being closely watched with much anxiety, quite apart from the result.

One of them gave cause for satisfaction; the other caused furrows to line the brow of the Pompey manager (Mr. J. E. Lever).

The uphappy aspect of the match was that the club's forward problem is no nearer solution than it has been during the past two or three seasons. The more encouraging fact was that the changed half-back line of Dickinson, Gunter, and Barnard (reading from right to left) "came off."

Frankly I was surprised at neither, but was pleased with Barnard's so-quick success at left-half, and the ease and effect with which Dickinson moved over.

With Gunter reaching heights which must have impressed the England selectors present, the half-back line has become once again a "real power in the land"—a sound core around which to build the Pompey of the future.

Had I only to take into consideration the first half in forming a judgment on the re-formed attack, I could only label it a miserable failure. Taking into consideration the second half, that criticism is modified to "by no means promising."

Credit marks go to Gordon for an improvement on the form he has shown in other matches this season, but that is as far as I am prepared to go as far as the inside trio is concerned.

Henderson, who shared in the all-round weakness of the Finney did not quite have things so completely his own way as in the encounter between the two at Fratton Park earlier in the season.

Even so, Finney's dominance was sufficient to be a decisive factor in the game, and one of the causes for the almost incessant one-way trek towards the Pompey goal in the first half.

The other was the Preston inside-right, Thompson (T.), whose interchanging with Finney, and understanding with Hatsell, who has taken on something of a roving game, was most effective; and the splendid play of Docherty at right-half.

The only reason why Preston did not pile up a strong interval lead was that McGhee was in storming form, and at this stage overshadowed even the efforts of the Pompey half-back trio.

After Escapes

In fact, strange as it may seem, Pompey came within inches of taking the lead themselves on the one or two occasions that Gordon, Robertson, and Rees came within heading or shooting distance.

In fact, it was just after one such escape by Preston that Thompson scored the first goal of his team's 2—1 victory, which certainly relieved some of their relegation fears.

Barnard's supreme moment came after ... efforts they were to make during the last half-hour.

He raced after an advancing Finney, showed just how to take the ball from him, and then set up a long run almost from his own 18-yard line to that of the home team.

Docherty—speedy, powerful—who was outstanding in a not-very-bright defence, tried to stop him, but even this fine player who must have given a great deal of satisfaction to the Scottish selectors present, could only cause a slight stumble.

On and on went Barnard, Preston falling back before him. Rees moved intelligently out to the left, and Henderson moved in.

Quick to see the chance, Barnard passed unerringly to the Pompey centre-forward, who in that second rose above his generally poor showing throughout the game.

He promptly transferred to Henderson, who controlled the ball with his left, and shot past Thompson (G.) with his right. Great work!

A few minutes later, Preston scored again, and held their lead to the end. I discovered afterwards there was more chance about Waterhouse's goal than I thought at the time.

Finney had beaten Mansell, and centred to Campbell whose shot might have gone anywhere except back to Finney. That, I thought, was the only fortunate aspect of the goal.

Afterwards, however, I learned ... when Waterhouse had shot and was deflected out of the goalkeeper's reach.

BARNARD
Quick success at left-half.

The best of Gordon was seen during the rest of the match, and two of his efforts deserved a better fate. In fact, right to the last minute, Pompey looked as though they might yet snatch a point.

Robertson should have equalized when, from close in, he hit the post with the goal yawning in front of him, and only Thompson to beat — a great chance presented to him by Harris.

Gunter went up in the closing minutes and came within inches of heading in from a Harris corner, and with Barnard moving up again and shaping for a shot which again might have saved the game in another second, the final whistle sounded.

Preston North End.—Thompson (G.); Cunningham, Walton; Docherty, Dunn, Forbes; Finney, Thompson (T.), Hatsell, Waterhouse, Campbell.

Portsmouth.—Uprichard; McGhee, Mansell; Dickinson, Gunter, Barnard; Harris, Gordon, Rees, Robertson, Henderson.

Mike **Barnard**

123 games, 26 goals (August 1951 - July 1959)

Preston North End 2 (Thompson, Waterhouse)
Pompey 1 (Henderson)

Division One, Deepdale, Saturday, March 24, 1956

Pompey: Uprichard, McGhee, Mansell, Gunter, Dickinson, Barnard, Harris, Gordon, Rees, Robertson, Henderson.

Attendance; 16,716

They were the days when the summer didn't mean time off for footballers, most would have to go out and find a job during a close season spanning three months.

Pompey were in Division One yet you would get the likes of Jimmy Scoular and Jack Froggatt working at Fratton Park after a playing campaign was over, while Johnny Gordon was a Redcoat at Butlin's.

As for me, I played professional cricket for Hampshire County Cricket Club.

Footballers' wages were in line with the skilled lads in the dockyard and, of course, there were no such things as pension funds or compensation for injury, so we had to find other means of earning money.

I was already on Hampshire's books before signing for my home-town club Pompey in August 1951 at the age of 18.

Admittedly the seasons would overlap by around a month, but for a while it wasn't really a problem juggling two sporting careers.

Footballers would return to their clubs for pre-season on August 1, yet the cricketers would still be in action until the end of August.

At the other end of the calendar, cricketers went back on April 1, while the football season didn't end until May 1.

The team - and sport - I represented just depended on the situation at the clubs at the time. People just seemed to accept it.

There were quite a few of us playing both football and cricket in that era, the likes of Dennis Compton, Arthur Milton, Derek Ufton, Stuart Leary and Willie Watson.

However, not many can claim they professionally played only for the football club and cricket county of their birth and I was very proud to appear 123 times for Pompey and in 276 first-class matches for Hampshire.

I also won the county championship in 1961 - the first title in Hampshire's history - although by that stage had left professional football and was turning out in non-league.

Born in Portsea, I attended Portsmouth Grammar School but after my first year wasn't officially allowed to play football, instead rugby replaced it in the winter with cricket in the summer.

That was a time when if you were instructed to do something you did it, basically it was 'That is how it is done here - so you must do as you are told'.

So I played rugby and cricket for the school team, progressing to Hampshire schools for both. In terms of rugby, I was good enough to play at that standard, although used to keep out of the way at full-back!

To make up for the lack of football opportunities at school, I joined Bedhampton Boys Club and most of our games were on Sunday morning, so Saturday was still free for rugby or cricket.

In the end I had to stop with the rugby and focus on cricket and football, but regardless of the sport I just enjoyed playing, no matter what the sport was.

I remember competing in the school tennis tournament, it sounds impressive but was a pretty poor standard, and also challenged for the swimming team.

It would be Hampshire who first signed me in 1951 and I would share digs with their groundsman Ernie Knights and his wife Bella, working on the Northlands Road groundstaff as well as playing.

Then came the switch to Pompey in August 1951, the club spotting me while I was on the books of Gosport. Suddenly, at the age of 17, I was a professional footballer as well as cricketer.

Jimmy Scoular was still playing at Fratton Park when I joined, an interesting character who was very talented but didn't have to be so crude with his tackling.

Still, he was very capable and if the ball came to him he used to sort of turn his back on it and trap it by sitting on it. He didn't have to be so dirty, though.

Jimmy Dickinson played 48 times for England because of his reliability, that was his strength.

He was also a strong player, a clean tackler, good in the air and somebody who played the ball early because he had the vision to spot people's runs very quickly.

In those days footballers were not allowed to drive until they were aged 18-20, but Jimmy had to have a car because he had to travel from Alton to come into training so was one of the first at the club to get a car.

He was such a quiet, modest man, an intelligent footballer, who did the right things early, was very consistent and reliable.

We had a truly exceptional player in Peter Harris, a high scorer of goals, especially for a winger. Those were days when the wingers would stay out wide, but he could come inside or play wider still.

I remember him moving to Hayling Island for the fresh air having contracted tuberculosis, forcing his retirement from the game in 1960.

Then there was Duggie Reid, goalkeepers used to dive out of the way of his shots, they were that hard, he was rugged and then took over as groundsman.

Yet if you asked any player from the Pompey side during the 1950s who was the best they had appeared alongside I have no doubt they all would have replied 'Len Phillips'.

He was a natural talent and marvellous. Everything you wanted in a footballer he possessed, the passing, the ball control, the intelligence which would ensure he knew where to run and get into the right positions at the right times, nobody had to tell him.

Len was that good, he really was, and should have played far more than three times for England.

I was an inside forward, a player who tried hard and worked hard at my fitness, getting the odd goal because I put so much in.

Once at Blackpool, Jimmy Dickinson, who was playing on the left-side of defence, came over to me as the inside left and asked if I could drop back a few yards to keep an eye on his man. It turned out to be Stan Mortensen!

Another very good performer I played alongside was Gordon Dale, a talented left winger on the ball and an absolute natural.

Now Dale, like all top players, had the ability to be quick over the first five yards, a yard start and he was gone. On occasions he would get the ball at his feet, anticipate the tackle and as it came in would lift it over the opponent's foot and carry on dribbling - I saw him do it!

By the time of my Pompey debut against Tottenham Hotspur on Boxing Day 1953, though, I had already made my bow for Hampshire.

That had arrived a year earlier in July 1952 in the form of a three-day match against

Glamorgan in Swansea.

At the time I was involved in National Service with the Army, but injuries paved the way for a call-up with the third day - the Friday - my 19th birthday.

It wasn't the best of starts, however, I made four and nought and bowled three wicketless overs, although did get a first catch and we won by 21 runs.

My next match arrived more than 12 months later against Warwickshire in August 1953, when I scored two ducks at Portsmouth and we lost by 129 runs.

National Service did impact on my availability in both sports for those first two years, there was no way out of it, and I still remember my soldier number of 22516646.

Strangely enough, most of the time I was stationed at Bicester in Oxfordshire, which was then an Army camp situated on the windy side of a hill and in mid-winter it was unbearable, so I didn't enjoy that!

Still, Spurs were my first opponents as a Pompey player when, at the age of 21, I was selected at inside-left in place of Charlie Mortimore, who was a Gosport lad.

In front of a crowd of 36,777, they took the lead after only 13 minutes, Sonny Walters running in from the touchline to strike an angled drive past goalkeeper Ted Platt.

The equaliser arrived in the final minute when Jackie Henderson fired in a right-foot shot from 30 yards and Charlie Vaughan arrived at the far post to head home.

Spurs' keeper, Ted Ditchburn, had been superb all game but not even he could keep that out and we had a deserved point.

The Football Mail that night wrote 'Although Harris was undoubtedly the danger man, as far as the Pompey attack was concerned, and Phillips the genius behind many Pompey moves - give a pat on the back, too, to Michael Barnard. He looked the most promising prospect so far tried at inside-left this season'.

My second season saw me play 31 times and score five goals as, under Eddie Lever, we finished third in Division One.

For the majority of the campaign we had actually been in a good position to take the title, sitting at the top of the league until well after Christmas, then fell away as the cracks started to appear.

Chelsea took the title - for the first time in their history - while we ended up finishing behind Wolverhampton Wanderers on goal average after winning only one of our last seven matches.

Funnily enough, Chelsea's manager was Ted Drake, who had played 16 first-class cricket matches for Hampshire from 1931-36.

Naming my favourite match is not an easy task, but it occurred the following season when, in March 1956, we travelled to Preston North End, who had Tom Finney in their side.

The Lilywhites were 1-0 up when I got a lucky break from a tackle with Tommy Docherty and played a ball to Derek Rees, who set up Jackie Henderson for the equaliser.

Walking back to the centre circle for the kick-off, Finney turned to me and said 'Well played son'.

Some may think it was a stupid thing to say, but it reflected his marvellous attitude and I accepted it because Tom Finney, yes Tom Finney, had said it to me. Although we went on to lose 2-1!

It worked out badly for our manager Lever in the end. The crowd were used to winning and, as it is now, when top teams lose a couple of games they get slated.

In those days it wasn't ex-players who became bosses, quite often it was people like Lever, who was a school teacher. A nice enough fella, but basically realised he wasn't the man for the job as he hadn't played the game at a high level and would leave in May 1958 and teach mathematics at Oak Park Boys School in Leigh Park.

Freddie Cox came in from Bournemouth to replace him and wasn't very good at Pompey, but by then for me the sports were clashing, while football had also given me quite serious injuries such as cruciate ligament damage and a torn cartilage, which happened in the same match!

In October 1956, I had already scored when Sunderland's Billy Elliott came in with a two-footed tackle on me but, as there were no subs, I was switched to the wing for the remainder of the game in a 3-3 Roker Park draw. I didn't play again that season.

My cricket commitments were also catching up with me and it got to the point where I could no longer get away with playing both sports, especially with me missing Blues matches to play for Hampshire.

Although my availability depended on who wanted me the most, I would find out that at Fratton Park there was always somebody around to play on a full-time basis, whereas obviously I couldn't.

Having been put on the transfer list by Cox in September 1958, my last Pompey appearance was a 5-1 home defeat to Newcastle United in March 1959, Ron Saunders getting our consolation goal.

The club would finish the campaign with nine successive defeats as we were relegated out of Division One, finishing bottom having conceded 112 goals in 42 matches.

That summer my contract was up, although back then you could not leave without the club's say so and they had to re-register me by a certain time to command a fee. However, they forgot and I was able to move for nothing!

I had the option of signing for Southampton, Ted Bates was their manager with the club in Division Three, but it was just the time Terry Paine and company were coming through and a revival was beginning to develop so it was tempting.

However, I was still playing cricket and, despite aged only 25, decided to go to non-league Chelmsford City in the Southern League who matched my maximum wage of £20 a week - and I could also continue with my cricket.

The Clarets were managed by my old Pompey team-mate Harry Ferrier and with Len Phillips and Gordon Dale also in their side there was a real Fratton Park feel to the club.

In March 1960 I would interrupt my honeymoon to play at home against Gravesend & Northfleet and scored four times in a 7-1 win!

Overall, I netted 43 goals in 129 games before leaving in 1963 for Poole Town, retiring the following season.

Meanwhile, my Hampshire career was going well and we won the County Championship in August 1961, led by an extraordinary likeable fellow called Colin Ingleby-Mackenzie.

He was a genuine character, very outgoing, who had the ability to get away with murder with the way he talked to some people, especially the girls.

Typical of Colin, when he died in March 2006 I attended his funeral and there were four horses pulling a carriage containing his coffin outside Lord's cricket ground followed by all the dignitaries you could think of from London and the Home Counties.

He was a good captain and sometimes declared an innings while we were batting leaving you thinking 'No, why have you done that?' and he would say 'Good odds, so declare'.

That was just the way he was, very talented, an excellent after-dinner speaker, very keen on the horses and bet every day. He was also one of the last people to see Lord Lucan alive, being friends.

My role in that title-winning side was to just do something useful, that's all.

Although, I finished that season strongly with a century and three half-centuries in my six innings on the way to lifting the title.

During my Hampshire years I made 9,314 runs at an average of 22.07, but should have scored more, although I suppose a lot of people can say that.

I was a right-hand orthodox bat and didn't usually bowl, although with most benefit matches on a Sunday before Sunday League games came in, I was allowed to turn my arm over in them.

My batting position was usually between one and six, for a while opening with Roy Marshall, a white West Indian with thick glasses who was a fine striker of a ball and I enjoyed partnering him.

Of that team there was also Peter Sainsbury, who also featured in the 1973 title-winning side, Alan Wassell was a slow left-arm bowler who married a girl from Gosport, while Butch White was a fast bowler who was quick in short spells and used to slog a few.

Jimmy Gray operated quietly in the background, Roy Marshall's usual opening partner and was very successful, as well as being a good golfer who would be a regular with Peter Sainsbury at Stoneham Golf Club in Southampton.

It was a good team and we deserved to win that title.

In the previous nine years only Surrey and Yorkshire had won it, so it was a remarkable achievement, winning 19 matches to pip the latter to the trophy.

There was a member of the Hampshire board who owned a jewellery shop in Southampton and as a reward for winning the championship we were allowed to pick a pair of cufflinks or a Rolex watch. I chose the watch.

At the end of the 1965 season I decided to retire, I saw the light. I was ready, unless you are doing really well you don't enjoy it as much and it was the right time to call it a day.

I wasn't getting enough runs or wickets or both, while there were up and coming people who needed to play instead of this 33-year-old.

People often ask me which sport I preferred. Well, I played professional sport, and, like every profession, if you are doing well you enjoy it more.

If you are struggling you don't enjoy it. It doesn't matter if you are playing cricket, playing football or in the office all day, it's the same thing.

Overall I have a lot of good memories, I consider myself very lucky in many ways.

umbro
PORTSMOUTH F.C.

16—THE NEWS, MONDAY, JANUARY 11, 1988

News Sport

Pompey defy all the odds

IT TOOK a breathtaking goal to carry Pompey to the victory their battered image desperately needed at rain-sodden Ewood Park on Saturday — but it also took a save which was a bit special from the final shot of a fiercely contested tie to avert a Tuesday replay.

The frantically-paced match was in overtime when substitute Mark Patterson's angled pass sent Simon Barker, the fair-haired midfield man coveted by a string of big clubs, surging on his own into the penalty area. But Alan Knight crowned an outstanding personal performance by spreading himself full-length to beat away the shot.

It was just about de-
ved for a gutsy display of
racter at the end of a
k when Pompey's repu-
on had been battered by
il of controversy.
he torrent of adverse
licity might have de-
yed many sides — and
that had not been
ugh, they had to blood
untried youngster in a
cial midfield role and
two players before the
half was out.
ut Pompey rode it all.
eir defence was dis-
ted by the loss of Paul
rdyman in the 19th min-
— and they took a fur-
body-blow before sub-
te Billy Gilbert had a
ce to settle in, Black-
pinching an equalizer.
en, ten minutes before
ime, Terry Connor
d off with a hamstring
and Alan Ball had to

BLACKBURN 1, POMPEY 2

he would have needed to make the save of his life to prevent Kevin Dillon's 35-yard strike settling the tie.

Referee George Courtney surprised most people by allowing Pompey's full-back to escape with a stern lecture for the challenge and in the end produced only one yellow card, booking Horne for one tackle on his man Barker.

Whitehead, abused every time he touched the ball after that incident, was the man who spared Darby a nightmare start, clearing off the line in the first minute after the youngster's attempt to nod a ball back to Knight had floated over the keeper's head.

But if Darby's nerves were jangled, they quickly settled. In the seventh minute his astute pass got Hilaire away for the first time — and Quinn skidded in at the near post to stick away

● GOAL HERO . . . Mick Quinn nips in to beat Blackburn defender David Mail and keeper Terry Gennoe to open the scoring for Pompey at Ewood Park on Saturday. — Photo sales no. B2112-1-2-3.

But hero Dillon vows:

NOW I'VE GO
TO GET AW

Noel **Blake**

August 1984 - May 1988 (173 games, 14 goals)

Blackburn Rovers 1 (Garner)
Pompey 2 (Quinn, Dillon)

FA Cup Third Round, Ewood Park, Saturday, January 9, 1988

Pompey: Knight, Whitehead, Blake, Ball, Hardyman (19 mins Gilbert), Dillon, Horne, Darby, Hilaire, Quinn, Connor (38 mins Fillery).

Attendance; 10,352

Walking out at Ewood Park in the FA Cup was my proudest moment as a Pompey player. It meant everything and still does.

For the first time in my career I was wearing the captain's armband, a massive responsibility entrusted in me by our boss Alan Ball.

When you are captain you are not just captain of the team, it is the entire club you are representing, a big thing and a tremendous honour.

I had filled in on occasions during my time at Birmingham City when the skipper was injured, but to be handed that armband by the manager officially is something I am immensely proud of.

Alan's wife, Lesley, God bless her, said to me 'You could be the first black captain to lead a team out at Wembley'. Little things like that stick.

There had been a few changes since promotion to Division One and that January 1988 fixture was only my fourth match back after missing the first half of the season through injury.

Kenny Swain had led us into the top flight but was now out of favour and no longer captain, while his replacement in that role, Mick Kennedy, had been sold four days earlier to Bradford City.

Before that Blackburn Rovers game, the manager informed me I was the right person for the job and lay down the challenge to rise to the responsibility - I kept the armband for the remainder of the season.

It got even better, we won that FA Cup third round match 2-1, playing really, really well in the process. You could say it is from a selfish point of view, but that was my all-time favourite Pompey game.

The manager named Lee Darby in midfield to replace Kennedy, an 18-year-old lad making his debut, and in the seventh minute he released Vince Hilaire whose cross was slid in at the near post by Mick Quinn.

Simon Garner thundered home a headed equaliser at the far post from right-back Chris Price's cross only 13 minutes later and we went in 1-1 at half-time.

Then, on 70 minutes, Kevin Dillon scored what can only be described as a worldie. It was a really good move between four or five players before a cross-field pass teed up Dill for a 35-yard right-foot volley into the net.

We were struggling in the league at the time and those FA Cup games kicked us on a little bit, sparking a mini-revival.

Next up in the cup we defeated Sheffield United 2-1, then saw off a Bradford team containing Mick Kennedy 3-0 to book a quarter-final spot for the first time since 1952.

Luton Town were the opposition and we lost at Kenilworth Road on the plastic pitch 3-1, Mick Quinn getting our goal. I still maintain if that had been played on grass we would have gone all the way.

I joined Pompey in August 1984 for £150,000 and it was down to Ron Saunders' advice. I trusted him implicitly.

At the time I was playing for Birmingham and during our pre-season tour to Holland I was called in by Ron. It was explained a few clubs had made enquiries for me, namely Everton, Manchester City, QPR and Pompey.

I didn't have an agent but trusted him as he had been my manager firstly at Aston Villa and then Birmingham, so I asked him what he thought.

Ron replied 'If I were your dad and advising you, I would say go to Pompey'. That was a big factor for me going there.

Birmingham's finances at that time meant I had to move on, they had already sold Pat Van Den Hauwe to Everton and Tony Coton to Watford - now it was my turn.

I am thankful to this day to Ron, I have never regretted that decision and had four great years with Alan Ball at a club which remains a special place for me.

Bally was a very demanding manager, very thorough, very professional, very strong, and liked his team to play a certain style, which we certainly did. He was a top, top manager in my view.

Training was good, we always worked with the ball apart from a Tuesday session which was a run and when you finished it felt you had no legs left, but we were a very, very fit side.

The first few months were eventful, there was my falling out with some of the crowd, but overall I have nothing but high praise for the club, my time there and the friends I made and am still in touch with.

I started the 1984-85 season reasonably well, but at the back end of October and early November had a little blip here and there. It was a spell where I made a few errors, costly errors, and then it kicked off and became a racial thing.

There was never a problem when I was out and about around the city, just on the pitch with 200 or so idiots shouting things from the stands, although nothing was ever thrown.

At the time I was still relatively young in terms of my career and as a person was still developing, coming to terms living in a different area away from my Birmingham roots.

That reaction affected me during games, no question about it. In those days, as a black player you expected it away from home but to get it from some of your own people wasn't a pleasant thing.

Not everybody did it, far from it, but I look back on my better times down there and equally the racism was part of it. Still, I rode the obstacles to overcome those people and eventually helped the club achieve something.

You have to remember the world was a different place in the 1980s, there was no Kick It Out campaign in those days, as a black player you had to stand on your own two feet and fight your corner. That was what it was like.

It was particularly horrendous against Huddersfield in December 1984. I had made an early error when dealing with a cross and they took the lead through Dale Tempest - that is when it went fever pitch.

However, I got the winner to give us a 3-2 success when I scored a great header from Kevin Dillon's cross, it was virtually from the edge of the box, but I didn't go over to the fans to celebrate.

The abuse had been going on for a game or two and the fans looked at my reaction to scoring and thought 'Hang on a minute, this isn't right'.

That was when most people realised what I was going through.

Then the good people of the city rallied round, the lads were terrific, the chairman - John Deacon - took a public stance saying it was unacceptable and those responsible would be banned. It started the change.

There was an outcry and we stuck together as a team.

I remember baskets of fruit would come to the club, there were letters of support, Lindy Delapenha was one of those who started writing to me, the club's first-ever black player.

He recognised I was having a rough time with the Pompey crowd and contacted me advising to keep my head down and keep working hard. To this day I have never met him, but it meant such a lot.

It was the only time I experienced racism from my own supporters, you don't forget it but you move on from it. I don't like thinking or talking about it to be honest, I try to never look back on it.

However, the good people of the city really made me feel wanted, I appreciated it so much when they came out and said it was not acceptable - and I kicked on as a player.

In my four years at Fratton Park, I won The News/Sports Mail Player of the Season twice on the bounce.

To do it once might be a fluke in some people's eyes. I am not saying it was, but to do it twice on the trot puts you into club history in more ways than one and that is a special thing for me.

In that first year for me at Pompey we finished fourth, despite a blip in January and February where we won once in seven matches.

Then we came back and went on a run and just missed out on the last day despite winning our final three matches, instead Manchester City went up in third spot on goal difference after defeating Charlton Athletic 5-1 at Maine Road.

That season would also produce a moment that is mentioned too often for my liking - my own goal against Wimbledon at Plough Lane.

It was October 1984 and, from our centre having conceded a goal, the ball came to me and I produced a back pass towards Alan Knight, only for him to be bent down rubbing his knee.

So the ball rolled into the empty net without a Wimbledon player having touched it. It was one of those things and we ended up losing 3-2.

Sometimes I get brassed off being reminded about that because I did many more very, very good things for the club, but people for some reason always go on about that. They never look at the fact I got Player of the Season for two years running.

In my second year at Fratton Park we did very, very well again, but still missed out on promotion from Division Two.

Bally brought one or two additions here and there, including Mick Channon for his experience. He didn't score the number of goals he would have liked - or we would have liked - but what a great contribution he made.

Channon had terrific experience, a great fella who was good friends with the manager and superb around the place for us younger lads.

I remember going to Norwich City in January 1986 and Knightsie was out with a broken hand so Andy Gosney was in goal and we lost 2-0. I'm not blaming Andy, far from it, we were collectively in a bad spell coinciding with Knightsie missing.

We were just not functioning so met for a clear-the-air meeting and got going again - only to narrowly miss out once more, this time three points adrift in fourth place.

For 1986-87 we brought in Paul Mariner and that signing was a big part of our subsequent promotion, he was someone who took the weight off Mick Quinn up front and shared the load.

We won promotion on a Tuesday night, even though we didn't have a game.

Oldham Athletic needed to win at Shrewsbury Town to take it into the final day and lost 2-0 - we went up without kicking a ball.

To celebrate we had a drink at the Cowplain Social Club before heading off to Kenny Swain's house in Denmead for a party, with the majority of the squad there.

For the next couple of days we had a celebration at the stadium and attended all sorts of functions here and there.

Then on the Saturday we played Sheffield United at Fratton and the title was still up for grabs but we lost 2-1, which was a bit of an anti-climax, but had gone up in second place behind Derby County.

It had been 28 years since Pompey had been in Division One but we were back.

We had come through after three years of challenging, in the main using the same group of players. That took some doing, you had to have that spirit otherwise you wouldn't have achieved a top-four finish three seasons on the spin.

When you look back we were destined to get promotion because we were too good not to. I know that sounds corny but we played some really good football over that period of time.

We were consistently up there and that takes a lot of doing, we were always in there. I thought we were destined to get it.

As a group of players we would socialise together and play together. Our team was more or less the same XI week in, week out, apart from suspension, injuries and a loss of form. We were settled and had consistency.

As for the defence, we conceded 28 goals in 42 games in the promotion season, the best in all four divisions, and that was down to the team ethos the gaffer instilled in us. When we lost we all lost, when we won we all won.

Bill Gilbert was my central defensive partner and we clicked, but still worked hard at it.

He was a technical player and should have gone on to play for England, I have said it a million times, he had the ability to play for the seniors in my view.

In the main I tended to attack things and Bill cleaned up around me. I wasn't a technical player, whereas he was, but we both were uncompromising and good in the air.

We believed in each other and trusted each other, it was a case of you look after my back and I'll look after yours.

There were occasions when we fell out, we weren't afraid to give each other a rollicking. If you are going to have a partnership it can't always be hunky dory, sometimes you fall out.

That's not only to do with making a mistake, it could be about how your decision-making wasn't right or you wanted things to be better.

We had very high standards. I made a few mistakes but in the main we hit it off, he is the best player I've partnered, without a shadow of a doubt. He was a quality footballer.

Mick Kennedy was, for me, also a top player, really underrated. He could play off his left-foot or right-foot and had a very good range of passing, but people only saw his game as a midfield hard man.

That was seen as his main attribute but Mick could play. He did like a tackle, though - and he could tackle!

The 1987-88 campaign would see us in Division One, but there was a different feel to the club.

Firstly, there were a lot of changes to the squad, we got promoted and new boys came in, a few alterations here and there, that happens, after all you need more experienced players at that level.

Some worked and unfortunately some didn't. There was Ian Stewart from Newcastle United, Mike Fillery came in from QPR and I thought did well, Terry Connor from Brighton & Hove Albion, Ian Baird from Leeds United, Barry Horne came from Wrexham, while Clive Whitehead arrived from West Bromwich Albion.

Then John Deacon acquired Portsmouth Basketball Club, which didn't help.

We were told by people at the club that finances for the football team were now going into the basketball team - to think I was actually a big basketball fan!

I don't know if Deacon had lost interest in us or not, we just had to get on with our jobs.

That was difficult for me as I picked up a knee injury in a pre-season game at Swedish side Leksand in July 1987 and didn't next play until halfway through the campaign.

Having worked so hard to get into Division One, to miss out for such a long time was absolutely gutting. At least I had played there before with Villa and Birmingham before joining Pompey, but having given everything over three seasons to get there it still hurt.

I didn't like watching games, I disliked the bit where people were saying 'When are you going to be fit?'. I was forever repeating myself and it wasn't about me, it was about the team.

So I stopped going to Pompey games and instead used to watch my old team-mate Mick Tait play for Reading. What a big, big player he had been for us, capable of playing anywhere, so versatile.

I eventually returned to the side on December 28, 1987 for a 1-1 draw with Watford at Fratton Park which left us in 19th place - exactly the same position we finished up at the season's end.

Playing that day I felt it just wasn't the same as what we'd had, I could see that. It just wasn't the same club and then February and March time there were one or two things wrong for me, some people had resigned themselves to relegation.

We didn't make the best of starts to life in the top flight, winning one of our opening nine matches, and struggling for long periods.

Then it started to break up. Mick Kennedy was sold a week after I had made my comeback, while Bill (Gilbert) went through a spell of playing left-back or right-back. That season we started only two league games together in the centre of defence.

That defence was the mainstay over those years when we were trying to get into Division One - and then it wasn't there anymore.

Malcolm Shotton came and went, sometimes Paul Hardyman would play, sometimes Kenny Swain played, it wasn't the same collectiveness we'd had the previous two or three years, the continuity had gone and we were relegated at home to Newcastle with one match remaining.

I remember returning from Old Trafford having lost 4-1 on the final day of the season and there were about four people who came back on the bus. That wouldn't have happened in previous campaigns, that team spirit and team morale had gone.

One young lad, who shall remain nameless, didn't want to play in that match because he had a party in London. As the captain I said to him 'What are you on about, you either want to party in London or play at Old Trafford'.

There were little things like that, it wasn't the same. When the old guard changes sometimes it is never the same.

Despite being out for half a season with my knee problem, when I returned I didn't miss another match. In fact, I had only been absent for one game in the previous three seasons and that was on a plastic pitch at Oldham because of a groin strain.

Up to that point I had made 117 consecutive appearances since my move from Birmingham.

My contract was up at the end of that Division One campaign, Jim Gregory had taken over as owner in mid-May 1988 and wanted to change the club around.

We had a conversation and I was told I was surplus to requirements and made available on a free transfer. Basically, the club's medical people felt my right knee was a problem.

I'd had bits and pieces done to it before, keyhole surgery and a couple of wash outs, while there was a problem with my cartilage which they wouldn't take out and as years went by it became bone-on-bone.

But I knew it wouldn't be able to finish me off. They got it wrong, no question about it, my final professional match was in my 40th year with Exeter City in February 2001.

Within a few days of leaving Fratton Park I had interest from seven or eight clubs, including QPR, Crystal Palace, Wimbledon, Watford and Birmingham City, but it was Leeds I joined.

I didn't want to leave Pompey and didn't like the way it happened, the issue of my knee was an excuse.

Okay, we got relegated and I was captain, but I felt with a few additions here and there we could have done something.

I don't think it was ever the same for Bally either after that. He had also grown up with us - and it had all changed for him as well.

Pompey is a special club and unless you have worked there you don't know how special the fans are.

It's a special noise. It's difficult to explain, when you are on the field it really is a wonderful place. When you are a home player it doesn't half lift you.

Brave Pompey jam Arsenal Cup machine

By REG BETTS

Portsmouth 1, Arsenal 1

Pompey brought the big-time atmosphere back to Fratton on Saturday with an inspired second-half onslaught which ... and finally broke down the Arsenal machine.

A crowd of almost 40,000, united in the emotional experience which is uniquely generated by summit football, saluted a Mike Trebilcock equalizer in the dying seconds of a magnificent contest.

Pompey richly deserved their fourth round replay at Highbury tomorrow night — and incidentally another fat bonus for the club and the players.

I will certainly not argue with the fans who voted Saturday's cup classic Pompey's finest hour for close on two decades.

Players normally living in down-town Second Division emerged as more than mere mortals — mighty tacklers, fleet-footed runners on rain-drenched turf, warriors who declined to accept defeat. Such is the inspiration of the F.A. Cup!

Through the first half Pompey's aggression kept the skills of Arsenal within bounds, but a Peter Storey penalty goal in the 15th minute added enormously to an already daunting task.

The transformation was sensational. With Norman Piper pushing forward and support coming from Fred Smith, George Ley, and David Munks, Pompey took control and handed Arsenal an almighty drubbing.

Sagging

Propping up a sagging defence, goalkeeper Bob Wilson handled the ball superbly and launched himself to smother shots ... Trebilcock and Ray Hiron.

In this tackle on Arsenal's Kennedy, Colin Blant shows the determination that gained Pompey a replay.

Havant's Pink Cup blues

Their reign as Meon Valley Football League champions already in jeopardy, Havant Youth waved goodbye to the Pink Cup they won last season with a series of defensive lapses which helped Park Lane Old Boys' to a 5—3 win in a second round tie at Havant Park, yesterday.

Sam Miller keeps up ... of success

Wetherby tomorrow

Judas is worth a bet at Wetherby

Norman **Piper**

356 games, 57 goals (May 1970 - March 1978)

Pompey 1 (Trebilcock)
Arsenal 1 (Storey)

FA Cup Fourth Round, Fratton Park, Saturday, January 23, 1971

Pompey: Milkins, Smith, Munks, Blant, Ley, Hand, Piper, Bromley, Pointer (73 mins Youlden), Trebilcock, Hiron.

Attendance; 39,659

As I jogged back towards the halfway line I noticed Pele beside me, glancing over with a smile before uttering 'Good goal, good goal, good goal'.

I will always remember that, this country boy from Devon playing against Pele. Oh my gosh.

It was a good goal too, a left-foot screamer across the keeper, although we still lost 8-3.

There was a record crowd of 77,691 packed inside the Giants Stadium for that NASL play-off first leg against New York Cosmos in August 1977.

My team, Fort Lauderdale Strikers, were managed by ex-Pompey midfielder Ron Newman and had Gordon Banks in goal, but were still hammered.

Among New York's scorers were Giorgio Chinaglia (three), Steve Hunt (two), Gary Etherington, Tony Field and a certain Franz Beckenbauer, not Pele though, nor Carlos Alberto. You could see what we were up against.

I had spent the summer playing football in America, although it overlapped with the start of our Division Three season, making me unavailable for the first four fixtures.

Still, when I was released from Pompey seven months later I would return to America for good.

It was my choice to leave Fratton Park in March 1978 following eight years, 356 games and 57 goals. You get stale after a while.

I needed a fresh challenge, I had just turned 30 and believed I had been at Pompey long enough and couldn't do any more. The manager, Jimmy Dickinson, agreed.

With hindsight, I wish I had stayed and got another club in England before moving to America, I should have played another two or three years back home. I would do it differently if I had the chance again.

Yet it was right to leave Pompey, this was a new opportunity, the money was quite good out there and in my short profession you have to get as much as you can, while you can.

Up until that fixture against Pele and Co, one of the biggest crowds I ever played in front of was 39,659 at Fratton Park when Arsenal visited in the FA Cup fourth round.

That January 1971 match is my favourite Pompey memory - a draw against the Arsenal side which would go on to clinch only the second double in English football in the 20th century.

Bertie Mee's team later that season won the First Division title and then defeated Liverpool 2-1 after extra-time in the FA Cup final, in the process completing the first double in the club's history.

However, we took them to an FA Cup replay and the Gunners were fortunate to beat us in the end, I thought we were the better team at Highbury.

They were a tremendous side, Pat Rice at right-back, Bob McNab at left-back, Frank McLintock, Georgie Armstrong, Ray Kennedy, Georgie Graham, John Radford, Charlie George and Bob Wilson.

We were 16th in Division Two and not expected to get anything from it. To stand any chance we had to be at our best and they had to play at 60 per cent.

As it turned out, the occasion was something special, quite an even game and we deserved the draw at the end achieved through Mike Trebilcock's last-minute equaliser to make it 1-1.

Radford was trying to clear the ball and could have played it back, but instead tried to turn with it and got robbed by Fred Smith who crossed it from the right.

It went through a crowd of players straight to Trebilcock at the far post who controlled and then smashed it into the net. He never used to miss those.

Recently I watched it on YouTube, you could see me jumping in the air when it went in, while the crowd went bananas, then Arsenal kicked off and the referee blew the whistle.

The atmosphere was terrific, almost 40,000 people in attendance with it pouring with rain and the pitch heavy and muddy.

We had fallen behind in the 35th minute through a Peter Storey penalty after Georgie Ley had punched the ball off the line.

I also had a goal disallowed. Ray Hiron had gone up with Wilson, the ball falling to me and I put it in, but it was chalked off for a foul on the keeper during the build-up.

It was a shoulder-to-shoulder challenge from Ray and unfortunate as it wasn't a foul, the referee was wrong.

Still, we had drawn against the number one team in the country and Fratton Park collected gate receipts of £18,002 4s.

The replay was postponed due to a water-logged pitch and it wouldn't be until 11 days after the original match that we lost 3-2 at Highbury in front of a crowd of 47,865 - after I had initially given us the lead.

On six minutes Nicky Jennings delivered a corner, it came out to the middle of the box and I struck a left-foot shot which went in-between the post and McNab positioned on it, I couldn't believe it.

Charlie George equalised on 13 minutes and then Peter Simpson gave Arsenal the lead on 32 minutes from an Armstrong corner.

Ley made it 2-2 and then Eoin Hand gave away a stupid penalty with a foul on Radford and Storey stepped up to shoot past John Milkins for the winner in the 84th minute.

We also had Brian Bromley sent off two minutes from time, except the referee had dismissed the wrong player, it should have been Ley after a scuffle with Pat Rice, but they were still great memories.

That was my first season at Pompey, although my May 1970 move nearly didn't happen after I backed out as it wasn't enough money!

I had caught Ron Tindall's eye while guesting for a Weymouth XI in a benefit match for their players Alex Jackson and Tony Hobson against Pompey in April 1970.

Weymouth lost 2-1, with Tindall making his last appearance as a player, but I had done enough to convince the Blues to make an offer to Plymouth Argyle for me straight after the game.

So I held talks with him and George Smith but it wasn't right so I walked out of the office.

They said 'Where are you going? Where are you going?' I replied 'I'm going home, I'm driving back to Plymouth, the money is not right.

So I returned to Home Park and the manager, Ellis Stuttard, was stood there with a fag in his mouth and said 'What the hell are you doing here?'.

'I'm not going', was my response, to which he said 'But you've got to go', so I said 'Well, why is that?'.

Studdard replied 'We need the money!'

Basically they had to sell me otherwise they would go under, so I went back to Pompey a few days later and we came to an agreement, signing for £40,000 which equalled the club record set in January 1968 when Trebilcock moved from Everton.

I would be getting £45 a week, plus £10 for an appearance and £10 for a win bonus - and that club would be my home for the next eight-and-a-half seasons.

Tindall was manager, with George Smith having stepped down the previous month and then taken up the role of general manager.

I would be his third signing in a week, following the arrivals of Fred Smith and Colin Blant from Burnley.

In all my years at Fratton Park, Ron Tindall would be my favourite boss, a nice guy, who was funny.

On Fridays we used to work on set pieces and one time we practised corner kicks from the Milton end part of the ground, but they weren't going very well.

So Ron picked the ball up and said 'This is the way it should be done'. He put the ball down by the corner flag and started walking backwards - then fell over the wall behind him.

He had disappeared from view and everyone started laughing. Then we saw Ron again, climbing up and also laughing, although I am not going to tell you what he said!

George Smith was an Army man, a really strict guy, and when I arrived from Plymouth wanted me to get a short back and sides haircut, not that I did!

During my first season, it was apparent he and Georgie Ley didn't get on, they were always arguing, with Smith accusing him of not being hard enough.

There was a little gymnasium behind the Fratton end and one day the players went in there and Smith and Georgie both had their boxing gloves on ready to go at it.

So I had a towel round my neck as the trainer for Georgie, while Mike Trebilcock wore a towel round his neck as Smith's trainer.

It was so funny, they really went for each other. I have never seen anything like it in my life, this player and former manager punching each other for three rounds of two minutes - and Georgie Ley won!

They shook hands afterwards and moved on, that was the way George Smith was.

Sometimes he would ask me the last time I saw my family, knowing they were still in Plymouth, and I would say 'Well, not for a while' and he would let me go down there and come back for training on the Thursday, giving me four days off.

Smith would be the same to other players, people who had families in Lancashire and the like, he was a great family guy. You respect somebody like that.

Ian St John was a bit different, he was a winner when he played for Liverpool but was a bit arrogant, it was do it his way or take the highway.

He moved me to right-back and at Bolton Wanderers on a Tuesday night in November 1975 it was 1-1 at half-time, but we were getting hammered.

So in the dressing room at the interval he turned round and shouted 'Have any of you got anything to say?'.

I replied 'Yes boss, I've got something to say, they are getting behind us, getting crosses in, we cannot play with a sweeper'.

Now Chris Lawler was the sweeper and not only past his best but not quick enough to get out there, so I added 'If we don't play with a back four we will get killed in the second half'.

St John snapped 'You are not doing so well are you?'. Sorry but don't ask the question if you don't want to know the answer!

In the second half Bolton got three crosses in and scored three goals - and St John never talked to me for two weeks. Unbelievable.

Whenever we played five-a-side in training he would make sure his side won, he was that kind of guy.

When I left, Frank Burrows was assistant manager to Jimmy Dickinson and wasn't one of the better guys I encountered at Pompey.

He was a hard man and would never say good morning to anybody. Every day he walked right into the treatment room and never said a word!

My Pompey debut was in August 1970 at Norwich City - and I netted a late equaliser in a 1-1 draw.

To be honest, I can't remember my goal, but will never forget the best I ever scored against Sunderland at home in January 1975, a cracking strike from the edge of the box following a Mickey Mellows cross in a 4-2 win.

When I joined, it was noticeable we didn't have a reserve team, it was something Smith had scrapped in 1965 when he had been manager, it was just a 17-player squad.

You don't think of it at the time but it clearly showed a club with no ambition, it was all about survival and eventually we would get relegated to Division Three under St John at the end of the 1975-76 season.

I am not saying we weren't good enough but just didn't have the squad of players and finished bottom, 12 points adrift of safety. It was a sad season.

The previous campaign we had finished 17th and drew 0-0 against Manchester United at Fratton Park as they won the Division Two title under Tommy Docherty on their way back up to the top flight.

During my time at Fratton Park I played all over the park, midfield, up front and even right-back in the end, which I quite enjoyed.

Obviously I arrived from Plymouth as a right-sided midfielder at a time when Albie McCann, a quiet lad, was the anchor man, with Brian Bromley in there as well and Nicky Jennings on the other wing.

I wouldn't say I was the best player in the world, but as an attacking midfield player I would get forward, get the rebounds and get the goals. At the Pilgrims I netted 37 times in 233 appearances so it was something in my game.

For Pompey I took penalties as well, although missed a couple. I remember one against Grimsby Town at home in April 1977 when I hit the post and we ended up losing 2-1 in what turned out to be St John's last Fratton Park match in charge.

During my Pompey years, Norwich manager John Bond tried to buy me but it didn't materialise, you don't know what has gone on, I have no idea what happened there. The club also turned down a bid from QPR boss Gordon Jago.

I was happy at Pompey, though, I lived in a bungalow in Milton Road, Cowplain, and there were always a good bunch of players at the club.

Those of us living in Cowplain - Nicky Jennings, Eoin Hand and Fred Smith - used to team up and share a car to training every day, there would be Sunday lunches, and many of the team would get together for a pint at the Green Dragon

Ray Hiron was a Pompey boy and Bobby Kellard was a good player, boy you wanted them on your team, I wouldn't want to play against Bobby in particular, he would kick everybody!

Mike Trebilcock was a good lad, a goalscorer who was either on it or he wasn't, hot and cold, and like all forwards there would be occasions when he would lose confidence.

Another decent player was Billy Wilson, who was short like me but a good tackler, could read the game excellently and got forward. Despite being a left-back mainly he didn't have a left-foot really, it was for standing on, he was really right-footed!

After playing in America in the summer of 1977 and facing Pele, Beckenbauer, Carlos Alberto and Co, moving there permanently appealed to me.

Ron Newman gave me that chance in March 1978 and I left Fratton Park for Fort Lauderdale once more, with Bobby Stokes departing in the same week ahead of the transfer deadline.

Footballers were going over to the States to promote the game, even if the real high-profile ones were getting most of the money, yet the country still wasn't really into it.

After a while, and many years, it has now got to the stage where there are good stadiums, good training fields, a great structure for the kids and unbelievable facilities.

Today we get three or four Premier League games shown live on television every Saturday, the coverage is better here than it is at home!

When I joined Fort Lauderdale Strikers permanently not only was Gordon Banks still there but Georgie Best had also arrived, somebody I regard as the best player ever.

Gordon had only one eye at the time following his car crash but was still a good player, he dominated the penalty box and his disadvantage didn't affect him whatsoever, he did fine.

Georgie would play for us for a season-and-a-half, what a player he was, he would just glide past opponents, but got mixed up with the wrong people.

Then there was me, a country boy from Devon on the same football pitch as Pele, Beckenbauer, Carlos Alberto, Banks and Best and playing in front of almost 78,000. Great memories.

Kappa
jobsite

Pompey 2 aet
Spurs 0

So much for unhappy endings as Piquionne and Prince prove there's life left in Pompey

Batting Blues force a dramatic script rewrite on the day many deemed was their last hurrah on the big stage, as NEIL ALLEN reports...

BACK WITH A BANG Prince Boateng marks his long-awaited Pompey return with a goal from the penalty spot after Aruna Dindane was hauled to the ground in the second half of extra-time at Wembley

MAN IN THE MIDDLE
Alan Wiley (Staffs)

Ricardo **Rocha**

97 games, 0 goals (February 2010 - May 2010, September 2010 - May 2012, November 2012 - May 2013)

Tottenham Hotspur 0
Pompey 2 (Piquionne, Boateng pen)
(After extra-time)

FA Cup Semi-Final, Wembley, Sunday, April 11, 2010

Pompey: James, Finnan, Rocha, Mokoena, Mullins (119 mins Hughes), Boateng, Wilson, Brown, Yebda (87 mins Utaka), Piquionne (112 mins Diop), Dindane.

Subs Not Used: Ashdown, Kanu, Basinas, Smith.

Attendance; 84,602

There are certain moments in your football career you can come back to and say 'That was me at my best'.

The FA Cup semi-final against Tottenham Hotspur in April 2010 was one such occasion.

That match I can honestly say I was at the top of my game. It was one of my best performances and a pleasure to be part of such a special, special day.

Until then I didn't show my best in a Pompey shirt, but in that Wembley fixture I believe I displayed my value, people could see what I was worth.

That was really important for me, especially against my former club. I wanted to prove to everyone I had enough quality to have had more of a chance at White Hart Lane.

I had a few problems with sending offs during my time at Pompey, it looked as though people were chasing me with the red cards, having picked up four in total over my 97 appearances, including two in my first three games!

During that FA Cup run I was suspended for the Southampton game and also the Birmingham City quarter-final, although thankfully played in the best ones - the semi-final and final.

That day against Spurs was my first time playing at Wembley and looking back can say it was my best-ever match in a Pompey shirt.

To cap it all, we won 2-0 to reach the final against Chelsea, while I was named man of the match. Such a special day for me.

To be honest, everyone played well and I can tell you Aaron Mokoena and I had an especially tough time up against good strikers like Peter Crouch, Jermain Defoe, Roman Pavlyuchenko, and even Niko Kranjcar, who was also moved up front a little bit.

Pompey were clearly the underdogs against Harry Redknapp's side, no-one was expecting us to win, after all we had been relegated from the Premier League the day before when West Ham had beaten Sunderland.

People thought it was going to be easy and the FA Cup was heading for a Chelsea v Spurs final, with us losing by four or five goals in the process.

For us it was everything or nothing - and you could see that in the way we played that day. We were together, playing our best, a team effort.

The public thought we didn't have a chance but we went there, gave our best, played a really good game and beat a team that was very superior to us.

I think the result was meant to be, it is one of those fates you cannot explain, you just feel it. Sure, we were talking to the media beforehand saying the usual platitudes about how we will do our best and were the underdogs, but deep down we actually were thinking it was possible.

Avram Grant didn't speak much, he would just say what he had to, and on that day instructed us to not be afraid, to go out and do our best. He explained it was a big thing for the club and how we mustn't let the fans down

Most of all, he convinced us we had enough quality in the team to win it.

It was a physical game, I remember all the moments in that match, I always do with every game I played, and it was hard, but we stuck together and knew we possessed the players to beat them.

A lot of people said we were always defending and Spurs had more chances, but in the end we played brilliantly and scored twice in extra-time through Frederic Piquionne and a Prince Boateng penalty.

I actually don't remember what Avram told us during the on-pitch huddle before the start of that extra-time, the adrenaline was so much that I was not hearing what he was saying. I was listening but thinking 'We need to do this'.

When that final whistle went the feeling afterwards was amazing. Suddenly people across the country were pleased for us, they could see we were a club having a lot of problems and had pulled off an FA Cup surprise.

A lot of our players could have been named man of the match and, to this day, I still remember celebrating with the fans at the end and our midfielder Hayden Mullins being by my side.

He just grabbed me and said 'Hey, man of the match' and I replied 'No, come on, you are just messing with me'.

Hayden was adamant and told me 'I'm telling you, it is true', but I said 'Hayden, don't do this, let's just celebrate the victory'. Then when I walked into the dressing room they came in with a Champagne bottle for me!

It turned out they had announced the man of the match on the Wembley big screens and put my picture up, but I didn't see it and thought Hayden was just messing with me.

Hermann Hreidarsson - who was injured at the time - wanted to open my bottle in the dressing room there and then but the guys wouldn't let him, 'He has to remember this forever' they shouted.

He didn't do it and I still have it with me. I am not going to touch it, it is a souvenir that is in a special place.

Instead of opening it, I stood in the middle of the dressing room and dedicated my award to everybody, from the players to 'Big' Kev McCormack, the kitman, they all deserved it, not just me.

The celebrations were mental, everyone was tired after going into extra-time but we knew how much it meant to all of us, to the fans and the club. It was fantastic.

The fact this happened against Spurs was wonderful, having made only 18 appearances for them during two-and-a-half years after joining from Benfica.

I always believed as a player you had to be professional in whatever you do, you have to do the best for the club you are representing, you should give 100 per cent no matter the situation you find yourself in.

At Spurs even when not playing I did that and, on the day I left, the director of football at the time came up to me and said 'Thank you for being as professional as you could until the end of your contract'.

I had reasons to be upset, they didn't let me leave earlier. I had offers but they didn't accept the money, they just left me in the corner.

They were paying me so I had to do my best in every training session, playing in the reserve team or whatever, so his words meant a lot because everybody was happy with my work there even though I didn't play.

Then less than a year after leaving White Hart Lane I had been part of a Pompey side to beat them in the semi-final of the FA Cup and was also made man of the match. Wonderful.

For the final against Chelsea the following month, Carlo Ancelotti's side were fantastic in the first half, they had the better chances, hitting the woodwork five times, while we were a little bit nervous to be playing against a team which had just won the Premier League.

We played very, very well in the second half, then with the match still goalless Boateng - who was such an unbelievable player - missed a penalty and Didier Drogba went on to win it for Chelsea in the 59th minute with the only goal of the game.

If you score that penalty you are winning and Chelsea would have all the pressure on them while we were defending brilliantly, so there is always that feeling things could have turned out differently.

That 1-0 defeat was difficult for me, I had lost finals in Portugal and obviously it is never a good feeling but I'd had five months at the club and wanted to pay back all those people who had been unbelievable towards me.

I started crying at the final whistle, I couldn't give the fans that amazing trophy and with relegation also that season my emotions leaked. That from somebody not normally emotional!

Boateng was also crying, having missed a penalty he felt all the emotions like me and everybody was saying to us 'Don't worry, you played fantastically, don't cry', but I really couldn't stop.

I had arrived at Pompey just 14 weeks before that FA Cup final and how that came about was a big surprise to me, especially as initially there was talk of me joining in the summer of 2009.

Before the start of the season an agent called and said it was a possibility I would be able to move to Paul Hart's side and play in the Premier League again, something I was definitely interested in.

But then after a few weeks there was a lot of confusion in the club because of the ownership situation so instead I went to Standard Liege, who were playing in the Champions League.

The problem was I had not played for a year because of my difficulties at Spurs and didn't feel right, while I couldn't settle in the city so was looking for the opportunity to go elsewhere and they agreed to cancel my contract.

Then a friend of mine called to say I could definitely go to Pompey - and this time I signed a few hours before the deadline on February 1, 2010.

As mentioned before, I had a few red cards during my time at Fratton of which two were for professional fouls and the other two were harsh, they were not right.

At Reading I was given a straight red after bringing down Shane Long and the same punishment happened to me when we played Sunderland at home, although the referee Kevin Friend initially sent off Hassan Yebda by mistake!

I told the referee it was actually me who had tripped Darren Bent, I had to own up and be honest, I wasn't going to let Yebda take the red card for me, definitely not.

At Cardiff City in April 2011, I was sent off after Jay Bothroyd head-butted me and left me requiring four stitches on my eye.

I didn't do anything, we were just arguing and the guy head-butted me, I started bleeding, the referee gave me the red card and we went on to lose 3-0!

When you know you have done something wrong you get the red card and you just go, but the worst feeling is when you don't do anything and get sent off. It really is the worst.

It was like that at Burnley as well when I received a second yellow, which was just unbelievable.

I let Jack Cork play a pass but he wanted the foul so went to ground and the referee sent me off!

That red card against Sunderland ruled me out of the FA Cup tie at Southampton, which was the following match, but I did manage to face them twice in the 2011-12 season.

We drew 1-1 at Fratton Park in December, but it was the return match at St Mary's in April 2012 which gave me so much joy - and left Southampton supporters more upset than us!

Sometimes I go on YouTube to see the fans' reaction to that David Norris goal in the 2-2 draw, it is just unbelievable, I get goosebumps every single time.

It was actually my ball into the box which lead to the equaliser, in stoppage time I put it in from the halfway line, Dave Kitson jumped up for a header with one of the defenders and it fell to David Norris to strike a fantastic left-foot volley.

What a moment, what a moment. You can see our wonderful fans celebrating behind the goal, you can see Kelvin Etuhu coming off the bench to celebrate with the supporters and he gets a yellow card.

They are moments you will remember forever.

I don't think I endeared myself to the Southampton supporters during that match, but when you have all the adrenaline and emotion inside, you can do stupid things.

People may recall me kicking the ball into a female fan but, I am being honest with you, I didn't actually want to do that, it was an accident.

I knew the ball was out and was trying to waste some time so my intention was to kick it against the advertising board, but I missed that and it struck a supporter behind the goal.

You can see on the footage I was apologising saying 'I am sorry, I am sorry' but they were shouting at me and wanted to come onto the pitch.

Then Southampton's Adam Lallana came up to me and said 'What are you doing?' and I replied 'I didn't mean that', but he kept calling me names - so I slapped him!

You do things which after the game you go 'What have I done?' but in the heat of the moment you can do some crazy stuff.

I was lucky, though, I was booked for that when it could have been another red card. It wasn't a big slap but people can go off for less.

Of course, when I was booked I was thinking I had to stick with it and make out I had done nothing so was shouting to the referee 'What have I done?' - but I knew!

At the end of the game I apologised to Lallana and he accepted that, you can fight them on the pitch but when it is over you are friends again.

The funny thing is for the first six months of my time at Pompey I lived in Southampton. Seriously!

My wife and family hadn't come over at that point so I rented a small apartment in Ocean Village, with Younes Kaboul and Boateng also living around that area.

One time I asked the club if they could help me get to Southampton Airport and they sent a taxi to pick me up from Ocean Village.

The driver couldn't believe I lived there and told me 'I am a big Pompey fan, I have come to Southampton to pick you up because it was you. If you were someone else I wouldn't have done that!'.

At the time I didn't know much about the rivalry between Pompey and Southampton - but he explained it to me very well and the following season my family and I moved to Fareham.

Still, six weeks following that St Mary's match I was released by Michael Appleton - and found out by reading The News!

He never said anything to me or Jamie Ashdown - who was also not offered a new deal - but I could feel in training he wasn't going to keep me on, so it didn't take me by surprise.

I was okay with it, I just wanted the best for the club and if the manager felt that meant going in another direction then that was fine.

What upset me was the treatment of Jamie, which was handled worse than me because he had been there eight seasons but no word was ever said to him, not even 'I am building a new team, doing something different, I wish you guys all the best and good luck'.

Appleton didn't say anything, I don't think he is the type of guy to do that. People are different, I don't wish to criticise him, it's the way he does things, he is a good manager and I always wish him well.

After that I had a few offers but they were for countries which would have been difficult for me to move to, especially with my kids eager to go back to the local school in Portsmouth.

Then in November 2012 my friend Guy Whittingham - a good man - was made Pompey caretaker manager and asked if I could help him out, I couldn't say no and was back once again.

It wasn't easy, we had a lot of games without a win but it was all because of the problems surrounding the club and it was a difficult season.

Everybody was getting a month's contract, the club was not stabilised, there were players coming in, going out, it was always a different team playing each week.

We were relegated to League Two at the end of that 2012-13 season and Guy wanted to re-sign me, which I was very interested in.

Talks were held about playing and also a director of football role, but terms couldn't be agreed so I wished them all the best and we went our different ways.

Looking back at my career, I wish when I first came to the Premier League I had gone to a club like Pompey and not Spurs because it is like a family.

Everybody will support you as a player, everybody will be there for you and at Spurs it didn't happen, it wasn't like that. Pompey is a wonderful club.

WS. MONDAY, JANUARY 9, 1950

AP TRIPS
Y RAIL
from
UTH & SOUTHSEA

Lackadaisical Portsmouth Held To A Draw

MORE THRUST NEEDED AT NORWICH

By THE RANGER

WE have to wait until Thursday to see whether Portsmouth are going further in the F.A. Cup competition, and if they play no better than they did against Norwich at Fratton Park, on Saturday, they will have little interest in the road to Wembley after their visit to Carrow Road.

There were many who thought Portsmouth had an easy task before them in meeting the Third Division club, and they may have been right, but the mistake was that Pompey thought on the same lines, and played like it. Norwich confessed that Portsmouth would be a hard side to beat. They, too, played like it, and their courage earned them the right to fight again.

I thought Pompey's experience would have served them better than it did in this game. They have played all types of football against all kinds of opponents and they ought to have known that Norwich would not go out without a fight. Yet on Saturday, as we have so often seen at Fratton Park this season, it was not so much the opposition as Portsmouth themselves that prevented them recording a victory.

Worst Since the Semi-Final

I GIVE Norwich full credit for their performance, one of the best of the day, but I think had Pompey settled down to anything like their real form they would have chalked up too many goals for the Canaries.

Pompey can thank their lucky stars Norwich were not ...

Pompey Had No Initiative

NORWICH are a nice Third Division side but there was nothing outstanding about them. I liked their defence which was well led by Norman Low, the son of Newcastle's old Scottish international, but Pompey had no initiative and were too easily put off the ball. Their passing was all adrift and there was not sufficient understanding in the forward line for the short passing to succeed. Norwich were much better at finding their men with either long or short ball.

They Should Win at Norwich

THE injury to Delapenha early in the second half threw the Portsmouth attack out of gear more than ever but it never shaped like a goal-scoring line and, taking the team through I thought they compared poorly as champions when placed alongside their Third Division opponents who ...

Wheatley had to have stitches inserted in a cut, and in the second half, Webber, who had been playing cleverly, was hobbling on the right wing, and the side was further disorganized. Brilliant goal-keeping by Black saved the Saints, who were also well served by the two reserve backs Wilkins and Ballard.

Tim McCoy, the Northampton centre-half, formerly with Pompey, blotted Wayman out of the game.

Ekner Breasts in Winner

HERE is the subject of a wise-cracking discussion on the homeward-bound Portsmouth Reserves' coach on Saturday night: Dan Ekner's match-winning chest, writes The Stroller.

With this mighty piece of anatomy Dan butted the ball into the Leyton Orient Reserves' net four minutes from time to snatch a 3—2 Combination Cup victory for Pompey.

Earlier Portsmouth had twice gone in front through Gordon and Reid, but Leyton came back and equalized both times with goals from Smith and Taylor.

On their first half showing, Portsmouth should have won hands down. "Shoot on sight" was the order and the Pompey forwards — Ekner, Gordon and Reid, especially — took it literally. Sometimes Ekner did not wait to see the whites of goalkeeper Welton's eyes before slamming the ball goalwards.

There was ...

REPLAY TICKETS

Portsmouth's allocation of tickets for the cup replay at Norwich on Thursday ... 750.

These, however, are available only to shareholders with privilege tickets ... season ticket holders.

Applications for tickets must be made personally ... Fratton Park to-mo... between the hours of ... and 12 and 2.30 and 4 ...

Prices of tickets are ... 5s., and 4s., and only ... per person will be avail...

Applicants must pro... their books at the time ... applying.

Services "A" ... Bournemouth

UNITED SERVIC... fairly zipped thr... Bournemouth defenc... Officers' Ground on ... and most of the first ... powerful back section ... clever display of pas... backing up, writes ... Judge. But lack of s... in taking and giving t... pass kept the first-ha... down to a try scored fa... wing man B. A. Lloyd ...

Full-back R. E. Kei... merly with London ... played a heroic ga... Bournemouth and th... wards crashed throug... good revival in the first ... the second half. Le... Moyes put on an unc... try to bring the scores ...

After that it was all ... again. Skipper D. S... scored a try which H. E... converted. Next c... splendid dropped go... little centre A. R. Richa... the final score was ... 14pt. to 3 when A.B. ... followed up to cross fo... try.

Wing man E. V. F. S... taken off the field wi... injury just before the ...

POACHER'S POCK...

Shirts with pockets ... wrist watches have be... on smugglers at S... Airport.

Lindy **Delapenha**

Eight games, one goal (April 1948 - April 1950)

Pompey 1 (Delapenha)
Norwich City 1 (Kinsey)

FA Cup Third Round, Fratton Park, Saturday, January 7, 1950

Pompey: Butler, Hindmarsh, Ferrier, Scoular, Flewin, Dickinson, Harris, Delapenha, Clarke, Phillips, Pickett.

Attendance; 42,059

The moment was obvious, I thought the referee couldn't miss it.

My first and only Pompey goal - and it was a carbon copy of the infamous Diego Maradona World Cup handball many, many years later.

Actually I did feel embarrassed, I don't like to do that type of thing, but it was something I couldn't resist.

Harry Ferrier made a forward lob from near the halfway line and the ball dropped into the penalty area.

I leapt in the air and the Norwich City goalkeeper, Ken Nethercott, came a little bit late. I knew he was arriving, it occurred to me he was going to bang me on the back so I put my hand up over my head.

The ball caught my knuckles, flew over his hand and into the back of the net, just inside the post.

The Canaries were in Third Division South, while we were Division One champions - and we had been thrown together in the FA Cup's third round.

On the day we didn't play well, my 28th minute goal was the only one we managed, with Noel Kinsey equalising on 60 minutes to give Norwich a 1-1 Fratton Park draw.

I cheated but it had stopped the embarrassment of a lower division team potentially beating us on our own ground. That was the way I saw it anyway.

When my goal happened the Norwich players made a strong appeal to the referee who, having then consulted his linesman, allowed it to stand. I couldn't believe it, but remained quiet!

The referee was a one-armed man named Alf Bond, who went on to officiate the 1956 FA Cup final between Manchester City and Birmingham City, but got it very wrong that day at Fratton Park.

That was my third successive game for Pompey after replacing the dropped Duggie Reid at inside-right - and I had scored my maiden goal for the club.

Mind you, in the second half I damaged my leg and had to go to outside-left to keep me out of the way, Reg Pickett coming across to fill. There were no substitutes back then.

We went on to win the third round replay at Carrow Road five days later, Reid recalled in place of an injured me to get both goals in a 2-0 win.

Next was a 5-0 victory at Grimsby Town and then we lost 3-1 at home to Manchester United in a fifth round replay so didn't get too much further after my goal.

Yet that Fratton Park fixture was the most dramatic match of the eight games I played for Pompey and the one that sticks in my mind as my favourite.

It was also my final Pompey appearance on home turf - and my penultimate for the club before departing for Middlesbrough in April 1950.

I spent two seasons with Pompey, becoming the club's first black player and the first Jamaican to appear in Division One.

When I left the West Indies my intention was to try to play professional football in England, but was then called up for National Service following the Second World War, so my career was interrupted for a little while.

Before joining the British Army I did have a trial at Arsenal, although it wasn't much of a trial. I travelled to Highbury, played both halves and didn't do too badly but not enough to impress the manager Tom Whittaker, although he did tell me to come back once my

National Service was over.

As it happened I was posted overseas in Egypt with the Royal Fusiliers and it was a blessing in disguise because it is there where a scout for Pompey and Chelsea spotted me.

I was stationed in Cairo and one day represented the British Army against the German Prisoners of War, in fact the Germans had a pretty good side at that time but we beat them 2-0.

Afterwards this fella came up and asked whether I would like to play professional football. I didn't even know he was there watching!

I told him that was my ambition and he replied 'Well, I'm working for two clubs, Chelsea and Pompey. I will give you a letter for both of them and you can take your pick'.

My friend in the Army, a fella called Horne, lived in Havant and when my National Service came to an end after two years he said to me: 'You've got this letter from a scout, you are going to England and have nowhere to stay, so come and stop with me and my family and then see Bob Jackson and see what comes of it'.

So in April 1948 I arrived in the city and stayed with his family for a couple of days before Bob Jackson, Pompey's manager, later got me into digs with a lady in Fratton.

Anyhow, I was given a reserve match in the London Combination against Bristol Rovers and played pretty well in a 3-1 win. In fact, Bob came into the dressing room at half-time to make sure I signed!

He had never seen me play before and decided he didn't want anyone to get me - suddenly I was a Pompey player.

I would go on to score quite a few goals in those reserve games because that is where I spent a lot of time at Pompey. I was a prominent member of the London Combination side.

What a great first-team that was, though, they won the Division One title two years in a row when I was there and the second time, in 1949-50, I qualified for a medal after playing six matches in the season.

I sent my medal home to Kingston, Jamaica, for my mother, Josephine, and she kept it, but when she died must have taken it with her because I really don't know where it went to. I wouldn't even be able to guess where it is now.

My positions varied, I could play inside left, outside left, outside right or inside right, but wouldn't call myself a centre forward, I was too small to be a centre forward.

I had rivals in the first-team who never seemed to get injured and never seemed to play really badly. Reid was one, Ike Clarke was another, Bert Barlow was another and Len Phillips was the other. I had very little chance of getting into the side unless there were injuries.

In my second season, Duggie lost a bit of form so firstly Dan Ekner and then me filled in for him, although he soon got his place back again when I picked up my injury against Norwich.

But they had too good a side and I wasn't there long enough to get into the team. I was scoring a lot of goals for the reserves, making a lot of headlines, but just couldn't dislodge these great names in Pompey history.

Duggie scored plenty every year and featured in my position on the inside right. He could also kick a ball as hard as anything, I have never seen a man strike a ball that powerfully.

It was actually more a toe punt rather than an instep shot, and he was also good with his head, my word he was good in the air.

Duggie was this strapping 6ft 2in figure and if you looked at him you would be afraid. He was a scary-looking fella, not dirty, very gentlemanly, quiet and very nice, but a strong fella with a frightening face.

Jimmy Dickinson was a gentleman, a perfect gentleman, the opposite to Jimmy Scoular!

He was extremely good, a good defender, good distributer of the ball and he, Reg Flewin and Jimmy Scoular were probably three of the best half-backs in the First Division at that time.

Scoular was a tough man, he wanted to fight on the field every day. He was a good man to have in your side because he was tough, strong and a good tackler but, at times overdid it.

He was a nice enough person off the field, pleasant, but on it I would say he was dirty. Once he was sent home from a Pompey summer tour of South America after being dismissed in a game against Fluminese and creating a fuss on the field.

That showed you how bad he was!

He is the only member of that team that I would say would play as they do today. I am not happy how they play today, too many players going over the top of the ball and jumping from behind, but that was Scoular.

Jimmy Dickinson wasn't like that, he was the perfect gentleman, but nevertheless a great tackler and excellent distributor of the ball.

Len Phillips was my good buddy, I courted the girl he married - Joan - for a while at Pompey, she was a lovely girl.

He was outstanding and I'm surprised didn't play more than the three times he did for England. He was good on the ball, a good goalscorer, a good worker of the ball, scored a lot of goals and made a lot as well.

Goalkeeper Ernie Butler was quite a tall fella, 6ft 3in, not too agile but certainly good with his hands and caught the ball when necessary.

Peter Harris was like a flying machine down the right, he was a dream on the wing, like greased lightning, a great goalscorer and what a crosser of the ball he was.

Jack Froggatt on the left was big and strong, a good header of the ball, Ike Clarke was a prolific scorer who played some days and Bert Barlow other days.

The full-backs switched around a bit, Phil Rookes at one and Bill Hindmarsh was the other, while Flewin was a big fella, good in the air, and worked well with the other two wing-half backs.

Those players could play in any Premier League side today, any of them, no problem, including myself.

There is not much that has changed as far as I am concerned, except probably the pitches are a little bit better, more level, and the balls have much improved, you don't have to play with the ball now, the ball plays for you, they are so good.

Bob Jackson was the manager and always wore a bow tie, he was never without it, and we would say when his team scored the bow tie would spin.

He had three fingers and a thumb on his right hand, the index finger was missing, and the players, particularly Scoular, would openly take the mickey out of Bob.

When he was speaking, Scoular would put up his index finger and waggle it around, so that was always the joke with the manager, although I don't think he actually knew!

I had a run in with Bob once, it was my own fault, I was a jolly old fella and used to like going to dances.

They held them at the Savoy, which was opposite the South Parade Pier, and I used to like going on the Friday night because they had Ted Heath and all these great bands coming down.

Obviously we would have a match the next day so I used to sneak in at the end of the evening, but then I think somebody once told a tale on me.

I was walking up the steps one night and as I am looking up who should be on the balcony staring down at me but Bob Jackson. I didn't stay long that night!

The next morning I walked into Fratton Park as we were playing in London as part of the London Combination reserve league and Bob collared me and said: 'Why were you at that club last night?'.

My reply was 'I am playing today, aren't I?'.

He said: 'You were but you are not now' and that was it, I was left out of the team!

Len Phillips was my friend, we went out quite a bit, he was a Friday night man as well but was fortunate he wasn't caught!

Being a black player living in Portsmouth at the time, people still ask whether there was any racism, but I handled it.

When anything was said I treated it as a stupid remark and sort of looked at them first and would give an answer back, not a rude or dirty answer, it would be a laugh because I have a good sense of humour.

So I used to answer the crowd in the way they spoke to me and they treated it as a joke and it ended up as a joke.

There was the odd one with a stupid remark - as I can also make a stupid remark - after all, we are all human beings.

It was fine in Portsmouth but then again I didn't play as much, I was on the field every week at Middlesborough so heard it a lot more there.

In my second year with the club, after the opening four matches I took Duggie's place as he wasn't playing too well and stayed there until we played at Aston Villa in September 1949 and came across a fella called Frank Moss. He wasn't too nice a player.

He was another Jimmy Scoular, but Scoular was a better player than he was, much better.

Moss knocked me in the air and I came down and the outside of both ankles were black, purple, green, blue, all sorts of colours, but thankfully not broken.

I had been playing well, but just couldn't get the ankles back to normal again, both ligaments were torn so I had to receive treatment all the time. They were purple for seven months, it really was a bad, bad injury.

Even when I returned from injury in December the ankles weren't properly back. Should you get a ball on the end of your toe you jumped through the roof, so that caused me to lose my place.

I enjoyed it very much living in Portsmouth, I loved the place, it wasn't as cold as the other parts of the country I would later live such as Middlesbrough, Mansfield Town and Hereford United.

Apart from football, I also played cricket and was a pretty good batsman, appearing in matches for the United Services. What a lovely ground Burnaby Road was, a lovely batting wicket.

I had a trial for Hampshire one summer, held in the Isle of Wight. I turned up on the first day and fielded and never got a bat so thought 'What the hell am I coming over here for a trial for?' and didn't go back the second day.

Worcestershire was another club where I had a trial after future England batsman Tom Graveney recommended me.

We had played together in the British Army, once we were together at the wicket and I put 129 on the board and he had made 50. In the second innings I had 50 and Tom had 133 so I was in good company there!

Anyhow, I went to Worcester but it had peed down all night so I got a sticky wicket and made seven runs before getting one that popped off the handle and was out.

I didn't like short-pitched bowling, I wasn't about to be hit in the eye and finish my football career. Football was my living and there were no helmets in those days so in the end I gave up cricket.

It was April 1950 when I left Pompey for Middlesbrough, but I wasn't sad because I knew I was going into a first team. Their manager, David Jack, had seen me play against them so was keen to sign me.

I would go on to score a lot of goals for Boro, including two in a 4-1 win at Ayresome Park against Pompey when Scoular tried to rough me up - he had no friends on the football field!

Wilf Mannion was playing inside right, although I wasn't expected to replace him even though that was my position. Instead I was converted to outside right and our partnership together proved outstanding, we really clicked.

I also met a young goalscorer and a hell of a centre forward called Brian Clough, whose best buddy was the goalkeeper Peter Taylor.

For three of my first six seasons I was leading scorer, then he came along and I was the second leading scorer!

Clough was one of these people that no matter what happened during a match he had to get a goal, he had a knack of being in the right place at the right time. The ball seemed to find him, he didn't find the ball.

If a shot ever hit the upright, the ball would come back and land at his feet.

We used to have a routine from corners and free-kicks where I wouldn't play the ball to him, instead I would put it into a position and he would run into that position to score.

For instance, I probably would aim for the penalty spot from the corner - I was an extremely good crosser of the ball - and he used to run there. Clough was also extremely good with his head.

Clough was very arrogant, absolutely arrogant, he called a spade a spade all the time, he wasn't afraid to tell you, but knew the game.

Taylor, for a goalkeeper, also knew the game. He knew where a centre forward was supposed to be and where a right winger was supposed to be and wasn't afraid to tell him.

I had no doubt eventually Clough would become a manager. I think that more or less started in those days together at Middlesbrough.

They were really good buddies, together all the time, everywhere, and talked football non-stop, that is how they knew so much.

Both of them were actually very unpopular at Ayresome Park because they were never apart. What Clough said went and what Taylor said went and the other players took a dislike to them.

I kept in touch with the pair, though, and Clough sent me his autobiography 'Walking On Water', which included how I used to always drive him around in my Ford Anglia, with one day me taking him to Stockton-on-Tees to get an engagement ring for his wife-to-be Barbara.

I sent back a message saying 'Brian, I used to do more than that, I used to make you most of your goals!'.

By the time I left Middlesbrough for Mansfield in June 1958 I had scored 93 goals in 270 appearances, playing alongside Clough in the last three seasons.

I left England in 1964 to return to Jamaica and am considered the best all-round athlete my country has ever produced, playing football, cricket, tennis, hockey and being a runner.

I suppose you can say I also showed I could play basketball in that FA Cup match for Pompey!

BLACKBURN ROVERS 3 POMPEY 3

MAGIC MAC'S FINEST HOUR

By MIKE NEASOM

McLoughlin takes his time

Praise for hero

MAN OF THE MOMENT ● Pompey's Alan McLoughlin

MATCH facts

Alan **McLoughlin**

361 games, 68 goals (February 1992 - December 1999)

Blackburn Rovers 3 (Shearer, Gallacher, Sherwood)
Pompey 3 (McLoughlin 3)

FA Cup Third Round, Ewood Park, Saturday, January 8, 1994

Pompey: Knight, Kristensen, Symons, Awford, Dobson, Daniel, Stimson (78 mins Russell), Doling (65 mins Durnin), McLoughlin, Powell, Walsh.

Sub Not Used: Horne.

Attendance; 17,219

It took a hat-trick against Blackburn Rovers for the Pompey fans to eventually accept me and my background.

You just can't walk into a football club from down the road and expect to win over the supporters straight away, it doesn't happen like that.

What you have to do is play not just one good game or 10 good games, but do it over a season and I believe the next two years following my February 1992 arrival from Southampton displayed increasing levels of performances and rising expectations.

As a team we were delivering. Admittedly, ultimately we didn't deliver the FA Cup or promotion, but the brand of football was entertaining and they saw me as part of that.

No matter who you are, goals are a great way of getting supporters on your side. I was scoring on a regular basis, playing well on a regular basis and displaying commitment to the club on a regular basis.

It was also about saying the right things, not being a prat, not referencing things you shouldn't, buying into the football club, learning about the city and what the fans expect.

In addition, I loved living there, whether it be in Warsash or Whiteley, it's a lovely part of the world to settle down in.

If you do those things you stand a far better chance of the fans accepting you, rather than acting ignorant and not bothering - and I went on to last almost eight years as a player at Fratton Park.

Even after my playing career had come to an end I would get the 'Scummer' comment now and again, usually from people beered up. Normally they do it slyly in a group, someone shouting it out.

I remember walking into the Chimes Bar a few years ago while working for The Quay radio station and seeing a group of lads as I made my way through. 'Alright lads.' I said.

'Alright Macca,' came the reply and as I made my way down the corridor heading to the Frogmore Road entrance one of them shouted 'Scummer'.

I started to carry on with the intention of ignoring it but stopped and thought 'Hang on, I'm not leaving it there'.

So I went back and confronted them, I think they were a bit surprised when I said 'Come on then, who shouted Scummer?'.

They shrugged and I followed it up with 'If you have not got the guts to say it to my face then don't say it at all. Come on then who is it?'. They were red faced and said nothing.

Then there was a time in the commentary box at Wembley for the April 2010 FA Cup semi-final with Tottenham Hotspur, one drunken bloke shouting something across at me.

They think it's funny and it does hurt a little bit. I would say 99.9 per cent of the fans know my heart is with Pompey.

I can't do anything about my Southampton past, joining them under Chris Nicholl from Swindon Town in December 1990 was the right thing to do at the time. It was eventually also the right thing to move away.

I could have taken an easier option, there were a host of clubs wanting to take me - but decided to come to Pompey.

Originally I arrived at Fratton Park on loan with a view to signing permanently so it was up to me if I stayed, I could have gone back to Southampton and waited for another club to come in but my family were happy down here.

Besides, I wanted the challenge to try to get us into the top flight, which is the ambition Jim Smith sold to me, and I decided to stay permanently.

Heading into an FA Cup third round visit to Blackburn in January 1994, at that point in my career I had scored a hatful of twos but never achieved the milestone of bagging three.

At the time I was having an unbelievable couple of months. In the November I had netted the goal which took the Republic of Ireland to the 1994 World Cup Finals and my form in terms of scoring and playing well was white hot.

We had been drawn away to Premier League Blackburn, whose record in December was absolutely phenomenal, undefeated including a 1-1 draw at Old Trafford on Boxing Day, and lying second in the table.

They had conceded eight goals in 12 league matches at home and were title contenders, transformed by Jack Walker's millions with Alan Shearer up front on fire boasting 20 goals at that point.

Before the match Pompey were seen as no-hopers, perceived as making up the numbers. Our own aim was to take Kenny Dalglish's side back to Fratton Park for a bit of a pay day. If we did get beat, though, let's not get spanked.

We went on to grab a 3-3 draw, while I recorded the only hat-trick of my playing career.

Blackburn took the lead in the 21st minute when Graeme Le Saux pulled the ball back from the byline down the left, it took a slight deflection off one of our players which delivered it to where Shearer was stood and he buried it with his right foot.

Alan Knight had no chance because the England striker had hit it so hard down to his right-hand side - now we feared at that mid-way point through the first half we may cave in.

That didn't happen, though, and in the 48th minute I picked the ball up in midfield, and played a great little one-two with Paul Walsh. Looking back at it now I actually had a turn of pace which was nice, allowing me to glide between David May and Colin Hendry!

I then saw the goalkeeper Tim Flowers coming, so feigned as if I was going to shoot, took an extra touch and pushed it into the net with my right foot to make it 1-1.

Rovers regained the lead in the 71st minute when Stuart Ripley's cross came in from the right and Kevin Gallagher was left unmarked to produce a right-foot finish.

We fought back once more, eight minutes from time Benny Kristensen crossed from the right, Darryl Powell flicking the ball on and I gambled.

As it came in I read the situation, managing to take the ball down to ensure I was clean through with only the keeper to beat.

I was so confident because the season had gone so well, there were no thoughts of blasting it, instead I opened the body up and stroked it into the bottom corner. I was at that level where I thought I could do most things well and had no fear.

If I am honest, as a team we were delighted with 2-2, if we could get back to Fratton Park with a replay then brilliant, if we lost 3-2 at a side like Blackburn then it is not the end of the world.

However, five minutes from time Dalglish's side got a third, Le Saux's left-wing corner eventually dropping to their skipper, Tim Sherwood, who had a slap at it and it flew through a crowd of players and past Knightsie.

I have looked back at it a few times and in his goal celebration Sherwood appears to be trying to have a pop at me over the way I celebrated our second goal!

As we traipsed back to the halfway line thinking that was it little did we realise there was still more drama to come.

With 30 seconds remaining, Ray Daniel knocked a long free-kick into the box, there were a few headers among a melee of players and I've anticipated where the ball might land.

After scoring goals over the years, you get a knack of learning to anticipate situations and mistakes, it becomes instinctive.

It was a loopy ball delivered in so I knew not to gamble too far because there would not be enough pace for it to carry on, then unbelievably it plonked straight in front of me.

Normally I might have swung at it with my left foot or took a quick shot with my right, but I didn't, I was completely calm even though I knew the Pompey fans were on my right and it was a hat-trick chance. The moment was surreal.

Once again there was no need to blast it, I had to repeat what I did for the second goal, use my confidence to stroke it into the corner rather than thrashing or blasting it past Flowers - and that is what I did.

Blackburn kicked off, the ball went back to the keeper, was booted upfield and the game finished. I had that elusive hat-trick and Pompey had a 3-3 draw.

At Southampton people had made decisions about me and there was part of me that day which said 'Look, I can do it at this level, I have just scored a hat-trick against the champions-elect'.

To all those who doubted I could perform at the top level, suddenly I had popped up and shown what I was capable of, that for me was pure elation.

As a kid there had been all those extra hours in training at Manchester United, the disappointment of subsequently being released, then the hard work at Swindon which was a really tough environment in terms of physicality.

There was Southampton and the shenanigans which went on when Chris Nicholl paid a club record £1m for a central midfielder but instead decided to play me on the left-hand side.

All those things came together to make it a special moment, especially considering how good Blackburn were at the time.

We actually weren't a bad side and went on to miss out on automatic promotion to the Premier League the following season because West Ham had scored one more goal!

Meanwhile, four days after that Ewood Park result, we collected a 2-2 draw at Old Trafford in the Coca-Cola Cup against Manchester United, Ryan Giggs and Eric Cantona scoring for them.

Still, in our Rovers replay 12 days after the first game, we were unlucky, Blackburn running out 3-1 winners with Jason Wilcox handling the ball into the net at the far post for their third a minute after I had pulled one back.

It was two years earlier when a reserve game at Staplewood helped pave the way for an escape route out of Southampton to Fratton Park - and the opposition was Pompey!

We ran out 6-1 winners in that February 1992 fixture, with Paul Moody scoring a hat-trick while I got the final goal. Mind you, Colin Clarke had to go in goal for Pompey after

Andy Gosney had been stretchered off, while Warren Aspinall received a red card for a foul on me.

Within two weeks I was with the Blues, Ian Branfoot having no objections to their enquiry - and I had no hesitation in accepting.

I so desperately wanted to prove Southampton wrong and if it meant going up the road to their arch enemy I was quite prepared to do it.

The amazing thing was they actually agreed I could also play in the FA Cup so there could have been a scenario where I was playing for Pompey against Southampton in the semi-final and potentially knocking them out despite being employed by them!

As it was, they were beaten 2-1 in a quarter-final replay at Norwich City, while we went on to lose to Liverpool in the semi-finals.

Jim Smith was a very good boss, a superb man manager and good tactician who worked players hard at set-pieces. I probably didn't appreciate him at the time in terms of how good he was, he got the best out of us and had a good eye for a player.

My debut was a goalless draw at Wolverhampton Wanderers, followed by my first appearance in Pompey colours at Fratton Park, with Tranmere Rovers the opposition.

As a Southampton player turning out for the club I took a lot of stick with plenty of shouts of 'Scummer' screaming around the place. It started with my every touch of the ball in the opening minutes and the abuse just continued.

It's amazing, though, how a goal makes people jump up and down and forget who you are and I scored on that home debut, after Chris Burns had earlier broken the deadlock in a 2-0 victory.

The comments didn't affect me, I was aged 24 and had a thick skin, it was the way I was brought up. Obviously I get nervous, but nothing fazes me.

My third appearance saw me get the winner against Brian Clough's Nottingham Forest the following month in the FA Cup quarter-finals, again at Fratton Park, on our way to the semi-final against Liverpool.

The following campaign in 1992-93, however, was the best Pompey team I played in and my favourite season at the club, without a doubt.

We were a good side, an exciting side, Fratton Park was buzzing that season, those magnificent fans were watching us play entertaining football week in, week out.

Guy Whittingham got his ridiculous amount of goals, Paul Walsh was alongside him, while I weighed in with 12. As an attacking three it worked fantastically well.

My job was to go and support Guy and I would sometimes play in the hole behind the pair of them, the system was quite narrow and for a while an alternative was to operate with a diamond with me at the top.

Walshie got The News/Sports Mail Player of the Season which was daft really. He was exciting, he was magical but anyone who scores 47 goals in a campaign - as Guy did - should get that award in my eyes.

Having said that, I can understand why he won the vote because he made the crowd get out of their seats and was the key player, although I still feel aggrieved for Guy that he didn't get it.

As for the league, that season goals scored counted rather than goal difference so one goal stopped us going up automatically, it was ridiculous.

We drew 5-5 at Oxford United in March 1993 after cruising 5-2 with 13 minutes to go, there was Sunderland in the penultimate match when we went down to nine men after Guy Butters was sent off for handball on the line, then Walshie went mid-way through the second half.

All we had to do was score goals, not worry about defending, and it was a 3-3-2 in that match in the end, we just went for it, Guy actually had two one-on-ones late on, one more goal could have been crucial. We lost 4-1.

In the last match of the season against Grimsby Town we went one down and came back to win 2-1, although Kristensen missed an absolute sitter, he decided to knee it and it went over the bar from close range.

At the same time, Steve Claridge was playing for Cambridge United, already relegated from Division One, and had a perfectly good goal chalked off at West Ham United, ending up losing 2-0.

That meant the play-offs, yet being without the suspended Walshie for both semi-final legs was a killer, an absolute killer.

We played Leicester City, Filbert Street was being redeveloped for the first leg so it was staged at Nottingham Forest's City Ground.

The Foxes won 1-0, Andy Awford and Kit Symons should have tackled Julian Joachim and taken him out on the halfway line, instead he ran through the middle of them to get the only goal.

Then a 2-2 draw at Fratton Park knocked us out on aggregate and we remained in Division One.

There was no Guy the following season, he had joined Aston Villa in the Premier League, and halfway through the campaign Jim brought in Gerry Creaney, who had his issues off the pitch.

The Scot got goals but was not as brave as Guy. Guy was the most fearless centre forward I ever played with, he never shirked anything and scored so many goals where he clattered the goalkeeper.

Nowadays he would probably be sent off, but back then challenging a keeper was allowed, he would then be lying on the floor in agony and you could tap the ball into the empty net.

Apart from finishing seventh with Terry Fenwick in 1996-97, we never again reached the heights of that play-off season, while in later years would twice stay up on the last match of the campaign, firstly at Bradford City in May 1998 and then at Huddersfield Town in May 1999.

During my time at Fratton Park, there were opportunities to leave and a £600,000 fee had been agreed for me to join Celtic at the end of the 1993-94 season.

My former Swindon manager Lou Macari was in charge of the Scottish giants, although I never requested the move, it was the club that accepted it.

At one point it appeared to be going through on deadline day, then the club sensibly thought about it and delayed it, stating if we didn't get promotion to the Premier League then the deal would be back on in the summer.

I was quite prepared to go to Celtic Park considering the size of the club and my Irish background, apart from Manchester United it was my other team; albeit something I would have done with a heavy heart.

Well, we didn't get promoted and in June 1994 while I was with the Republic of Ireland squad at the World Cup finals in America it was agreed Lou would come out to see me to sort out things, he was also wanting to recruit Colin Calderwood at the time.

Then he got the sack, it hadn't been a great year for Celtic. I hope that was the case anyway and it didn't happen because he said he was buying me!

Years later I played in an England v Republic of Ireland Legends game with Bryan Robson at Craven Cottage and he told me when he was Middlesbrough boss they had a £650,000 bid turned down and couldn't understand why - I had never before heard about that one.

Now I know Bryan from my days at Manchester United, he had no reason to lie to me, so I was quite taken aback by that news. There must have been some specific reason why.

These things happen, though, and if they had come off obviously I wouldn't have been at Pompey for so long.

There were other teams in for me later in my Pompey career, clubs such as Port Vale, QPR and Swindon, but I refused to go as in my eyes they weren't as good as where I was at, they didn't excite me.

It was a big thing playing at Fratton Park in that atmosphere, if an atmosphere at another club wasn't going to stimulate me then I wasn't interested.

When I did leave in December 1999 I was gutted with the way it was handled. It wasn't the fact I was sold which upset me but the manner and how certain people did it.

I would certainly hope this football club nowadays wouldn't treat a player how I was following two months short of eight years, 361 games and 68 goals.

There were 18 months left on my contract and I was told if I didn't leave I would never play for Pompey's first-team again.

Milan Mandaric had just taken over as owner and I suppose you don't become a multi, multi, multi-millionaire by being nice to people. He wouldn't talk to me, the one person dealing with this and taking the time to speak was David Deacon.

At that point you realise you are just a commodity, a saleable asset, and they needed to raise money to pay off Alan Ball and his coaching staff who had all just been sacked. Besides, they deemed £260,000 good money for a player approaching 33.

Tony Pulis was coming in as manager, understandably he wanted to bring his own team in, but I wasn't over the hill, I was still more than capable of playing for Pompey. Although he made no effort to speak to me because he wasn't yet in charge.

I don't blame him, it was instigated by the powers that be at the club at the time and Mandaric wouldn't say anything to my face, which didn't stand well in my eyes, it was all via Mr Deacon.

I respect them as business people and what they have achieved, but you should have the guts to speak to that person face-to-face to tell them, if I don't get that I don't have respect for you.

Straight talking has got me into trouble sometimes and people think I am a bit curt on occasions but at least they know where I stand. It's in jest sometimes, I like to think I am friendly, but I also take my job incredibly seriously.

As a football player I fell out with team-mates because I didn't think they were giving enough effort and that is just how I am at the end of the day.

What made it even worse about the way I was treated was the fact Bally had promised me a testimonial, then Mandaric came in and wasn't going to entertain that.

At one point Mr Deacon was instructed to tell me I wouldn't be getting a benefit game, but if I was it would be against Havant & Waterlooville or an equivalent team at Fratton Park.

No disrespect to those clubs but it was just the petty nature of the time, there was no need for it, no need to treat people like that.

I haven't ever spoken to Mandaric, although he made the fatal mistake of waving to me once when I was in the commentary box working for The Quay.

Terry Brady, who I know, was sat next to him and waved at me, with Mandaric then following suit even though I don't believe he realised who he was waving at.

Regardless, he got two fingers straight back at him from the press box at Fratton Park!

To this day he probably doesn't know I was giving him the Vs, but I was too far away to tell him what I really thought, which I would have done if at all possible. Believe me.

MONDAY SOCCER PARADE

ACE HATELEY HAS A BALL AGAIN

POMPEY 4, GRIMSBY 0

FOR HATELEY read Hat trick . . . that's the new name which may shortly be pinned to Pompey's tall dark destroyer of a centre-forward after the most spectacular week of his career.

MIKE NEASOM at Fratton Park

● GOAL . . . Mark Hateley rises to head home John McLaughlin's corner kick for the second goal of his hat trick. Photographer: Eric Masterman.

Wark axed by Scots

Foster is staying

Mabbutt in but doubtf

Mark **Hateley**

44 games, 25 goals (May 1983 - June 1984)

Pompey 4 (Hateley 3, Tait)
Grimsby Town 0

Division Two, Fratton Park, Saturday, November 5, 1983

Pompey: Knight, McLaughlin (46 mins Morgan), Howe, Tait, Sullivan, Webb, Doyle, Dillon, Rogers, Hateley, Biley.

Attendance; 12,906

My dad didn't speak to me for four months after I signed for Pompey.

We had an enormous argument, a proper fight, because I had decided to drop out of Division One with Coventry and into Division Two.

The Sky Blues had wanted me to stay, Bobby Gould had just taken over from Dave Sexton but I was adamant I wanted to leave and Bobby Campbell sold me the club.

I was 20 years old and we had so many centre forwards at Highfield Road I ended up being out on the left wing most of the time.

In my mind I needed to get away and prove myself in the position I felt I was strong enough at. I always was a centre forward and it was about getting your chance to establish yourself in that role.

My dad, Tony, had been a striker with Aston Villa, Chelsea and Liverpool and wanted me to stay in the top flight. He insisted it was hard enough remaining in Division One, never mind dropping out of it willingly.

He obviously wanted the best for me and at that particular moment didn't feel the move to Pompey was right. I was also playing for England under-21s, so to him it was all wrong.

The argument was a phone call, in fact a lot of phone calls, which ended up with the phone getting slammed down and basically an 'I will show you' type of thing.

Thankfully I made the right decision, I didn't make too many wrong decisions in my career and that particular season turned out to be a ridiculous year for me.

I had a few other offers in that summer of 1983, including Watford under Graham Taylor, but as soon as I spoke to Bobby Campbell and chairman John Deacon in a Luton hotel at the end of May 1983 I was sold on it, absolutely, and signed.

An arbitrated fee would later put it at £190,000 - a club record - and it was just the perfect match. About four months later when the goals were going in my dad started to talk to me again!

We were two peas in a pod, he was pretty much the same as me, if we fell out, we fell out, we didn't care who it was with.

On New Year's Eve in 1984 I was on a winter break from AC Milan and held a party at a house I owned in Nottingham, which my dad came to.

Obviously we had seen each other since the move to Pompey but I walked up to him and said: 'Before you say anything, I told you so, I told you it was the right move to make'.

He replied: 'Aye, but I was never going to tell you that!'. That was it, well and truly buried.

My one year at Pompey was the basis of my whole career, it provided the foundations. Without Pompey I don't think I would ever have achieved what I managed to do.

I scored 25 goals in 44 games during that campaign, not a bad return for a young lad, and by the summer was an England international and an AC Milan striker.

There was also a spell when I scored two hat-tricks within five days - both at Fratton Park.

The first was against Cambridge United on November 1, 1983, a mid-week 5-0 victory during which Ernie Howe and Mick Tait also netted.

It was the second which was my favourite Pompey game, however, and the only time I registered consecutive hat-tricks in my career.

The opposition that Saturday was Grimsby Town, just two days before my 21st birthday, and we grabbed a 4-0 win, Tait again joining me on the scoresheet as we moved into seventh spot.

The funny thing was around my birthday I always used to get goals, I have no idea why it turned out that way, it was just one of those things.

If I was stuck in a dry patch through October I was never worried because my birthday was coming on November 7 and the goals would get going again.

The player marking me for the Mariners was Chris Nicholl, also their assistant manager and a big, big tough boy who had previously played for Southampton, Villa and Northern Ireland.

During that game I remember him saying to me 'Clear off will you, I am sick of you scoring goals against me', although not nearly that politely.

You see in May 1982 I had also scored a hat-trick against him when I was in the Coventry side which played at The Dell on a Tuesday night and left with a 5-5 draw.

Nicholl obviously remembered me from that match and that is why the hat-trick against him was even sweeter, especially as he was a decent player.

To be honest, I don't actually recall much of that game against Grimsby!

It's strange how your mind plays tricks on you because I thought I had totalled nine or 10 goals in the three matches over that particular week - it turns out the third fixture was actually a goalless draw at Carlisle.

I suppose that is what football does to you, one game rolls into another and another and all of a sudden you are scoring every week in your mind, but it's not quite like that.

There were that many games I played in and goals I scored, it's too far in the past now for me to recall plenty of them. Besides, I have never been a great collector of memories of goals because I never ever saw myself as a goalscorer.

Believe it or not, I always perceived myself as a goal provider for other players playing with me, that is the way I looked at the game.

I thought the goals were a bonus, but it wasn't imperative that I scored, it was more important people around me netted and that is how I viewed myself - as a provider.

Still, we had sackfuls of goals in that Pompey team under Bobby Campbell during the 1983-84 season. Sheffield Wednesday went up in second place yet had scored one fewer than our tally of 73.

In contrast, we finished 16th but were exciting to watch because there was just as much chance of winning 4-3 as losing 4-3, while there were some really good players in the side as well.

We had a great goalkeeper in Alan Knight but he had an aged back four in front of him and the rest of the team was very attack-minded.

Kevin Dillon was such a good player, he was born before his time, a player who had passes picked in his head before anybody could ever dream about them, I thought he was that good.

In attack, Alan Biley was wonderful to play with, he had tasted higher levels, performed with big players, operated under good managers and had the experience you would think a young lad would thrive on - and I did.

He made my job easy and if you flip the coin around the other way I think we both made each other's jobs easy in the particular way we played.

There was Alan Rogers, who crossed the ball for my first Pompey league goal during a match at Fulham in the third match of the season. He did that step over, went to the byline and then hung it up at the far post.

Neil Webb was also knocking around there, it was an absolute pleasure to be in that team, we were very creative, that's the way Bobby wanted us to play - we just couldn't defend.

That is probably why the chairman John Deacon looked at the situation and the players we had and believed we should have been at the other end of the table challenging for promotion, especially with the number of goals we scored.

Bobby got the sack on the eve of the final match of the campaign. Pompey had been jumping up leagues left, right and centre with two promotions in four seasons and he obviously thought with the side we had it should have continued.

I enjoyed working with Bobby, he wanted to play the game properly and pretty much asked everybody to be themselves and express themselves when on that football pitch.

He actually took me from being a Division One centre forward-cum-left winger and turned me into a player who could perform in Serie A and serve as England's number nine - within a year.

Only Chelsea's Kerry Dixon and Newcastle United's Kevin Keegan scored more than me in Division Two that season - and they both played for promoted teams!

What Bobby did was add another dimension to my game by making me angry. Not angry in terms of going around kicking everybody, but by bringing out a certain element of intensity to everything I did in a game.

It was definitely for the better, I was more aggressive all over the park, working my way around, the way I held the ball up, defending and the way I attacked the ball. That is where the surge of goals came from that year, the little bit that needed to be brought out of me.

I knew it was there but hadn't previously come to the front. I have always had an aggressive nature and I suppose it is how you apply that aggressive nature to any sport or line of work.

You can channel it in the right ways and the wrong ways and Bobby obviously got me to channel it in the right way and it took me onto scoring goals, playing in the England side which won the 1984 European Under-21 Championship and then going on to appear in the Maracana all in the space of one year.

Having said that, in April 1982 I was sent off for England at Hampden Park in the 1982 European Under-21 Championship semi-finals' first leg and banned for three games for violent conduct, including the two-legged final against West Germany.

Scotland's full-back Ray Stewart had kicked me in the nuts in the last minute of the game so I turned round and lamped him, earning me a straight red card.

I told you that anger was always there!

My time at Pompey, though, was like the blink of an eye, an incredibly fast year, arguably my best-ever in football in terms of getting from A to B.

It was ridiculously quick, like one of these Roy of the Rovers stories, and if you wrote it all down you would think it a complete flight of fantasy.

I scored in Pompey's final match - a 5-0 win over Swansea City - to take me to my 25-goal target and then five days later was representing the under-21s in the first of a two-legged European Championship final against a really good Spain side.

We won 1-0 in Seville, Mel Sterland grabbing the goal, then a week later defeated them 2-0 at Bramall Lane in front of a crowd of 11,478, Howard Gayle and me the scorers.

The door opened for me there and then, I was in the right place at the right time and with the under-21s' win still fresh in everybody's memory progressed into the England senior squad.

On June 2, 1984, I appeared as a substitute for Trevor Francis in a 2-0 defeat against the USSR at Wembley for my debut and everybody knew the next squad was going to South America as a trial run for the Mexico World Cup in 1986, looking at the climate and different playing surfaces.

There were injuries and three days later I was on a plane heading for a three-match tournament involving Brazil, Uruguay and Chile but, being this young Division Two footballer, I thought I was going to be pushing skips rather than playing.

I believed I would just be going for the experience as a lot of young players did on international trips, see a bit of the country, watch how the big boys work - little did I know I would be starring in the opening game!

In the middle of all this, Alan Ball was appointed Pompey's manager on June 5, but I never had chance to meet him in his new role before the move to AC Milan happened at the end of the month.

Bally had been in charge of the youth team and I would see him in and around training. He was probably the most frustrated youth-team trainer ever because he wanted everybody to play the way he played - one touch.

It was five days after that appointment when Bobby Robson came up to me and told me I would have my first England start against Brazil in the Maracana.

The stadium was only half-full, the grass was about eight inches long to cover up all the ruts, bumps and bobbles, it was a total anti-climax for a ground considering what the name Maracana conjures up upon its very mention.

It was a massive stadium, albeit ancient and crumbling - and we are still the only England team to ever win there!

Myself and John Barnes were born on November 7, although I am two years older, and we both picked up a goal and an assist in that famous 2-0 victory.

Barnesy scored first, the ball was pumped up to me and I caught it on my chest, brought it down, swept it out to him on the left-hand side and the rest is history.

If you look at the goal, Tony Woodcock makes a great run across all of the defenders to take them away and leaves me completely unmarked, I was screaming at Barnesy to pass the ball to me because I would have had a five-foot tap in.

Then he did the next dummy, puts the goalkeeper on his backside and hits the back of the net, before elbowing me right in the jaw as he celebrated!

My goal came after half-time, Barnesy did his step over, got to the byline and hung it up a million miles in the air for me to head home at the far post. I say to him even now I don't know how I got on the end of that awful cross!

It was very, very similar to my first league goal for Pompey against Fulham, except Alan

Rogers was John Barnes on that day.

That goal goes out all over the world and suddenly I was signing for AC Milan 18 days later in a £915,000 move from Pompey.

I would have thought the Maracana goal did it, you don't know how things work abroad but they obviously had done a background check, saw how many I scored that season in Division Two and also for the England Under-21s.

I didn't really say goodbye to everyone on the south coast, it was an absolute whirlwind, 100 miles per hour.

I returned from South America, came back to the club literally for half-an-hour to sign some forms, didn't even have time to pack properly at my house in Langstone before jumping straight onto another plane and flying to Milan to sign.

That is how fast and furious it was, it was just one ridiculous day after the next, crazy.

Sometimes you take a punt on a younger player and that is what AC Milan did on me, it was great for both of us. They completely deconstructed my whole game as soon as I got there and built me up into a European centre forward.

With the playing style I went over there with, I would never have survived in Italian football and the manager, Nils Liedholm, was an ex-centre forward who had captained Sweden in the 1958 World Cup.

He was full of wisdom, while a young Fabio Capello was working with the youth team and had just started coaching.

Most afternoons the pair of them would take me out with a goalkeeper and completely strip my game before building it up again.

They showed me where to be if certain players had the ball, how to receive the ball, where to run and where not to run, where to challenge and where not to challenge, right through the fundamentals and basics of being a top European centre forward.

The raw uncut version was always there and they added a lot more to my game, a lot more awareness, a lot more knowledge and a lot to my technique which later probably benefitted Arsene Wenger at Monaco and then certainly Graeme Souness and Walter Smith at Rangers.

We won the French title at Monaco in 1987-88 under Wenger, me finishing as the league's third top scorer with 14, behind Jean-Pierre Papin and Patrice Garande.

He was a good young manager at that stage, very intense and everything was done with a stopwatch. Everything was about timing for Arsene!

When you think about it, you drop down a league, score 25 goals, get to play in an under-21 final, represent England in the Maracana and on your first start score, then sign for AC Milan 18 days later. It's just madness.

And it was all down to ignoring my dad.

THE NEWS, MONDAY, FEBRUARY 28, 1983

Pompey on sick parade

Bobby Campbell will hold a sick parade before he names his Pompey side for tomorrow night's meeting with Wigan at Fratton Park (7.30 p.m.).

Saturday's match with Bournemouth left Campbell with what could be the greatest injury problems he has faced in his 11 months in charge of Pompey.

Already deprived of centre-half Ernie Howe with a cracked knee cap, Campbell could find himself without his other two front-line central defenders.

Steve Aizlewood is nursing a nose broken yet again, while Andy Rollings has severely bruised muscles in his right shoulder. Yet both could play.

Rollings, relieved that his fears of a broken collar bone were dispelled by a post-match X-ray, is prepared to ...ore the discomfort if he is needed.

"It's much better than it was on Saturday night — if it ...ntinues like this and Bob feels he needs me, then I'll ...ore the pain and play.

"I felt sick on Saturday after I'd come off when Aiz was ...ed. I wondered whether I should have stayed on, ...ugh my balance was affected by the injury."

• NIGGLED AWAY

Aizlewood is also prepared to risk further damage ...ose which has suffered more than its fair share of ...tion from its owner's willingness to put his head ...the danger is thickest.

"...this is as bad a break as I've had, but if Bob ...e I'll be there," he said.

...round off his problems, Campbell must also ...g doubt about centre-forward Billy Rafferty's

...injury which has niggled away for some time ...red up in the first few minutes of the ...h match and by the end the big Scot, whose ...s such a crucial ingredient of Pompey's ...moving with considerable discomfort.

"I've a few problems, but in this game you ...ept those and not whine about them."

"...g to be a difficult match. We're the leaders ...e shot at and Wigan were thrashed at home. They're professionals and their pride will ...t. Someone has to pay."

...o brother ...aged 76

...ull back Billy Smith has died in his ...at the age of 76.

...brothers and one of them, inside ... They were both in the ... City in the 1934 F.A. Cup

... history with the ... A third ... City side beaten

... in June.

● He stoops to conquer ... Quick as a flash, Pompey's Alan Biley heads the ball goalwards ...

● The ball eludes Bournemouth goalkeeper Ian L...

... much to the delight of Biley and the ... Pompey and cele...

TRIUMPH OF THE BRAVE

Bournemouth 0, Pompey 2

Anyone wondering whether Pompey had one of the all-important but intangible qualities necessary for success — character — should have been among the seething crowd at Dean Court on Saturday.

As an invasion from Fratton fans drew more to the match than Manchester United could attract for a Milk Cup glamour tie back in the autumn, Pompey proved that the steely determination to get out of the Third Division is there.

BY MIKE NEASOM

Everyone has known they have the quality and the ability for a long time. Now there is no doubt Bobby Campbell has also got the calibre of men the marathon of an English season demands if it is to be rewarded.

If ever there was an occasion when lesser souls would have crumbled this was it.

DAMAGED

Pompey were forced to reshuffle their defence for the first time midway through the first half, rejig it again immediately after half time, and ultimately were reduced virtually to nine men.

The first ...

had another two or three. It was great and so were the crowd. I thought it was a home match."

Ultimately, Pompey eased home on the back of Aizlewood's first-half penalty and a typically sharp piece of goal-area work by birthday boy Alan Biley.

Biley, celebrating his 26th birthday, snapped up his 20th goal of the season midway through the second half finally to convince Bournemouth that there was to be no escape from Pompey's thirst for revenge.

RECORD

miscued his shot from Graham's cross.

STRAIGHT

Within seconds of his departure, Pompey were ahead. Alan Rogers, always a thorn in Bournemouth's side, was brought down by the splendidly competitive Tommy Heffernan. Aizlewood, having seen goalkeeper Ian Leigh start to dive to his right in anticipation of the usual shot, drove straight and true from the penalty.

Referee Downey almost allowed Bournemouth to level in the 33rd minute when he ...

passed the half without having to make a testing save.

His one awkward moment came before Tait and Ellis had got their act together. A delicate, floated shot by Graham drifted over him and just wide. That apart it was all hollow threat from the home side.

Pompey, in fact, looked far more dangerous, and aided by lack of communication between goalkeeper Leigh and his defence, always threatened to tighten their grip on the points and that record.

MISUNDERSTANDING

Eventually they did in the 76th minute from a corner gifted by more Bournemouth defensive misunderstanding. Rogers curled the kick into the ...

LINCOL... BOW T...

Mob violence and death threats h... Blades and his board of directors.

After a weekend of turmoil, the direc... decided to step down en bloc.

On Saturday, the chairman needed a police escort home after the home match against Plymouth, and his property ...

Former chairm... cial director He... said: "After giv... years ...

Alan **Rogers**

190 games, 17 goals (May 1979 - January 1984)

Bournemouth 0
Pompey 2 (Aizlewood pen, Biley)

Division Three, Dean Court, Saturday, February 26, 1983

Pompey: Knight, McLaughlin, Aizlewood, Rollings (26 mins Ellis), Sullivan, Webb, Doyle, Tait, Rogers, Rafferty, Biley.

Attendance; 13,406

Rainer Bonhof laid on Gerd Muller's goal which ensured Germany lifted the 1974 World Cup following a 2-1 victory over Holland.

He was also the inspiration behind what has often been said was my trademark - the step over.

It was the summer of 1975 when my club Plymouth Argyle embarked on a pre-season tour of Germany, during which on a day off we attended a match between Borussia Mönchengladbach and Cologne.

Borussia had Bonhof turning out for them, a German international midfielder who in front of my eyes produced a trick I had never before seen. The step over was used three or four times and on each occasion I studied it ever closer.

So I came back home to Plymouth and practiced it and practiced it in training. It took me a year, I fell over the first time I attempted it, but in the end became pretty proficient.

I would drag the ball with my right foot as I was running along and then step over it and knock it with my left and it worked every time.

There was no television back then analysing everything, so it was largely a surprise to the opposition full-back. You could call it my party piece!

In May 1979, Steve Davey - who I had played with at Plymouth and was now at Pompey - rang and asked if I would be interested in moving to the south coast.

Before I signed, I sat with Frank Burrows in the South stand looking at the pitch and he said: 'If you do your trick you will have 15,000 Pompey fans swaying one way and all fallingfor it and they will love it. Just keep doing the trick, they will love it'.

There has got to be an end product, there is no point doing it and then putting the ball out of play. All you needed was a yard, then you could get the ball in.

Once I played a game with Fred Binney, who was a prolific goalscorer for Plymouth, and smacked a ball right across the face of goal. I thought it was a great cross but he gave me such a rollicking.

He told me it was so fast he couldn't get there, instead I should be looking to pass the ball across - and from then on I thought about it. As you get older you work out what is best.

Crossing was my strength, but because of the margin of error it was more difficult to pick out a player so I would purposely underhit it slightly so it would be a great near-post ball, or would slightly overhit it and it would be over the keeper and Billy Rafferty would be coming in at the far post.

It was my lack of accuracy which made them such good balls, if you know what I mean.

My percentage was to try to hit the keeper because if they were slightly underhit they were great balls and slightly overhit they were also great balls.

There are occasions when I think to myself I should have imposed myself on more matches, sometimes I allowed myself to drift out of a game, but I was a winger, give me the ball and I am fine.

In my four-and-a-half years at Fratton Park, it was the February 1983 match at Bournemouth which stood out as my favourite.

We felt invincible that day, we just knew we were going to win, and that was rare. I recall looking around that Dean Court dressing room and thinking 'There is no way we are not going to beat these today', we were so confident.

Bournemouth were definitely intimidated by playing us, and you felt it.

A lot of teams got intimidated at Fratton Park, that Division Three season we beat Lincoln City 4-1 and Chesterfield 4-0, there were a few other drubbings also dished out.

In that 1982-83 campaign we won nine consecutive home league matches from October to February, you could tell the opposition couldn't get off the pitch quick enough.

As a team under Bobby Campbell we were building a head of steam and all of a sudden word was getting around this was a good side, the first in years worth watching, you sensed it around the club.

Heading to Dorset for that fixture, we had won six successive matches and a seventh would create a Pompey club record during their 60 years in the Football League.

So the pressure was on. The Cherries weren't a bad side actually, but it was probably the one and only time I ever knew we were going to triumph. It was an unbelievable feeling.

Our fans had taken over the ground, there must have easily been 10,000 Pompey supporters in an attendance of 13,406, and they were fantastic.

Sure enough, we went on to win 2-0 with a really good professional performance and a Steve Aizlewood penalty and Alan Biley header settling it in our favour.

To be totally honest, I was outstanding that day, I played really well, I have got to say, and had a hand in both goals.

I was playing with a lot of confidence at that time and we were going to win that game. If Bournemouth scored three we were going to score four. I just knew.

During the game I actually should have got three penalties, the one that was awarded arrived in the 26th minute, subsequently scored by Aizlewood.

The secret of earning a penalty was to take it up to the full-back and knock it to one side, not too far, just close enough so he thinks he can get it. You are almost inviting him in for the challenge.

Then you know he is going to make that lunge for the ball so you just touch it on and he can only catch you.

At Dean Court the ball broke to me and I pushed it to one side and their right-back, Tommy Heffernan, put in the challenge and I touched it on.

I do wonder whether there is a subconsciousness where you go down as a self-preservation because if you don't you could end up getting hurt.

It is almost like self-defence. Some people go down as a form of protection because if you stay on your feet and your studs are in the ground you actually end up getting hurt, so you need to raise your foot off the turf slightly.

You are not diving, you are looking after yourself.

We were dominant that day, it was just a matter of time before we got our second and in the 76th minute Biley touched home Peter Ellis' nod down from my corner.

That was it, seven consecutive wins - and there was Champagne on the coach on the way back if I remember rightly.

We would go on to win Division Three with 91 points, a record number at the time, losing nine matches in the process.

It was my second promotion in four seasons at Fratton Park, but that was a better team than the one from 1979-80.

The first promotion season under Frank Burrows was more free-flowing, it had more goals from midfield in Joe Laidlaw and Terry Brisley, while Colin Garwood was also prolific.

Whereas Campbell's team had Biley, who got 26, Billy Rafferty weighed in with 19, but I didn't get many that particular season, certainly Bobby Doyle wasn't a goalscorer, neither was Mick Tait.

Neil Webb had the capability and later became a goalscorer, but he wasn't that year.

However, we were a stronger team, having a bit more quality, with myself, John McLaughlin and Aizlewood the only key players who appeared in both sides.

Alan Knight was a far better keeper than Peter Mellor, who you felt always had a mistake in him, Colin Sullivan was stronger than Archie Styles, Brisley was great at what he did but in truth Webb was a better player, you can go through them all.

Plus I was a little bit older so wiser as well, a better winger in my mind, more consistent.

I always had a languid style, not blessed with blistering pace but quick enough to get by and as a winger my job was to get the ball into the box, scoring goals never came into it, I never thought I was a goalscorer.

My mindset was to take players on rather than passing it, I enjoyed that side of it.

Another memorable match was at Division One champions Liverpool in the fourth round of the League Cup in October 1980, one of only two occasions I felt the hairs on the back of my neck stand up when I ran onto the pitch.

The other was at Newcastle United in October 1983 when they beat us 4-2 in Division Two and went on to win promotion that season with Kevin Keegan, Peter Beardsley and Chris Waddle in the side. The atmosphere was phenomenal.

This was Liverpool, though, a club who had been my favourite team ever since the 1965 FA Cup final when they beat Leeds United and then went on to become even stronger. I loved them.

I was a mad Liverpool fan who lived in Plymouth and when Bournemouth hosted Liverpool in the FA Cup third round in January 1968 I went with my father.

The scoreline was goalless, but as a 13-year-old in a Dean Court crowd of almost 25,000, it was fantastic.

That night in 1980 with Pompey, I can honestly say as a team we weren't intimidated by Liverpool, we quite enjoyed it because we were the underdogs and not expected to do much against a team undefeated at home for almost three years.

There was that ticker tape reception as well, they reckon 12,000 Pompey fans were there in a crowd of 32,021.

At Anfield, when leaving the dressing room you go down some steps and then scale some other steps to come onto the pitch - then it hit us. The Anfield Road end on the left was a sea of blue and white ticker tape.

There was ticker tape in the Liverpool end as well but it wasn't as good!

We were actually the better side on the evening, though, we outplayed them, we outperformed them.

When we equalised and made it 1-1 it struck me 'We've got a chance here'. Then they regained the lead through David Johnson 60 seconds later and added two more in the final 10 minutes.

At that point we were chasing the game and then they caught us on the sucker punch, the third was clearly an offside goal from Johnson, blatantly offside, and the final scoreline of 4-1 was so unjust.

I actually played quite well that night, I was up against Phil Neal and a handful for him, crossing the ball which Alan Kennedy turned it into his own net for an equaliser in the 36th minute.

Davey fed me down the left and I took on Neal on the outside and passed it across, it went through Ray Clemence and Alan Hansen - and Kennedy came in at the far post trying to turn it around for a corner but instead put it into his own net.

I celebrated and Derek Showers, who would have been close to Kennedy at the time, was trying to claim the goal but clearly it wasn't!

We played really well and all enjoyed it. We weren't expecting to go there and do much, just play and see how we got on.

Aizlewood was missing that night with a foot injury picked up the previous game against Oxford United, which was such a shame, he hadn't missed a match that season up until then and what a player he was.

We called him 'Big Baz', nobody knew why. John McLaughlin and him both came from Swindon Town to join Pompey in the summer of 1979 and because Mac called him 'Baz' everybody did.

Baz was a bit of a bruiser but always good for a laugh. He would cut his eye and then start limping, he couldn't help himself, it was natural, he had to limp!

He was always injured, like the old soldier out of the trenches. It was comical in the end but that was the way he was and that made him a figure of fun in that respect.

Having said that, he was terrific, brave, fearless, never pulled out of a challenge and a really good all-round sportsman. Somebody who had so much ability.

Baz was a natural snooker player - and played cricket. There was a side called Havant Wednesdays in the off-season, four or five of us Pompey players would turn out for them at Havant Park and he once came along having not played for a few years and took two fantastic catches.

We asked where that had come from and he replied 'I didn't play to a bad level, you know'. That was him, he always kept things quiet.

At Baz's funeral I found out from his brother, Mark, that he could have been an international rugby player as he was good at rugby as well! He was just a natural sportsman.

He had a terrific right foot and between the pair of us we worked out a routine by the 1982-83 campaign that involved Baz knocking the ball inside the full-back I was playing against. I was already off and running so received the ball over the top to launch an attack.

The number of times we went from defending to counter-attacking through that method was fantastic.

He was outstanding, the rock of the defence, although it wasn't until I moved to Southend United that I realised what a hell of a player he was.

They had a couple of centre halves who weren't winning the ball or passing to me, I was used to it at Pompey and there were a lot of things they were doing differently.

Baz wasn't a natural captain, he wasn't vocal, not even in the changing room, he was quite a reserved sort of fella. What he did, though, was lead by example.

He had that consistency, an eight or nine out of 10 every week. If you were a manager going to bed on a Friday night you'd think 'I'll get a nine out of Baz tomorrow', whereas if you'd thought about me I might get a 10 or I might get a six!

Fratton Park was a great place to be involved with and there were plenty of characters who worked there such as Gordon Neave the physio, who was never up-to-date and seemingly forever stuck in the past.

You would say to him 'What do you think about Margaret Thatcher?' And he would say 'Who is she?' You would reply 'She's been Prime Minister for the last two years.' 'Has she?'

Once Lewis Collins was in Babes In The Wood at the Kings Theatre over the Christmas period and came to train with us.

Everyone recognised him, The Professionals was one of the best programmes on TV at the time and when Gordon brought him into the dressing room he announced 'I am sure this man needs no introduction'.

So we said 'Who is it then, Gordon?', knowing he didn't have a clue, and he said 'It's Lewis Carroll'. Of course the dressing room fell around with laughter.

Then Lewis Collins leant over and we heard him say 'Collins is the name' and he said 'Sorry about that chaps, it's Colin Carroll'.

Gordon's nickname was 'Gotcha'. The changing room was at the far end of a long passageway and he could look along right the way to the other end of the stand to see players coming in late and fine them.

You had to be in at 10am and he used to time it, so you would look around the corridor and see Gordon's head 70-yards away and then it would disappear. That meant you had three seconds to run into the changing room otherwise the head would come out again and he would shout 'Gotcha'.

Duggie Reid had retired as groundsman the season before I arrived but was still around the place and wasn't he strict. You daren't even put your foot on the pitch, it was like sacrilege.

It was a great surface to play on which was even more impressive because in those days pitches were completely different. From Christmas the goalmouth to the halfway line and back to the other goalmouth was a diamond of mud. The grass was on the wings, though, which was great for me.

Duggie didn't talk much, he was a quiet bloke, you wouldn't want to upset him - 'Get off my pitch' he would regularly shout.

As mentioned before, Frank Burrows was my first Pompey manager and as hard as nails. I had faced him when he was playing for Swindon and he was so similar to Baz, never shirked a challenge and would go straight through people.

He possessed this ferocious temper, there was a fear factor, but he was fair, as long as you performed for him he loved you.

I remember playing at Chesterfield in March 1981 and at half-time he wasn't very happy at being 1-0 down and sent us out with a flea in our ear. It got worse, not better, we ended up losing 3-0!

After the game he came in and started off on one, raging and smashing a cup against the wall.

At the top corner of the changing room at Saltergate there was a loudspeaker and in those days some grounds would announce the results, Arsenal 1 Aston Villa 2, that sort of thing.

We thought that was going to be our saviour and stop him in full flow - but it didn't.

'Gordon switch it off,' he instructed Gordon Neave. He replied 'Yes gaffer'.

So Gordon has grabbed the lead and is following it but starting to panic 'I can't find the switch, gaffer'.

'Gordon just switch it off,' but he can't! So Frank stepped onto a bench, grabbed the lead and just yanked it out of the speaker. He was fuming!

The following Friday after training we went to pick up our wages as usual and were instructed by the lady in payroll that the manager would instead be handing them out. That was a first.

We were told to head up to his office one-by-one and I went in and all of a sudden he looked huge in his chair, while mine had no springs in. He definitely had the psychological advantage!

He said 'Do you think you deserve these wages after last Saturday's performance?' and I actually said 'To be honest gaffer, you have said to me that if I put in three quality crosses in each half I have done my job. Well, I counted 10.'

He thought about it and said 'I'll give you that one, there you are then, you've got away with that. Don't tell anyone'.

Burrows had to give you your wages, but wanted to make you feel small!

Bobby Campbell was not my favourite person, although he was a really good coach and did bring in good players. He was organised, but there was an underhand way with him.

In one of our first training sessions there was a routine we called shadow where you would play against nobody.

Alan Knight would throw the ball to John McLaughlin, who gave it to Bobby Doyle, who knocked it back to Colin Sullivan, and so on.

The idea was to get a shape and then move up with the pitch ending with a cross or a shot, basically trying to get us to develop an understanding of where you are meant to be in relation to each other.

One time McLaughlin rolled the ball to Ernie Howe and all of a sudden a voice shouted 'Stop'.

Campbell said 'Ernie, you do not want the ball'. He replied 'What do you mean boss?'

'Your job is to win it, you don't call for the ball, I don't want you to have the ball and if you do have the ball give it to your nearest team-mate'.

Well Ernie was a good defender but couldn't play really.

Anyhow, we started training again and McLaughlin was on the ball and passed it again towards Ernie.

'Ernie, what did I tell you?'. In other words we had to miss Ernie out because he wasn't good enough!

In October 1981, Burrows had signed David Crown but I quite liked the competition. If I was too assured I could lapse back so that gave an edge to my game, it left me thinking I had better get my skates on.

I missed three games that season and won four consecutive player of the month awards in the Sports Mail on the way to getting promoted that season.

In the 1983-84 campaign, I had found myself out of the side for 10 matches, my only appearance during that time being a substitute against Shrewsbury Town, but received a recall for the FA Cup fourth round tie against Southampton in January 1984.

They won 1-0 through Steve Moran and I actually played quite well that day - I bet it seems I never had a bad game - but I gave Mick Mills a bit of a torrid time.

Regardless, that proved to be my final Pompey match.

Alan Ball was in charge of our reserves for a period of time and I got on well with him, I knew he liked me as a player and as it turned out recommended me to Bobby Moore, Southend's manager.

Moore rang me at home and to be honest I wasn't really listening. This was Bobby Moore on the phone - he was the bee's knees!

The clubs had agreed a £20,000 fee and he wanted to meet me at Waterloo station. Then he asked on the phone what I looked like!

It turned out he had never seen me play and had gone purely on Bally's recommendation. That was good enough for him.

I said 'Bob, if you stand in the middle of Waterloo station I might just recognise you!'

He was a little bit similar to Jimmy Dickinson, just too nice. People like that had it in their nature to be lovely to people, but in the cut and thrust of football you need to have that edge to your personality.

Moore had no ego, it never occurred to him somebody might recognise him.

When he was sacked in the summer of 1986 he was replaced by David Webb and the first thing the new manager did was call me in and said he'd twice tried to sign me, once as boss at Bournemouth and once at Torquay United.

Then he added: 'Now I am manager here I have got to let you go, you are on too much money!'.

I loved it at Pompey, absolutely loved it, two promotions and many, many happy memories.

OKI
PRINTING
heFA
CUP
e·on

POMPEY: WE'VE WON THE CUP

Kanu's goal and Campbell lifting the Cup are memories that will live forever

by NEIL ALLEN at Wembley Stadium

POMPEY ... 1
Kanu 37
CARDIFF ... 0
Att: 89,874

Grown men were in tears, caught up in the torrent of emotion cascading down those steps as Sol Campbell lifted the famous old trophy

Kanu makes the most of Peter Enckelman's first-half error to hand Pompey their first FA Cup final success in 69 years

MAN IN THE MIDDLE

Hermann **Hreidarsson**

123 games, eight goals (May 2007 - January 2012)

Cardiff City 0
Pompey 1 (Kanu)

FA Cup Final, Wembley, Saturday, May 17, 2008

Pompey: James, Johnson, Campbell, Distin, Hreidarsson, Utaka (69 mins Nugent), Mendes (78 mins Diop), Diarra, Muntari, Kranjcar, Kanu (87 mins Baros).

Subs Not Used: Ashdown, Pamarot.

Attendance; 89,874

My first rendition was 'Blue Suede Shoes', a song you can dance to a little bit, which will also take the attention away from your voice.

Then I gave it a go with 'An American Trilogy'. Now that was ambitious, there was more laughter than applause, I have to admit.

We were eating at an Italian restaurant in Bray, near our hotel for two days, The Oakley Court in Windsor.

The next day we would be playing at Wembley in the 2008 FA Cup final against Cardiff City.

That night, though, we were relaxing, although I was wearing my Elvis Presley costume stood at the front taking part in a little karaoke.

Harry Redknapp had tipped me off, it was his idea, but we kept it between us so when I came out of the toilet dressed as the King it surprised everybody.

It was designed to take peoples' minds off the main event by keeping the atmosphere relaxed and fun. It was a good idea, the night before the cup final we were enjoying ourselves.

We wanted that trophy, nobody remembers who comes second in the FA Cup final and anything that could prepare us to achieve that victory was important.

So I got up to belt out a couple of songs, although not very well, with other members of the team and club staff also taking turns. It was a lot of fun.

John Utaka and Kanu did a double act singing Bob Marley & The Wailers' 'No Woman, No Cry' and were actually quite good.

Well Utaka was good, Kanu was mixing it up trying to turn it into a rap song, shouting something or other which nobody could understand.

The next day I had 50 family and friends coming over from Iceland, I had tried my hardest to get more tickets but that was all the club were going to give me!

The maximum was 20 per player, however I managed to sneak a few more from players who weren't using all their tickets which was handy as suddenly I was very popular with people back home. I cannot think why!

The FA Cup is massive in Iceland. Like any other Scandinavian country, actually probably more with us, we follow English football and there are a lot of Liverpool and Manchester United fans among us.

I remember watching the FA Cup final year after year, it was always an occasion, my first being Tottenham Hotspur against Manchester City in 1981, Ricky Villa scoring a fantastic goal in the replay.

As a boy, you always pretended you were a player in the FA Cup final when kicking a ball about in the fields. My team was Manchester United and I was mostly Bryan Robson, the number seven.

At the age of six I was given a Red Devils scarf and a shirt and although they didn't win many trophies around that time you stood by your team.

So to beat them 1-0 in the quarter-finals in March 2008 was interesting. Afterwards I received some weird phone calls from the family who are all Manchester United fans!

They were congratulating me in a sort of backhanded way, saying 'Hmmm you were lucky there weren't you?', and I was replying 'Hey for crying out loud, United have won 800 trophies, give us a break will you!'.

We stopped Manchester United doing the treble that season, they won the Premier League, they won the Champions League, but Pompey won the FA Cup.

After defeating a team like that we knew it was a massive opportunity to get ourselves into the history books, especially when Barnsley knocked Chelsea out later that the same day.

We were the favourites then for sure and knew it. We wouldn't get a better chance, yet were focused on the job in hand to make sure we fulfilled that opportunity

On that cup run they were close games all the way, of the six matches we played we won five of them 1-0.

The only one we didn't was a 2-1 victory at home to Plymouth Argyle in the fourth round, Lassana Diarra and Niko Kranjcar the scorers.

I also remember at Preston North End where David James saved a Simon Whaley penalty in the second half and we scored the winner in stoppage time when Darren Carter netted an own goal from Niko Kranjcar's corner.

We totalled 23 clean sheets that season, the team was strong defensively as a unit, that more than anything else got us to lift the FA Cup for the first time in 69 years.

Nothing could be taken for granted, though, everyone saw that as recently as the 2013 FA Cup final when Wigan Athletic beat Manchester City 1-0. Anything can happen on the day and you always have to perform for the occasion.

Regardless, the feeling heading into that final against Cardiff was the cup was ours to lose, then the atmosphere hits you and at that point we were definitely going to take the trophy home.

To be a part of what happened next was a dream come true in a sense and the only major trophy I ever won during my 15-and-a-half years in England.

I vividly remember the first half with a cross coming over and I'm going towards it trying to head it away when Jamo comes running out of his penalty area.

He absolutely clattered me, the top of his head bashed against my face and I had broken my right cheekbone.

The doctor came onto the field but I told him not to let anyone know, there was no way I was coming off!

I knew straight away it was something more than a knock, I could feel the pain, but the adrenaline took over and I forgot about it straight away.

With it being the last game of the season, I had a few months over the summer to heal properly, without anybody realising what had happened. Although I had a black eye for a bit.

Then in the 37th minute Kanu scored, just like he did in the semi-final against West Bromwich Albion, and with us being so good defensively we knew we had a great chance to keep that advantage.

Looking at that game, Lassana Diarra was probably our man-of-the-match, he was great for us the whole time and we expected him to be at the heart of things defensively and offensively.

He was always ready to receive the ball and could look after it so well, managing to calm things down whenever we needed.

Diarra was brilliant, you wondered how Chelsea and Arsenal couldn't find a way to use him when he was on their books - then he went to Real Madrid from us the following season.

When that final whistle went the relief was huge, it is wonderful knowing you have achieved something in football and I am still the only Icelander to have won it, none of my fellow countrymen have managed that.

You dream of being at Wembley and lifting a trophy, that day will stay with me for the rest of my life, it is something to forever cherish.

We went back to the hotel and had a few toasts there and then a lot of players stayed at the hotel to be with their families before everyone met up at a bar in London which had been pre-booked for some more toasts.

The next day was the open-topped bus around Portsmouth and that was something else as well. I loved those two days, great memories.

The FA Cup was my first major trophy in England so to be able to celebrate it with all the people who made the club what it is was special - and I certainly made the most of it, I can guarantee that!

People may remember on that day I was high on life, so happy, a little bit of singing and dancing on the coach.

It was a happy day, I was celebrating something really, really special, nothing to do with alcohol of course. I'm a happy person!

Really, I didn't have that much to drink, we didn't have a lot of beers on the coach although if there were any I definitely drank them!

I was probably still drunk from the night before and thought I would be part of the entertainment, at one point pouring beer over a policeman's helmet. Well, it was a great opportunity.

He was actually trying to drink it as I attempted to get it into his mouth, but there was no harm done, everyone was so happy, everywhere we looked people were smiling and cheering.

It was unbelievable, there were people everywhere, on top of lamp posts, climbing up traffic lights, as far as the eye could see. Anyone related to the city of Portsmouth were there, nobody present will ever forget those scenes.

At one point I tried to throw our owner, Sacha Gaydamak, off the stage but I was in good spirits just messing around a bit, it was the usual stuff, nothing new there.

Harry shouted at me at the time but I didn't really get told off afterwards, people were just in that sort of mood, as long as you weren't being too silly anything goes. It was all a lot of joy.

Besides, I had the wife and kids there so I was on my best behaviour - she drove me home though!

That 2007-08 campaign was my first at Pompey and incredible, it was just a great team and we were always hard to beat. It was a pleasure to be in a side like that with so many great players, good lads overall, making wonderful memories.

You look at those players, Diarra, Niko Kranjcar, Sylvain Distin, Glen Johnson, David James, Sol Campbell, I could list everyone from that squad.

It is hard to win a cup in this country unless you are the three or four clubs who splash out millions upon millions each season. So to do it with Pompey was brilliant, I was lucky to be part of that.

We got the freedom of the city for that, it allows me to have a rifle and a cow or something. There is a piece of paper which says so, I like the idea of doing that in Portsmouth.

The next season we had Europe to look forward to for the first time in the club's history, although I would start only two of those Uefa Cup matches.

The first was a 3-0 defeat at Braga which would prove to be Harry's last match in charge in October 2008, while I also scored against Heerenveen in a 3-0 win under new boss Tony Adams.

Unfortunately I was an unused substitute against AC Milan in the 2-2 draw at Fratton Park, it was a wonderful atmosphere though.

The 2009-10 season I played in all four rounds leading up to the FA Cup semi-final against Tottenham, then snapped my Achilles 16 days earlier against the same opposition at White Hart Lane.

It was disappointing to miss that Wembley game, but would have been even more painful if I hadn't played there three times previously.

During a four month period in 2008 we had faced West Bromwich Albion, Cardiff and then - in the Community Shield - Manchester United, without conceding a goal. That's not a bad record I suppose!

I was still there on the bench and part of it against Spurs in the April 2010 semi-final and then for the final against Chelsea, wearing my silly boot, and it was touching to hear the fans sing my name.

That semi-final win was a great occasion, as massive underdogs we had won 2-0 through Frederic Piquionne and Prince Boateng and there was a lot of celebrating in the Wembley dressing room afterwards.

Ricardo Rocha got man of the match and our manager Avram Grant took the bottle of Champagne off him and gave it to me, so I tried to open it but Ric wanted to keep it for his collection so I let him off.

I am going to have to visit him one day in Portugal and drink it!

When I snapped my Achilles in March 2010 I was almost 36 and thought 'Oh no, this might be the end of it' but to come back - and as quickly as six months - was really pleasing.

I would play another 31 matches for Pompey, by then in the Championship, and it later meant something to quit the game in 2013 on my own terms, when I was ready.

It was January 2012 when I left Fratton Park for Coventry City on a six-month contract, I didn't want to go, circumstances changed and the manager Michael Appleton didn't want me.

The idea was to go and play more football, I wanted to give it a try at Coventry but played only twice more, got injured and returned to Iceland with IBV at the end of that season.

I did manage to keep the team-customised A-Team Reliant Robin, though, awarded to the week's worst trainer. It is at a friend's house in England and I'm still trying to take it over to Iceland.

Hopefully one day I can get it over and it can be the first Reliant Robin in Iceland!

I loved my time at Fratton Park, in my four-and-a-half years we had the whole rollercoaster ride, near the top of the Premier League, winning the FA Cup and then dipped down with financial problems and some hard times.

It's a time of my life where I made some absolutely great friends and met wonderful Portsmouth people, the whole experience was fantastic.

I get the impression the fans liked me. They are enthusiastic about their team and understand their football - so obviously like good footballers like me!

My background of working in the fishing factories in Iceland taught me you have to work hard in life to achieve and I always believed in giving it my absolute all in everything I did.

I was always quite physically fit and that was probably my strength, it was about making the most of my football career.

When the Pompey Supporters' Trust were looking to raise money in April 2013, David James and I jumped at the chance to bring IBV, the team we managed, over for a friendly and 6,780 fans came out to watch. I got a bit of a run out as well.

When Guy Whittingham was sacked in November 2013, Jamo and I applied for the job, I would have loved to have come back.

We were in a healthy working environment, bouncing off each other, and wanted to keep that partnership going and on a higher level, but it was not to be.

We were meant to be going in for an interview but the club rang me and were honest and said they didn't want to waste anyone's time, especially as I would have to fly over from Iceland. Maybe there was an extra message there.

I accept that. I would rather them be straight. I understood where they were coming from.

When I left Pompey I always said I would love to come back here and be part of the club. Maybe there will be a better time for me later on.

During my 20 years in football, Pompey was definitely my favourite time. It was not always clear skies with us but that first season, especially, stands out massively.

POMPEY 1 STOCKPORT 0 / Supporters pump up the vol...

FANTASTIC FANS KEEP THEIR HEROES GOING

...to a victory which they hope will signal the start of the climb away from trouble

■ Team at last played with the passion to match that shown by their fans

...ker Steve Claridge rises to head home his first goal for Pompey

...s and Quinn maul Reading

Nationwide Division 1

Above: Returning striker John Aloisi takes a tumble

Left: Goalkeeper Aaron Flahavan gave a commanding performance

Right: Sammy Igoe gets into a tussle with Stockport's Kevin Cooper

THE HERO

THE VILLAINS

Pompey 1 Stockport 0

POMPEY FANS HAVE THEIR SAY IN BLAST OFF!
Page 33

turning point

Andy **Awford**

371 games, three goals (August 1986 - November 2000)

Pompey 1 (Claridge)
Stockport County 0

Division One, Fratton Park, Tuesday, February 17, 1998

Pompey: Flahavan, Pethick, Whitbread, Awford, Cook (63 mins Allen), Carter, McLoughlin, Vlachos, Igoe, Aloisi (63 mins Svensson), Claridge.

Sub Not Used: Perrett.

Attendance; 8,622

That morning I couldn't walk down the stairs, instead I had to bum shuffle along the steps.

At the time I was aged 28 and when you get to that stage it is clear your body is yelling it cannot do this anymore. I decided to retire.

The previous day I'd played in the centre of Pompey's midfield for the 1-1 draw at QPR, lasting the entire 90 minutes.

That November 2002 fixture would prove to be the last of my 371 appearances for the Blues.

I'd had a catalogue of injuries throughout my career, as people know, and it just took its toll, I couldn't do it anymore.

When I look back it wasn't one particular injury which finished me but a number, such as two broken legs, a knee problem, while I nearly broke my neck at Sheffield United.

You always get your niggles but those four were my main injuries and the body's tendency for overcompensating to cope was playing havoc.

In truth, I had lost a bit of desire as well. I wasn't the fittest of players, I had to work really hard at my fitness levels so I was getting to the Paul McGrath stage of not training and trying to play at weekends.

My body was telling me I couldn't train all the time so then my performance level dropped and I was feeling down - then I thought 'I've had enough'.

It was hard calling it a day, of course it was, it's like chewing your right arm off. What do you do when you stop playing football? To have to reach that decision was horrible.

I took a Sports Studies degree following retirement and part of the psychology component addressed both physical and mental burn-out - and I've sat there thinking 'That was me'.

My body was saying enough was enough, I believe my head was as well, my mind was struggling with it, I couldn't perform out there properly.

I could have played at a lower level maybe for two or three years but didn't want to, so quit playing and moved into a scouting role at the club under then-boss Steve Claridge.

Then 11-and-a-half years later I was first-team manager.

I loved every minute of playing for Pompey, worked with some great managers and appeared in front of the best supporters in the country. I wouldn't swap any of it.

The game which sticks out most is Stockport County at Fratton Park in February 1998, without a shadow of a doubt.

Now I'd played in some big Blues games, the 1992 FA Cup run, various great escapes, I even sat in the crowd against AC Milan and that night chanted along with everybody else.

But, for me, nothing can compare to that evening against Stockport, it still gives me the goosebumps thinking about it.'

Having arrived at the club in the summer of 1986 I've seen how superb the fans are. As a schoolboy going to watch the games it was always exciting - yet that night against Stockport something changed.

It was the start of a new level of support. We've always had a very good atmosphere, yet that evening it went up a notch and has remained there ever since.

That fixture was something special, I have never known a crowd make so much difference towards winning a football match. It was an amazing night in Pompey's history.

The Wall of Noise it was called and I've got friends who were visiting somebody in St

Mary's Hospital that same night and couldn't believe the noise.

Apparently, when there is a goal at Pompey you can hear the cheer from the hospital, but they said it was a constant noise that evening, like we had won the FA Cup.

There was no big build-up to the fixture, I don't remember Alan Ball saying anything he wouldn't normally talk about, I just believe the fans realised we needed their help desperately.

We were nine points adrift at the bottom of League One, Stockport were a place above us, it was a big game and the opportunity to close the gap - which we thankfully did.

Jeff Peron sent a cross in from the left in the 15th minute and Steve Claridge scored from a header.

We defended the Fratton end in the second half and there was no way they were scoring, never in a day, and amid it all the chant of 'Alan Ball's Blue and White Army' rang out from the first minute to the 95th.

The noise seemed to increase as the game wore on. When playing you are in the zone anyway, you hear the noise, of course you do, but you are concentrating on the football.

However, I remember in the second half it was getting louder and louder, bigger and bigger, and all from a crowd of 8,622 containing barely any Stockport followers.

I am sure people will say it was like that at Northampton Town in May 1980, Tottenham Hotspur in the League Cup in 1985, the convoy at Anfield in the League Cup in October 1980, I've heard Alan Knight talk about all those games and other supporters can connect with those memories.

For me, though, that was the first time I had experienced it at that level and at the final whistle didn't actually want to leave the pitch.

Afterwards we sat in the changing room saying 'That was something wasn't it?'.

Stockport kicked off our Great Escape, that was the start of building a momentum. We needed that victory like never before, we were going to drop into Division Two otherwise.

We later beat Huddersfield Town 3-0 at home, Barry Horne was playing for them, but were still in 21st spot heading to Bradford City on the final day of the 1997-98 season and needing to win.

I remember being told in an interview we hadn't won at Valley Parade for more than 71 years and responding with 'It has got to change sometime'.

It did, we triumphed 3-1 through two goals from John Durnin and Sammy Igoe and it was a great trip home.

As soon as I got on the coach, Neil Sillett, our physio, handed me a beer, one of many, while Bally ended up needing a new suit after being covered in Champagne from top-to-toe.

I have always said you shouldn't celebrate staying up, but as a player that season was a big relief and prompted a little bit of celebration.

We stopped at a pub for an hour on the way back and when returned to Pompey ended up in The Marmion for a party with 'Touchline' Tony Male doing the DJing. I didn't get much sleep that night!

I was delighted for Bally, who had come back to the club just over three months earlier and managed a side which had some good players but underachieved massively.

He had been boss of Pompey when I had signed almost 12 years earlier, in fact he first came across me while I was on a week's holiday with my parents at Butlin's in Minehead!

I was aged 10 at the time, Bally was taking the soccer school there and kept my name in his head as one to watch in the future.

About four years later I was involved in England schoolboy trials at Moreton-In-The-Marsh and was spotted by Dave Hurst, Pompey's head of youth development.

My dad tells me the first thing I did was let the ball go under my foot in the first minute and the opposition scored, although I can't remember it. Regardless, Dave rang my parents after the game.

At the next round of England trials in Bromsgrove, Bally turned up with Dave and remembered me from all those years before, but he had competition from five other clubs for my signature.

Manchester United, Arsenal, Aston Villa, Coventry City and West Bromwich Albion were also chasing me as a 14-year-old and each in turn had me for a schoolboy week, hoping to impress me, but most of all my parents.

When I came down to Pompey for a stint I loved it, absolutely loved it.

It was quite late in the August and a mate of mine, Mickey Turner, was already on Pompey's books and an England schoolboy captain. However, I also really enjoyed it at Arsenal and Coventry.

In the end I got it down to John Sillett's Coventry or Pompey, having decided I would probably get more of an opportunity at a lesser club than Arsenal. Looking back at it, Tony Adams and David O'Leary were there while Martin Keown and Steve Bould later came in so I was right!

My eventual decision was, of course, Pompey and when I signed as a schoolboy in August 1986 they were in the old Division Two.

From the ages of 14-16, I would continue my schooling in Worcester and come down to Fratton Park every school holidays, such as Easter, Christmas and half terms, to take part in training while playing for the club at weekends.

Having also played for the reserves on occasions, my dad was approached by Worcester City asking if I could play for their first-team on Saturdays - but I was Pompey's player.

The club thought it would be good for me to play men's football in what was my last year at school and the arrangement meant I wasn't required to play for our youth team, instead turning out for Worcester.

That is where my FA Cup record comes in, appearing as a substitute in their match against Boreham Wood aged 15 years and 88 days.

When I turned 16 I could join Pompey full-time and signed apprenticeship forms, but by the time I penned my first professional contract a year later in the summer of 1989, Bally had been sacked and John Gregory was manager.

Of course, one of the highlights from my time as a Pompey player was the 1992 FA Cup run to the semi-finals, yet while we are all fond of those Liverpool fixtures because we played so well, we didn't actually win.

You only really want to remember the games you are successful in.

Don't get me wrong, the semi-finals in April 1992 were fantastic occasions, everyone was proud of the way we took on a top Division One side - but we didn't win.

We should have done, though. We should have won the first game at Highbury and should have won the replay at Villa Park.

We didn't. While I have fond memories of it, it is still tinged with that sadness that we didn't quite get there and I have happier memories of other games, like Stockport, where we did win.

When you look back at the Highbury game, it was extra-time and we were 1-0 up through Darren Anderton's 108th minute goal with four minutes to go and, once we settled down after the opening 20-25 minutes, had enough chances to have sealed it.

We hadn't given Liverpool a kick all afternoon, we were up against top world-class players but they had run out of ideas, we were in the lead and should have closed the match down and it would have been game over.

Then in the 115th minute, Steve Nichol received the ball well inside our half and went on a run. The game plan was we sat in, invited them on and the nearest man to the ball would go on and press when they got to 30-35 yards away from goal.

He went through one challenge, then another, and he's running at me.

If I am honest, I was hasty, I flew out and caught him and even now my memory of it was he had gone past me as well and I needed to do something about it.

I came out a little too quick, I should maybe have stood my ground a little bit to hold him up, but my actual thought was if I don't bring him down here he is through.

Looking back at it, there was probably more cover than I realised, but I had made a deliberate foul and got booked for it.

There was still a lot of work for Liverpool to do from the free-kick, but you have John Barnes on the ball and he's 25-yards out and probably the last person in the country at the time you wanted in that position.

We had done our homework, the wall was lined up, my role when defending free-kicks was the charger from the wall, the player that if it was knocked short would get out and block the ball.

So I am on my front foot in case they knocked it, trying to edge a couple of yards to get out and close the ball down, but instead they have gone direct and I remember seeing it go over my head.

Knightsie actually saved it, it was a great save. Even now I laugh with him and tell him he should have tipped it around the post, but to get his fingers on it and touch it onto the inside of the left-hand post was an unbelievable stop.

The problem was we didn't follow in and Ronnie Whelan put the rebound in.

It was heartbreaking. I remember Warren Neill coming across to me saying 'Focus, we have got to make sure we don't lose', it was the right thing to do, a few of us younger lads were thinking 'Oh no, how could that have happened?'.

There was still a minute to go and we had to make sure we didn't get beat, we were all over the place and distraught. I don't remember much after that kick-off.

In the dressing room after the final whistle we were all blaming ourselves, people were upset and a few tears were shed.

Knightsie was gutted because he should have got across to the shot quicker and saved it better, I felt guilty because I gave the free-kick away, Guy Whittingham said he should have pulled down Nichol on the halfway line rather than let him get that far, Kit Symons was blaming himself because he should have told me not to run out there to Nichol.

Jim Smith just said 'Shut up the lot of you' in his little way. 'You have been absolutely magnificent, go and beat them in the replay, it has gone now'.

The gaffer dealt with it superbly. We had a game at Tranmere Rovers on the Tuesday - two days later - and then a Fratton Park fixture with Grimsby Town, so had to focus on those before going again for the replay at Villa Park.

In the Highbury dressing room he convinced us if we played like that again we could beat Liverpool, he made it positive.

I'm not a great believer in luck, I think you make your own, but Whelan taking out Mark Chamberlain in the first five minutes was important. In this day and age the referee doesn't even look at it twice, it's a red card.

Back then when you could tackle we thought it was a red card, we were screaming at the referee, but Whelan stayed on the pitch and scored the equaliser.

So it was onto Villa Park for the replay eight days later on a Monday night, we were dominant, had a great game plan once again and Alan McLoughlin hit the bar from six yards. Yet he wasn't even on the pitch when it came to the penalty shoot-out with the scoreline goalless.

I was meant to take the sixth, but was no penalty taker. I had only ever taken one before back in my youth-team days - and scored against Leyton Orient at Eastney Barracks in front of one man and his dog.

Graham Paddon, who was Jim's assistant, was gauging the situation and said to me 'Do you fancy it? You are going to go sixth'. I said 'Okay'. Well, you had to.

It didn't come to me in the end, Martin Kuhl knocked one wide, Kit scored, Warren Neill had his saved and John Beresford shot wide, whereas Liverpool scored their first four. We had lost and still had Warren Aspinall to take one.

Obviously the overriding factor was massive disappointment and frustration because we were so close and I actually think we would have beaten Sunderland in the final. I laugh with Paul Hardyman about it now, who played for Sunderland, although he completely disagrees!

That summer would be the closest I ever came to leaving Fratton Park when a bid was accepted from Chelsea.

Well it was the only interest as far as I know, the sole occasion I was contacted by the club to say they had accepted a bid. There may have been others, I don't know.

Anyhow, in June 1992 my wife, Mandy, was celebrating her 21st with a party at our Clanfield home when the phone rang.

Now I'd had a few beers and when I picked up there was a Chelsea director on the other end telling me they had agreed a fee with Pompey and would I meet them at the Guildford Posthouse the next day, which was a Sunday.

So I ran downstairs, got my dad to take over the call and stopped drinking immediately!

Unsurprisingly I didn't sleep much that night and at 8am on the Sunday Jim Hutchinson, a Pompey director, phoned and said: 'Andy there is a snag with the deal, don't go to the Guildford Posthouse because it would be a wasted journey for you, wait until you hear from me again'.

The gaffer, Jim Smith, was on holiday in Portugal so I contacted him and said 'What's going on?', I was a young lad aged 20 and didn't really know, I needed some advice.

He told me to speak to Chelsea, and seeing as I didn't have an agent instructed me to take my dad along and find out their plans.

In the end the deal broke down, to this day I don't know why.

Talking to Jim as a friend, he is still very guarded about it, my belief is he thinks he shouldn't tell me because it's not my place to know.

My view is Chelsea agreed to a double transfer for me and John Beresford but he didn't want to go there, he had his sights on Newcastle United under Kevin Keegan after failing a medical at Liverpool.

Then it was a case of adjusting the fee just for me, but nothing could be resolved. That is what I think anyway, I am still not 100 per cent sure why the deal collapsed.

So I stayed with Pompey, went into pre-season, brushed off the Chelsea talk and was quite happy to stay, I was enjoying my time.

Then in September 1994, West Brom's Gary Strodder broke my right leg in four places and I was never quite the same player after that.

Before that injury I was quick, over five or six yards I was sharp, but after the first leg break lost that yard of pace and that probably stopped me going and playing higher up because you have to be an athlete as well.

Not that I begrudge playing for Pompey until November 2000, it's my club and I love it.

vopence

ke
ce
n

t Torquay
the cham-
ndon, this

Lose
e to
ham

plenty of
nst Totten-
Park, and
save from
er.
the greater
combination
Dunmore
to give the
ack strongly,
yed magnifi-
er.
troke of luck
missed point

VICTORY
I. CITY

a shock when
had attacked
break against
and gone near
al times, City
in the 18th
scoring with
om close in.
ered another
minute when
through their

POMPEY SPIRIT WINS THE DAY

Pompey's inside-right, Gordon (right), leaps towards the Wolves' goal but the ball is deflected.—F.M. 0138

Newman Goal Beats Wolves

(By NIMROD)

Brave, weary Pompey held on grimly to their single goal lead against storming attacks from the fresh Wolverhampton Wanderers at Fratton Park, and caused great jubilation among the supporters with a fine victory.

WITH the stitches still in the cut above his left eye, received in last week's match at Bolton, Newman played at outside-left for Pompey.

It was stated before the match that McClellan, injured yesterday, was unlikely to play for the rest of the season.

Weddle moved to inside-left and Henderson led the attack.

Wolverhampton made one change from the side which beat West Bromwich Albion on Monday, Murray coming in at

Nimrod's Comment

POMPEY'S thanks must go out to a great-hearted defence, the spirit of which centred on their great skipper, Jim Dickinson, who was here, there and everywhere, inspiring his colleagues.

* * *

For fully the first half-hour of the second half, with the Wolves bringing their big guns—their brilliant wing-halves Flowers and Slater—into constant action, Dickinson, Rutter, and the rest of a gallant defence stood firm and solid.

* * *

Behind them, once again, young Barnett was coolness itself. In fact, he seemed rarely in any difficulty, a further fact which reflects great credit upon the Pompey defence.

* * *

Try as they would, Wolves could not break down that fighting spirit and, in the closing stages, the Pompey forwards, handicapped by Weddle's injury, came back into the picture.

* * *

The home attack certainly did their stuff in the first half, at the end of which they deserved more than their single goal lead.

* * *

The whole team thoroughly deserved the ovation which greeted them as they came off the field.

Ron **Newman**

120 games, 23 goals (January 1955 - January 1961)

Pompey 1 (Newman)
Wolverhampton Wanderers 0

Division One, Fratton Park, Saturday, April 20, 1957

Pompey: Barnett, Wilson, Mansell, Phillips, Rutter, Dickinson, Harris, Gordon, Henderson, Weddle, Newman.

Attendance; 31,111

The double decker bus would travel from near my Fareham home to St John's College in Southsea, going through Portchester on the way.

On the days you missed it, you had to catch the next one which took the longer way round, but it did have its plus points.

This different route had a stop outside The Seagull pub and living on the other side of the road was my big hero - Jack Froggatt.

You would get to see his house and he was always working in his yard doing something or other, but one day the bus stopped, I looked over from the top deck and he wasn't there, which was disappointing.

Then there is a clump, clump, clump on the stairs, I thought it was the conductor looking for money, yet who should it be but Jackie Froggatt!

My eyes were falling out, he looked over, acknowledged me and sat next to me. I was in a different world.

I was looking down at my skinny little legs and there were his right next to me, built like tree trunks. I don't think he even said hello to me, but I didn't care, I was going to be a professional footballer just like he was, although it was going to take a bit of time to do it.

Everything Froggatt did was great, he played on the outside-left like me, up and down that wing, and I always tried to copy him growing up. For that particular schoolboy he was the one.

By the time I joined Pompey in January 1955 Froggatt had left, departing the previous year for Leicester City after 304 games and 73 goals for the club, in addition to 13 caps and two goals for England.

Unfortunately I never had the opportunity to tell him that story before he died in February 1993 at the early age of 71, although his widow did later tell me he would have found it amusing.

Pompey was my team, it was my dad's team, it was my grandad's team, it was my great grandad's team, my wife's family were the same.

I watched games at Fratton Park, although coming from Fareham to matches was never easy. My Uncle Charlie lived near to the ground and my dad, Algernon, would take me round his house to meet up and go to the match.

I was very young at the time and we were allowed to stand up, but were actually half the size of most people in the crowd. In no time at all there would be three of us youngsters picked up and passed over their heads down to the front to see all the action. Little could I have expected that years later I would make 120 appearances and score 23 goals for them.

Before I could join Pompey fully, though, I worked as a carpenter in the dockyard, followed by a drill sergeant for two years in the Army based at Hilsea.

I lived in Johns Road along the Gosport Road in Fareham and would wait for my bus at 6am every day to go to the dockyard, they were tough times but it was what I had to do.

We would have an hour break and I used to play football outside the men's toilets. There were guys there smoking cigarettes and I could knock a cigarette out of their mouths by kicking the ball. I say that because I actually did it once and the chap chased me all around the harbour!

In the evening I would come home but to keep fit used to jump off my bus halfway from

Fareham to Gosport and sprint all the way to my house, which was some two or three miles. It was quite a long distance but the way I used to keep fit.

In the summer of 1954 I was selected to be part of the regular Reds v Blues fixture at Fratton Park, while still employed in the dockyard.

The previous season I had played several reserve games and this regular match was an opportunity to assess some of the best local players around. I couldn't wait to put my brand new shirt and shorts on.

So Eddie Lever came into the dressing room before kick-off, pinned the starting line-up on the noticeboard and didn't say a word to anyone.

Everybody was pushing and shoving, 'Who is playing, who is playing,' but my name was not mentioned, what was going on?

So I said 'Excuse me, I am not on a team' and was told 'We've got too many, you can come on in the second half so go up into the stands with the others and then come down at half-time'.

I returned at the interval and a lot of people were looking to see if they were continuing to play or had been put on a different team, but once again there was no Ron Newman mentioned. I hadn't got a single bit of mud on me, I was terribly depressed as you can imagine.

At the end of the match I approached the manager and said 'Excuse me Mr Lever, I didn't get a game, my name wasn't down'. His reply was 'Sorry about that, we had too many players, where are you going to play this year?'.

Well, it had been my intention to play for Pompey, so that was that. However, I had two friends playing for Woking at the time and they had been eager to get me to join their club.

I was never keen on the travelling but was now stuck with no team to play for that season so gave them a call and signed.

Now as I working in the dockyard, I was also playing for their football team and out of the blue was asked to play up in London for the Civil Service. I didn't even know they had a side!

So I travelled up there and, having blonde hair, stood out as we won. At the end of the game I was sat down having a cup of tea when this old man came up to me and said 'Do you mind giving me your address?'.

No problem, but who was he? He informed me he worked for the Football Association - and about two weeks later this letter with a fancy England badge came through the letterbox. I had been selected to play for the FA against the British Army.

Obviously I accepted and before the game the coach told us there were loads of managers and coaches in the crowd to watch us play - and I went on to have another pretty good game by all accounts.

Afterwards who should come up to me but Eddie Lever who says 'Young man, don't we have you on our books?'. I replied 'Well, you did but you didn't use me!'.

He then asked who I was playing for at the time and when I responded with Woking he asked me to give him a call the next time we didn't have a fixture.

We got to Christmas and an old buddy of mine, John Bell, who was a fellow carpenter in the dockyard, was urging me to ring Lever as I didn't have a game one weekend. I replied

'I would rather talk to God, I can't talk to him'.

He persuaded me in the end, although I still stood at home in front of that phone for ages trying to pluck up the courage to speak to Pompey's manager. Eventually I rang him, got straight through, and he agreed to give me a few games. I was quite proud of the way I handled it.

Not that many people had phones in those days but dad was in the repair business so had to have one. Good job really.

I ended up playing three trial games, the last at Bournemouth, and was signed by the club in January 1955, just weeks before I married Olive at Portsmouth Cathedral.

I was now a Pompey player and a few months later made my debut in a 2-2 draw at Charlton in April.

My second match was a first-team debut at Fratton Park against Chelsea, a side which would go on to beat us to the Division One title by four points the following month in that 1954-55 campaign.

The game finished goalless and there were 40,230 in attendance. When I was running I had my hands on either ear and was banging my head, it was going 'Woh woh woh woh woh' as I was running.

It was really weird, I had never heard of it before, racing up and down at Fratton Park I kept thinking what was this strange noise in my ears? Of course, I hadn't played in front of that many people before, I didn't know if it was normal!

I had brought my own boots to the club when I arrived, my dad had got them for me from Woolworths and I regarded them as the best boots I had ever seen.

I loved them, they had these big toe caps on which I used to hammer and hammer so you could feel the ball smoother.

In the end, though, there was nothing left, they were on their last legs and all torn up - I was at a Division One club with basically no football boots.

So I asked our centre forward Jackie Henderson what I should do and he advised I went to see Eddie Lever. Jackie was right, Eddie told me 'Don't worry young man, go to the sports shop', so I did.

I left with my first pair of Adidas boots, they were beautiful, I could have gone to church in them. They were pretty expensive but the man serving said 'You don't need to pay, you play for Pompey, they are yours'.

I was jumping up and down along the street and when I returned to Fratton Park the next morning headed into the boot room where there were these little, square open boxes you put your boots in to be cleaned.

So I put mine in there and went outside to do some running, yet when I came back my box was empty, my boots had gone!

'Where are my shoes?' I asked one of the trainers who replied 'They've been taken away, you can't have them. You are in the reserve team, you can't have these, these are for first-team players'.

So once again I found myself with no boots - and back I went to see Eddie Lever who insisted the trainers returned them to me.

They weren't very happy with me when I delivered his message, but what could I do? It was a bad thing they did, no question about it, and just because I wasn't playing in the first-team at the time. It was terrible.

The players made me so welcome, though, and treated me really well.

I thought Jimmy Dickinson was right next to God, but he was also right next to me - I changed beside him in the dressing room.

Don't ask me why, but he nearly always did and I would be putting on my shoes staring at him, watching what he did. I was this young lad and well aware this wonderful footballer was paid exactly the same as me!

That's right, in those days everyone received the same amount and when I first started we were both getting £15 a week!

In addition, I would receive £4 for a win or £2 for a draw, while in the off-season there was a £1 retainer. Meanwhile, I also had a £3 10d contract to play for any of the reserve teams.

It changed, of course, in January 1961 when what had been the maximum wage of £20 a week was abolished in the game following pressure from the players - then the money started to come in.

Up until that point, the only time Jimmy got more money was when playing for England, earning £50 per match.

Ron Saunders was another team-mate and he was very good, built for football, very strong, very powerful, great in the air and a natural goalscorer.

Like Gerd Muller, who I later managed for Fort Lauderdale Strikers in America, he was built to be a centre forward, using his body so well and I was always pleased when I saw him in our starting line-up.

I played with Harry Harris for three years, he arrived at Fratton Park after me and I left before him, and he was a get up and get them type of player, all over the place, he would knock peoples' heads off if he had to.

He was strong but not strong as in the same way as Saunders, Harry seemed to be more busy all over the field.

Harry would play inside-left to me and would get the ball and play it brilliantly inside the full-back towards the Fratton end - yet there was only one thing wrong with that. Who was going to get it?

That's right, me! Dear, oh dear 'Harry, I am not Superman' I would say to him!

So I am flying and he is hitting these balls harder and harder and they are going to the goalie most of the time, but that was my job, I had to run and people didn't realise how fast I was.

On the other flank, Peter Harris would be flying down the right-hand side, turning it, cutting and dropping the ball to the back post, he was brilliant.

Now the opposite winger's job was to make contact with his crosses at the back post and guess who that was? Yes, me again, making all the runs.

People talk about midfielders doing all the running but it is the wide players because you are sprinting all the time. In comparison midfielders were jogging!

It took a lot of energy to play as an outside-right or outside-left and that is how I got my nickname at Pompey, 'Mr Perpetual Motion,' my game was about work-rate and energy.

I recall playing Manchester City at Fratton Park in January 1958 and we were getting our backsides spanked, we just couldn't get the ball and the fans were getting angry.

At the time I was young and thinking 'This is not good, what shall we do? I know, I'd better get the ball back,' so I started chasing it and looked pretty silly.

Their player knocked it over there so I started chasing after him, another then played it over there so I went over there and I have gone all over the field, but what I did notice was the ball was getting closer until in the end I won it back!

The crowd went crazy because they just wanted somebody like me to put it right and I always thought that was one of the most important things that ever happened to me at Pompey. When I did that it worked and I realised what you could do to please a crowd.

We went on to win that match 2-1 as well, Ray Crawford scoring twice.

There was one game in March 1959 when we played Birmingham City at Fratton Park which finished in a 1-1 draw and I was marked by England right-back Jeff Hall.

On the Monday I received a phone call telling me to stay in bed as there would be a doctor and some other medical people coming round to my house.

It turned out Hall, who had done a hell of a good job marking me, was in hospital with polio and they wanted to test anyone he had come into contact with, including shaking hands.

The whole thing was scary. They put knuckles onto my chest and then I had to lower my nose onto my thumb, which if I could manage meant I didn't have the disease. Thankfully I was cleared.

Poor Hall, 13 days later he died aged 29, it was so sad for football.

Steadily I was making more appearances with the passing of each season but by the 1956-57 campaign we were struggling against relegation from Division One and it continued over the next two years.

Initially it was a strange feeling, the players there didn't really know much about that type of experience in football.

We had people like Jimmy Dickinson, Reg Pickett and Peter Harris who had won the title, while in 1954-55 under Eddie Lever we had finished third, missing out on the runners-up spot by goal difference.

A lot of the latter team were still around during those relegation battles, including myself, Norman Uprichard, Alex Wilson, Jack Mansell, Johnny Gordon, Mike Barnard, Gordon Dale, Jackie Henderson, Ron Rafferty, Derek Rees and Phil Gunter.

It would be during the 1956-57 fight to stay up when I scored my first-ever Pompey goal, in the process helping keep us in the top flight. The funny thing was, I had been let out of the Army to play.

We were battling relegation and had three matches in four days over the 1957 Easter weekend.

The first was on Good Friday and I didn't feature in a 1-0 win over Cardiff City at Fratton Park, but replaced Mike Barnard at outside-left the next day for the visit of a Wolverhampton Wanderers side which contained England internationals such as Billy Wright, Bert Williams, Bill Slater, Dennis Wilshaw and Ron Flowers.

It was my 10th appearance, Johnny Gordon drove in a low cross and I shot into the roof of the net in front of the Fratton end for the game's only goal.

I played with stitches in a cut above my left eye sustained a week earlier at Bolton Wanderers and The Football Mail headline that night read 'Pompey spirit wins the day'.

For us it was a do-or-die fixture or we went into Division Two and I was also playing five games a week in the Army. Everybody wanted my body!

At the time I was stationed at RAOC Hilsea, which is now housing but used to be the home of the Royal Army Ordnance Corps.

I had got into the Army late anyway because I had been in the dockyard and with a wife and child was determined to be stationed in Hilsea.

I was told the only way I could do it was to be a drill instructor, so I went to Aldershot, among 120-odd guys, and ended up being one of only 12 to qualify so managed to come back to the city.

My first job was looking after all the kids who had just joined, there would be 18-20 of them in one big shed and I had to get up at 6am, make sure they cleaned their teeth and during the day helped them get a decent meal. Basically I was in charge of them.

I couldn't play football then, there was no allowance for it, the Army was taking all my energy and all my breathing so I had to keep finding little schemes to get time off to play football.

Then after a year there was a job going to run the sports store, which I managed to get. It also ensured every other week I would get permission to go to Fratton Park to train.

So I had permission to play against Wolves that day in April 1957, enabling me to have the game of my life, scoring the goal of my life to keep Pompey in Division One - then the very next day I'm back in the Army.

It just so happened the following day there were some big-time military people coming round to inspect the whole of Hilsea barracks. All the big cheeses were there and everything had to be spick and span.

So I've got all the shoes polished and the socks and shirts in order when they all traipse into the sports store.

Then this big colonel said: 'Tell me this, didn't I read somewhere this weekend that a player from this area saved Portsmouth from relegation?'

'Oh yes, it was Corporal Ron Newman, he was the one,' came the reply and they couldn't wait to push me forward to introduce me.

They couldn't leave me alone after that, they were really chuffed at what I had achieved and having the write-up in the newspaper. I was God's gift to Hilsea Barracks at that time!

Anyhow, the following day was Easter Monday, I was again given permission to play and kept my place as we achieved survival with a 2-0 win at Cardiff, Peter Harris scoring both goals, the first finishing off my cross.

We ended up in 19th place with Charlton Athletic and Cardiff instead going down, but the relegation fight continued.,

The following season we finished 20th and, at the end of it in May 1958, Lever left as manager and was replaced by Bournemouth's Freddie Cox ahead of the 1958-59 campaign when we finally did tumble out of the top flight.

Cox had been very successful at Dean Court and started talking about different systems, when previously we had always played with three at the back as it was easier to get players offside.

There were new ways of thinking coming into the game in this country following Hungary's 7-1 destruction of England in May 1954 under Walter Winterbottom. The previous year the Hungarians had won at Wembley 6-3.

Rather than play the usual WM formation of those times, Hungary withdrew the centre forward further back and England couldn't cope with that.

Being young I tried to understand Cox's ideas, it seemed okay and I did what I was told, but great players like Jimmy Dickinson and Peter Harris were dead against it, they were older and it was all new to them.

Now I am not blaming those guys, I cherished working and training with them, but I believe Freddie had it right and could see the future and where it was going.

Still, the other guys didn't want to change the system they had been playing for years and it got awkward, some didn't like to do it that way and I guess messed things up a bit, leading to our relegation.

It continued not to go well under Cox, we also struggled in Division Two, slipping to the bottom in our second season, and players started to be sold, although the manager wasn't the one doing the selling.

That included me, going to Leyton Orient for £10,000 in January 1961, although I didn't want to leave.

It was a done deal, Orient wanted me, Pompey didn't, so I said 'Okay' and I left Fratton Park.

I had a terrible time there because it wasn't Pompey, everything felt so unusual. Nothing could be as special as playing for my club.

Admiral

● WE'VE DONE IT – Martin Kuhl, John Beresford, and Andy Awford salute the Fratton fans

● WE'VE DONE IT – Chris Burns is mobbed as he fights his way to the dressing rooms

PRICELESS 'JOKE'

By MIKE NEASOM

Mac on the mark as keeper blunder proves so costly

Pompey 1
Forest 0

THE GOAL, of course, was little short of a joke – the kind of error a schoolboy goalkeeper would be loathe to contemplate.

But what a priceless strike it was by the outcast from The Dell.

Alan McLoughlin was the man in the right place at the right moment as Mark Crossley fumbled and dropped an inswinging free kick by John Beresford with Fratton's first FA Cup quarter-final in 43 years just 107 seconds old.

Yet, as the fans behind the distraught Forest goalkeeper celebrated the gift, the men on Pompey's bench knew mixed emotions.

They were as delighted as the Pompey supporters to find themselves in front – but they feared that the lead had come too early.

They wondered whether their side, with so many young men unused to the expectations of a full house with Wembley's twin towers peeping invitingly over the horizon, might have the inner resilience and corporate discipline to preserve that shock lead for

In the end, though, those fears were unfounded. There were anxious moments of course, none more than when Stuart Pearce, the man whose introductory challenge on Darren Anderton had created the situation in which Crossley's handling betrayed him, met a cross from Nigel Clough with what seemed a perfectly-placed header.

All that did was to provide Alan Knight with the stage to produce the afternoon's outstanding save.

Inevitably that left Pompey's longest-serving player with a glow of satisfaction as he attempted to assimilate the warm feeling of finding himself in his first Cup semi-final of a career which has seen him go for

bending away from me, and then I noticed Pearcie coming on a late run and started to go back. Fortunately I was able to take off and knock it away.

"In the end, I suppose it was pretty important – apart from that I didn't have too many difficult moments thanks to the way the lads in front of me played.

"But as a goalkeeper I could feel for Mark. I was glad he made the mistake, but I know how he must been feeling.

"Every goalkeeper makes one from time to time and when you do, you just have to hold up your hand and accept what's thrown at you – but to do so in a match like that must be awful."

Acclaim

But if Knight was to make that crucial save and another scrambling effort

● IT'S THERE – Alan McLoughlin wheels away after scoring, chased by Pompey colleagues Colin Clarke and Darryl

man of the season acclaim a year ago, while Chris Burns battled and battled and McLoughlin buzzed waspishly about, chivvying and chasing

experience.

Inevitably, of course, there were moments of controversy; referee Steve Lodge's decision to dismiss Forest's Brian Laws for his late

I'm ready

Alan **Knight**

801 games, 0 goals (July 1975 - January 2000, January 2004)

Pompey 1 (McLoughlin)
Nottingham Forest 0

FA Cup Quarter-Final, Fratton Park, Saturday, March 7, 1992

Pompey: Knight, Neill, Symons, Awford, Beresford, Kuhl, Burns, McLoughlin, Anderton, Powell (64 mins Aspinall), Clarke (75 mins Whittingham).

Attendance; 25,402

We were the gremlins, transforming at night after having a drink.

Of course, in the Steven Spielberg film it was water which sparked the change into mischievous creatures - with us it was alcohol!

Vince Hilaire coined the nickname during one of our regular drinking bouts together and it stuck.

Our manager, Alan Ball, had earlier told us we turned into gremlins on the football pitch, but Vince and the rest of us thought it more appropriate as an off-the-field comparison.

In terms of team spirit, that was the closest group of players I was ever involved with during my four decades at Fratton Park.

We had missed out on promotion twice, yet Bally kept the nucleus of that squad together and we finally reached the top flight for the 1987-88 campaign, although it ended being a little bit of a let-down.

The owner, John Deacon, became more interested in his basketball team and selling the club, leaving the manager stitched up with no money to add to the team, while Mick Kennedy was sold halfway through the season.

Steadily the group broke up and went its separate ways, as happens in football. It was a shame, but they were great days.

Looking at those players, I wouldn't say Vince was a hard-core drinker like some of us, he would have the occasional whisky and Coke and get a bit tipsy, but that was it.

The funny thing is when he arrived from Luton Town in November 1984 he was a good boy, didn't drink, would sit indoors and watch TV at night, knew all the soaps - then he met us!

Vince is Vince and hasn't changed, he's always got a story to tell and is a very affable geezer. A bit difficult sometimes to pin down, but that's Vince.

Kevin Dillon was something quite special as a player, but a bit of a moaner and he and Kevin O'Callaghan would have a row or a dispute about absolutely anything.

They would argue over who had the best lawn, who had the better boot deal, who had the best tracksuit, those two could moan for Britain. It was a funny relationship, but they still got on well.

Then we had Noel Blake, a big, strong central defender who stuck to what he was good at, heading it, kicking it, knew his limitations and surprised everyone by going on to become a top-level coach.

Alongside him Billy Gilbert was an outstanding player, a very talented footballer. They complemented each other perfectly a great partnership in which Billy would get the ball and play it out with that superb passing range of his, while Blakey was the muscle.

Billy liked to do the social side, he has a wicked sense of humour and doesn't suffer fools, definitely one you didn't want to cross on or off the pitch. I believe he could have gone on to play for England, a very underrated footballer.

Blakey off the pitch was reasonably quiet until he had a drink, like the majority of the gremlins really.

There was one evening when I turned up at Martine's in Guildhall Walk and spotted him in a car park which used to be across the road from the nightclub.

He had ripped off his shirt exposing his bulging biceps and was throwing three or four blokes around in the car park. He had lost the plot a little bit, but that was Blakey, you could push him so far but shouldn't cross the line with him.

Mick Kennedy loved his drink - as did we all - and was good at getting the lads together and generating that camaraderie which was the cornerstone of the squad.

You would never get him attending the PFA Awards, though. He felt he had upset too many of his fellow pros over the years and thought he might be singled out!

Another part of the merry group was Mick Tait, whose ability to drink Kronenbourg 1664 is legendary, it never seemed to affect him, he had hollow legs.

I still live in Clanfield and everyone from that area still remembers him, yet he is a very quiet, unassuming guy and when they talk about heart in football he epitomised that. What a player.

Don't think I've forgotten Mick Quinn either, although he forgot to tell anyone he was on a driving ban when he joined the club in March 1986 and ended up in prison!

I remember in November 1987 the police turning up at Moneyfields while we were training and arresting Quinny for driving while disqualified, but it had actually been Clive Whitehead at the wheel giving him a lift!

They looked like Harry Enfield's Scousers so you could see how the Old Bill had got confused!

That gave Vince an idea and he went out and got a load of Quinny masks with strings on - and we surprised everyone by wearing them in a team photograph for the club Christmas card.

Obviously being the manager Bally didn't really go out with us, although sometimes on an away trip he would drag me out for a drink, with Vince coming along as well.

Apparently he used to like socialising with goalkeepers and used to have a few drinking sessions with Peter Shilton in his Southampton days - 'Grab a goalie' he used to call it. That kind of socialising doesn't happen anymore, players are athletes nowadays. Whether that is right or wrong I don't know, although I do feel sometimes there are sides which lack that team spirit.

You don't have to be each other's best mate, but you need to possess respect for a team-mate and on the pitch be prepared to die for each other.

When there were seasons in which we struggled at Pompey that spirit was probably what got us out of trouble in the end. We had a close-knit bunch of lads and, no matter their ability levels, we would fight and scrap to get us out of trouble.

That is why following my debut in 1977-78 I played in only one relegated side.

There was a massive drinking culture which was a huge part of all the teams I played in at Pompey, yet it stopped with the arrival of Harry Redknapp in March 2002, a short while after my retirement.

To be honest, I wouldn't change my years involved in that culture, even though I paid the price for it a little bit later on through my alcoholism.

I was very lucky that in the teams I featured in there was always a good bond between the players and with that gremlins group I believe the supporters saw that. Bally had brought in the 'Work hard and you can play hard' mantra.

The path which led me to Fratton Park began in July 1975 upon signing schoolboy terms, although initially I was a 13-year-old training with Fulham and QPR.

On Tuesday evenings I would be at Fulham and Thursday nights with QPR, then one day at Fulham's training ground in Kingston Upon Thames a scout called Reg Locke approached my parents asking if I would be interested in attending a week's trial with Pompey.

I didn't know where Portsmouth was, didn't have a clue, but found out they were in Division Two at the time with Ian St John as the manager, Billy Hunter his assistant and Tony Barton the chief scout.

So I accepted, working under the youth-team manager Ray Crawford, but got really badly homesick having never been away from my parents before, although still completed the week.

With my 14th birthday approaching, Pompey wanted me to sign schoolboy forms and I was half expecting Fulham or QPR to say something, especially as when I returned telling them the situation.

Instead they said 'Okay, good luck'. I thought they might have wanted me to stay!

Things were going well at Fratton Park, then when I was approaching 16 and looking to secure an apprenticeship, West Ham United came in for me at a time when Jimmy Dickinson was first-team manager and Ray Crawford his assistant.

Jimmy had accepted because Ron Greenwood had come down to talk in person to him about a deal, I think he was more in awe of the Hammers boss than anything!

The deal involved me and Clive Green going to Upton Park with one of West Ham's players coming the other way, but they couldn't afford his wages anyway. So instead Greenwood offered £5,000 for me in compensation.

At that point Ray got involved, despite being on holiday, and insisted to Jimmy I shouldn't be sold - and he agreed.

West Ham was the club I supported, the club my dad supported, but the move fell through, I signed as an apprentice in July 1977 and on the final day of the 1977-78 season made my first-team debut at Rotherham United in a 1-0 win, although we had already been relegated.

It wouldn't be until November 1979 before I returned to the side when Frank Burrows put me in for Peter Mellor for a few games, although I would start ahead of him in the 1981-82 campaign as Pompey's number one.

I played 51 of the 52 matches during that Division Three campaign - and stayed in the side for quite some time after that.

Of the 801 matches I played for the Blues, I was lucky enough to feature in promotion games and the Liverpool semi-finals, but the pick was the March 1992 FA Cup quarter-final against Nottingham Forest.

Alan McLoughlin scored from close range in the second minute after Mark Crossley had dropped John Beresford's right-wing free-kick and we held out for the 1-0 win, despite being under quite a lot of pressure without me being overly worked.

Recently I watched the extended highlights of that match on YouTube and it reminded me how we took a lot of knowledge from it into the semi-finals, playing with two banks of four and looking to hit on the break.

The match also sticks out for me because the save I made from Stuart Pearce's header was the best of my entire career.

It was a cross wide on their left from Nigel Clough in the 17th minute, whipped in, and the England left-back had made the run across the penalty spot and glanced a header which was speeding into my left-hand corner.

That was until I managed to get across and fingertip it wide with my left hand.

A moment such as that is purely instinctive, then it sinks in and you think 'well, that wasn't bad'. Then you start contemplating maybe, just maybe the luck will be with you that day.

Unfortunately good luck wasn't with us in the semi-final replay against Liverpool, a fingernail on the ball, it hits the post and goes along the goal before Ronnie Whelan taps in. Just little things like that.

Still, our 1991-92 FA Cup campaign began at Alan Ball's Exeter City and we were lucky to beat them 2-1. Then it was a 2-0 home win over Leyton Orient before winning at Middlesbrough 4-2 in a replay.

At that point a little belief started to run throughout the side and Brian Clough's Forest side were the visitors to Fratton Park, a team which had lost 2-1 in extra-time to Tottenham Hotspur in the final the previous season.

Jim Smith's game plan involved us being difficult to break down and then hitting them on the counter attack through Darren Anderton and Mark Chamberlain, while with the likes of Colin Clarke and Guy Whittingham at our disposal we always knew we could score goals.

It didn't quite pan out like that, we scored a fluke early on and then managed to see the game out by defending for our lives.

There was the big story that Crossley had been locked in a police cell until 5am the previous day after a shop window had been smashed following a night out drinking. Then he made that costly mistake.

Regardless, of what had gone on with him, Forest came to Fratton thinking it was a done deal, I got the feeling they believed they just had to turn up, although admittedly had quality all over the park with the likes of Pearce, Des Walker, Roy Keane, Nigel Clough and Teddy Sheringham.

Crossley's mistake was a bit of a wake-up call and they were reduced to 10-men in the 65th minute when Brian Laws was sent off for a late two-footed challenge on Beresford.

We had to defend for long spells but, in saying that, I wasn't called upon to make save after save, I was there sweeping up and played fairly deep. They couldn't play in behind us and we managed to nullify them quite well.

I felt at that stage in my career my talking and organising was probably a bigger part of my game than my shot stopping and we had a really good understanding as a defensive unit. It is something you work on in training and comes from understanding each other's strengths and weaknesses.

When Stephen Lodge sounded the final whistle, Pompey had reached the semi-finals of the FA Cup for the first time since 1949.

Over my time with the Blues I was part of three promotion-winning sides and while Bally's team was my favourite group, the best team was Bobby Campbell's which won the Division Three title in 1982-83.

That squad strolled the league, they were head and shoulders above all the other sides, possessing fantastic players like Neil Webb, Alan Biley and Kevin Dillon.

Although Bobby Campbell deserves credit for building that team, it was Frank Burrows before him who turned the club around, made it professional and put some discipline in there, also adding the fear factor.

During Frank's Division Four promotion season in 1979-80, I played eight matches, deputising for Mellor when the need arose through injury.

That was my first experience of success, even if we had gone up by the skin of our teeth, and I always remember how me and fellow ex-apprentice Keith James hadn't been selected for the last game at Northampton Town in May 1980.

So instead we waited in The Pompey pub for the lads to return and when the result came through I have never heard anything like it. The euphoria was incredible, the club had been in decline for years and the outpouring was just unbelievable.

Then there was the open-topped bus around the city, there were all those people lining the streets and I had never seen anything like that in my life. That has stuck in the memory big time.

The third promotion side, of course, were the gremlins, winning the right to play in Division One having finished as runners-up to Derby County in 1986-87.

As mentioned earlier, we worked so hard to get there and then Mick Kennedy was sold in January 1987 - it was a decision not greatly appreciated by a lot of the lads at the time.

It was tough on Bally because there was nothing he could do about it apart from resigning and nobody wanted that to happen, although he threatened to do so a few times.

It was all ripped away from us and so very disappointing - and then Jim Gregory came in as owner at the end of the season.

During that campaign I got my face smashed by Eric Young against Wimbledon, they were my nemesis, my local team who were in the Southern League when I was at school and we used to have battles against them all the time.

I would miss the last four games of that season, with Andy Gosney deputising, so my time in the top flight didn't last too long!

Looking back at individual matches, there were those I had what I would call worldies such as a goalless draw at Southend United in the League Cup in September 1981, a goalless draw at Plymouth Argyle in November 1981, a 2-0 win at Oldham Athletic in November 1984, they were games when we were under pressure all the time.

There was also at Sheffield United in December 1986 where we were down to eight men against their 10 and hung on and hung on until Paul Mariner, who dropped back to fill in as an emergency centre-half, scored an own goal in the 69th minute and we lost 1-0.

Of the managers, Jim Smith was one of the best, he was spot on, while his number two Graham Paddon was a good coach who didn't get a lot of attention but kept him in check along with the physio Neil Sillett because he really could go off on one!

Jim's footballing brain and tactical knowledge were superb, while the players respected how he said it as he saw it and clearly knew what he was talking about.

I didn't mind Terry Fenwick, we got on okay, it was just difficult for him working under Terry Venables and being inexperienced was a problem in itself. As a bloke, though, I cannot give him too much stick.

On the other hand, John Gregory loved himself.

After making my Pompey debut, only twice did I come anywhere near leaving Fratton Park, the closest being in January 1985.

In those days we used to change at the ground before travelling over to the Rugby Camp and one morning I was walking down Frogmore Road to hear Bally banging on his office window, which these days is the Montgomery Lounge.

He was shaking his head and wearing a big grin - apparently there was a big thing in The Daily Star that day saying 'Alan Knight is going to Arsenal'.

It seems they had been watching me as John Lukic was unhappy being number two to Pat Jennings and wanted to move to get regular football.

Still, we went to training and all lined up with Bally dividing us into groups to warm up before he turned round to me and said 'Knightsie I need a word with you', so all the lads go 'Woooooooo'.

He told me Arsenal had put in a £170,000 bid: 'I've told the club I don't want you to go but you have got to go, it's a great club, the best club I ever played for, the chairman has accepted it and if you need help with anything I will help you with it'.

I was then offered the option of training or going home, but I wanted to train.

So I told all the lads and they were saying well done, fantastic, then I rang home to speak to my first wife: 'I am going to Arsenal, I'm going to come home and sit by the phone'.

So I sat there, and I sat there. Nothing happened.

The next day I picked up a national paper and it was Bally slagging Arsenal off saying they were bang out of order. 'I had my star young keeper coming to me asking if he was going to Arsenal, Arsenal shouldn't have put that in the paper, it disrupted him'.

Now I had no idea what was happening so I went in and said to him 'What the hell is going on?'.

I was told the chairman wanted too much and it had fallen through. That was that.

Cheers, I thought, thanks a lot, I had the right hump at the time, it had made me look a mug and all the lads were taking the mickey.

After that there were a couple of times when I had contract disputes and was transfer listed, basically new deals I had been promised didn't materialise, although I suppose everyone thought 'Knightsie wants to leave again'.

I found it difficult to understand how someone could promise you something and then four months later completely deny the conversation ever happened. That was my naivety, I suppose an agent would have sorted it, but I didn't have one in those days.

There was another time when I came close to leaving in March 1997 when Terry Fenwick was manager and Terry Venables was in charge of the club.

Eddie Niedzwiecki, a coach at Chelsea, rang me up as they had a goalkeeping crisis and asked if I would go there on loan and sit on the bench.

Well, I had only just got back into the Pompey team after twiddling my thumbs for a while but this was a Premier League club who could name substitute goalkeepers - you couldn't in Division One - so of course I was interested.

The problem was Pompey wanted a loan fee, Chelsea said no and instead went for Craig Forrest from Ipswich.

The thing is, the lad came on as a substitute 36 minutes into his first game against

Newcastle United when Frode Grodas got injured! He played three times in a month in total.

That summer we were on pre-season in Norway and Venables gave me the classic 'There's always a moment in a player's career when their time is up' and raised the possibility of going to Australia to play.

It was fine, I had seen in the past players blanked, cold shouldered and frozen out when not agreeing with people in charge - but he never brought it up again!

Towards the end I was always battling towards to keep my place, various other keepers came and went, and it was time to jack it in during the summer of 1999.

I was made goalkeeping coach, but Bally, give him his due, found out I was close to making 800 appearances so brought me on as a late substitute in League Cup matches against Torquay United and Blackburn Rovers at the start of the 1999-2000 season to ensure I got there.

My final appearance came in January 2000 at the age of 38 when Aaron Flahavan and Andy Petterson were injured for a trip to Norwich City, so I got the nod ahead of Chris Tardif. We ended up losing 2-1.

However, I also came out of retirement under Harry Redknapp when there was an injury crisis, stepping up from goalkeeping coach to be an unused substitute at Aston Villa in January 2004 for a 2-1 defeat.

I was very lucky to go on for as long as I did, I was reasonably injury free and am paying the price for it a little bit now, that is football's lot, problems with knees and hips, bashes on the bonce.

I was fortunate to do something in the main I did enjoy, even if it did mess me up mentally a bit, but I suppose we are all like that in football!